# assessing reading

## MULTIPLE MEASURES 2nd Edition

*for kindergarten through twelfth grade*

*Arena Press* *Novato · California*

Arena Press
(a division of Academic Therapy Publications)
20 Leveroni Court
Novato, California 94949-5746
1-800-422-7249
www.AcademicTherapy.com
www.HighNoonBooks.com

Consortium On Reaching Excellence
in Education, Inc. (CORE)
1-888-249-6155
www.corelearn.com

International Standard Book Number: 978-1-57128-464-8

24 23 22 21 20 19 18 17 16
28 27 26 25 24 23 22 21 20

Library of Congress Control Number: 2008920094

2008 edition

**CREDITS**

Editors: Linda Diamond, B. J. Thorsnes
Contributing Authors: Orna Lenchner, Ph.D., Michael Milone, Ph.D., Jacalyn Mahler
Contributing Editor: Deliah de la Garza
Book and Cover Design: Lucy Nielsen
Special acknowledgment is given to Jim Arena, Nancy Martin, Ph.D. and Bonni Gatter at Arena Press

**Data forms for *Assessing Reading: Multiple Measures* are available for download at: http://www.corelearn.com/Resources/Free-Materials.html**

**ACKNOWLEDGMENTS**

For each of the selections listed below, grateful acknowledgment is made for permission to reprint copyrighted material as follows:

San Diego Quick Assessment of Reading Ability is excerpted from The Graded Word List by Margaret La Pray and Ramon Ross, in *Journal of Reading*, v.12 (4), 1969. Copyright 1969 by M. La Pray and International Reading Association. All rights reserved. Reprinted by permission of the publisher.

MASI-R Oral Reading Fluency Measures passages are from Multi-Level Academic Skills Inventory – Revised, by K. W. Howell, M. K. Hosp, J. L. Hosp, and M. K. Morehead. Copyright 2007 by K. W. Howell. All rights reserved. Reprinted by permission of the author.

Spanish Verbal Language Scales is excerpted from Dos Amigos Verbal Language Scales, by Donald E. Critchlow. Copyright 1969 by Academic Therapy Publications, Inc. All rights reserved. Reprinted by permission of the publisher.

Performance criteria for fluency and fluency scores: A discussion, by K. W. Howell. Copyright 2007 by K. W. Howell. All rights reserved. Reprinted by permission of the author.

Assessment-driven instruction: A systems approach, by L. Diamond, in *Perspectives*, Fall 2005, pages 33-37. Copyright 2005 by International Dyslexia Association. All rights reserved. Reprinted by permission of the publisher.

# CONTENTS

# Introduction to Assessing Reading

**Phonological Awareness**

- CORE Phoneme Deletion Test
- CORE Phonological Segmentation Test
- CORE Phoneme Segmentation Test

**Decoding and Word Attack**

- CORE Phonics Survey
- San Diego Quick Assessment of Reading Ability

**Vocabulary**

- CORE Graded High-Frequency Word Survey
- CORE Vocabulary Screening

**Comprehension**

- CORE Reading Maze Comprehension Test

**Fluency**

- MASI-R Oral Reading Fluency Measure

**Assessments in Spanish**

- CORE Spanish Phonemic Awareness Test
- CORE Spanish Phonics Survey
- CORE Spanish Spelling Inventory
- Critchlow Spanish Verbal Language Scales

READING IS THE MOST IMPORTANT SKILL TAUGHT IN school. For many students, however, it is neither easy nor straightforward. *Assessing Reading: Multiple Measures* contains a collection of formal and informal reading assessments for use with students in Grades K–12. These assessments assist the teacher in targeting areas of strength and weakness, in monitoring student reading development, and in planning appropriate instruction.

Unlike large-scale achievement tests, the majority of these assessments can be administered individually. Each assessment was selected because it measures an important research-based reading skill and because it is quick, reliable, and easy to use. Each assessment provides clear and accurate individual student information.

The assessments included in this book are designed to measure specific skills critical to successful reading. Some of the assessments are curriculum-based, while others are criteria-based, depending on the purpose of the assessment. Similarly, some assessments target specific skills, some are instruments for broader screening, and some can be used for both types of assessment. Spanish assessments are provided for the early grades where many students may still be in bilingual programs or may be receiving Spanish primary language instruction before transitioning to English programs. Profile Forms and Class Records found in the Appendix provide an easy way for teachers to summarize assessment results.

In an effective reading program, assessment informs instruction. This is true for large groups as well as for individuals. Different assessment instruments serve different purposes. The specific purpose determines the particular instrument selected and when in the instructional sequence it is used.

In the primary grades, reading instruction includes teaching discrete skills. These specific skills and strategies tend to be "enabling" skills, providing the foundation for long-term outcomes such as fluency and comprehension. Because of the need for mastery of these underlying skills, effective reading assessment in the primary grades is frequent and specific.

In Grades 4–12, assessment plays a role in monitoring progress as well as in identifying causes of reading difficulties, especially for struggling adolescent readers. Unlike primary grade assessment, which begins with the most discrete skills, reading assessment for older students often starts broadly and then becomes more discrete in order to pinpoint particular reading subskills that might cause reading difficulty. As a result, assessment becomes increasingly more specific in nature.

To meet students' various assessment requirements, schools should organize their assessment toolkits around four broad types of assessment: screening, progress monitoring, diagnostic (specific skills) assessment, and outcome assessment. In all cases, teachers need to understand the expected targets of mastery for individual skills in order to identify students at risk of difficulty and to tailor instruction to meet identified needs.

## Types and Frequency of Effective Assessment Systems

| | Screening | Progress Monitoring | Diagnostic Assessment | Outcome Assessment |
|---|---|---|---|---|
| **Kindergarten** | • Beginning of year, middle of year, and end of year<br>• Can be the same tool used for progress monitoring<br>• Often curriculum-based like DIBELS or AIMSweb | • At least three times a year<br>• More frequent, to guide ongoing modification of the curriculum, particularly for students falling behind peers<br>• Curriculum-based measurement and curriculum-embedded measurement | • If student fails to reach progress monitoring benchmarks<br>• Tools that identify specific skill gaps | • At end of year or major instructional sequence<br>• State or district assessments<br>• Can be same tools used for screening |
| **Grade 1** | • Beginning of year and up to three times yearly<br>• Can be the same tools used for progress monitoring<br>• Often curriculum-based like DIBELS or AIMSweb | • At least three times a year<br>• More frequent, to guide ongoing modification of the curriculum, particularly for students falling behind peers<br>• Curriculum-based measurement and curriculum-embedded measurement | • If student fails to reach progress monitoring benchmarks<br>• Tools that identify specific skill gaps | • At end of year or major instructional sequence<br>• State or district assessments<br>• Can be same tools used for screening |
| **Grades 2 and 3** | • Beginning of year and up to three times yearly<br>• Can be the same tools used for progress monitoring<br>• Often curriculum-based like DIBELS or AIMSweb | • At least three times a year<br>• More frequent, to guide ongoing modification of the curriculum, particularly for students falling behind peers<br>• Curriculum-based measurement and curriculum embedded measurement | • If student fails to reach progress monitoring benchmarks<br>• Tools that identify specific skill gaps | • At end of year or major instructional sequence<br>• State or district assessments<br>• Can be same tools used for screening |
| **Grades 4 through 12** | • Beginning of year and beginning of term<br>• Can be the same tools used for progress monitoring<br>• For Grades 6 through 12, use prior year ending assessments | • At least 2 to 3 times a year<br>• More frequent, to guide ongoing modification of the curriculum, particularly for students falling behind peers<br>• Curriculum-based measurement and curriculum embedded measurement | • If student fails to reach progress monitoring benchmarks<br>• Tools that identify specific skill gaps | • At end of year or major instructional sequence<br>• State or district assessments<br>• Can be same tools used for screening |

## Types of Assessment

The Effective Assessment Systems chart on the previous page describes the types and frequency of assessments that should occur.

### SCREENING

*Screening* tests provide information about the knowledge and skill base of the student. They are useful for determining the most appropriate starting point for instruction and for planning instructional groups. Screening tests usually include formal and informal measures with clear mastery targets. In this book, there are screening tests for phonological awareness, phonics, fluency, comprehension, vocabulary, and spelling. Testing systems such as DIBELS and AIMSweb provide assessments that are both screening tests and progress monitoring tools. For older students, tests such as the *Test of Silent Contextual Reading Fluency* (Pro-Ed) may function similarly.

### PROGRESS MONITORING

*Progress monitoring* is ongoing. Examples of progress monitoring assessments are teacher observations, informal or formal tests, and curriculum tasks. Progress monitoring is used to determine whether students are making adequate progress, and also to determine whether instruction needs to be adjusted. Progress monitoring measures include curriculum-embedded assessments such as unit tests, which measure the extent to which students have learned the material taught in a specific reading program. They also include general or external measures for assessing critical reading skills such as phonemic awareness, phonics, fluency, vocabulary or comprehension, or for predicting success in meeting grade-level standards by the end of the year. Curriculum-based measurement (CBM) is an assessment tool that is often used for progress monitoring because it emphasizes repeated measurement over time. DIBELS and AIMSweb are some examples of ongoing progress monitoring systems. Ongoing progress monitoring may also include diagnostic tests that pinpoint the causes of a particular screening test result or a particular observed reading problem.

Progress monitoring serves to guide the specific focus of instruction. These tests are given at least three times a year to all students in the primary grades. It is recommended that students who are beginning to fall behind their peers be assessed at least monthly, while students who have fallen considerably behind be assessed more frequently—every two weeks or even weekly. As with many progress monitoring instruments, further diagnostics may be necessary to inform accurate interpretation of results from these assessments.

#### DIAGNOSTIC (SPECIFIC SKILLS) ASSESSMENT

*Diagnostic* (specific skills) *assessment* can also be used for screening or progress monitoring. These tests identify students' specific strengths and weaknesses. Specific skills assessments should be given whenever a student is suspected of having difficulty learning what is being taught. Many of the tests in this book can serve as specific skills assessments.

#### OUTCOME ASSESSMENT

*Outcome assessment* is often used at the end of major units of instruction and at year's end. It provides data about exiting accomplishments and is useful for planning the next major segment of instruction and for determining changes to a school's curriculum. It also provides programmatic information for large groups of students. Outcome assessment usually leads to outcome evaluation, which represents a final judgment about a school's curriculum or about an individual student.

### Why Assess?

Reading is a complex process. Fluent reading is made up of two major domains: (1) the ability to decode or recognize individual written words, and (2) the ability to comprehend text as a whole unit. In order to identify student progress, to prevent reading difficulty from becoming entrenched, and to provide help to students with reading difficulties, teachers need to utilize assessments that isolate these two major components.

Many students fail to develop the decoding skill necessary for automatic word recognition because they are not aware that spoken words are composed of units of sound, or phonemes (Torgesen 2002). Because phonemic awareness is a strong correlate of reading skill, it is the basic (precursor) skill to be assessed in beginning readers (Ehri et al. 2001; Bishop 2003). Decoding skill can also be directly assessed through tests of real and pseudowords (Share and Stanovich 1995; Carver 2003). Assessing student knowledge of high-frequency words is also useful, because recognition of words that appear often in printed text is crucial for comprehension (Zeno et al. 1995). According to Adams (1990), poorly developed word recognition skills are the most pervasive and debilitating source of reading difficulty.

Research consistently supports the relationship between reading fluency, which is the accurate reading of text at a conversational rate with appropriate prosody, and reading comprehension (Rasinski 2004; Hudson et al. 2005). Slow, laborious reading taxes the reader's capacity to construct an ongoing interpretation of the passage. For this reason, fluency tests, which measure both rate and accuracy, are critical assessment measures.

Tests of reading comprehension measure comprehension of passages and whole text—the ultimate goal of reading. Such tests measure higher-order skills through the use of multiple-choice questions, open-ended questions, or maze passage techniques. To demonstrate comprehension, the student must bring to bear word recognition proficiency, syntactic knowledge, background knowledge, comprehension monitoring, and reasoning skills. Finally, vocabulary warrants assessment because it is so closely correlated with comprehension. Studies of reading comprehension conducted in 15 different countries show that the correlation between vocabulary and reading comprehension ranges from .66 to .75 (Thorndike 1973; Joshi 1995; Biemiller 2005; Nagy 2005).

## When to Assess

The Assessment Sequence for Students in Grades K–3 begins with assessments of the most discrete skills. In contrast, the Assessment Sequence for Students in Grades 4–12 begins with the most global skills. The Diagnostic Plan for Upper Grades provides a diagnostic sequence for identifying sources of reading difficulty as well as instructional recommendations. The Assessment Sequence charts on the following pages are guidelines for a suggested testing schedule. It should be noted that many of the measures on the charts can be replaced by teacher observation, informal checklists, and materials that come with a basal reading series. Also note that not all students will need all assessments.

## References


Adams, M. J. 1990. *Beginning to read: Thinking and learning about print.* Cambridge, MA: The MIT Press.

Biemiller, A. 2005. Vocabulary development and instruction: A prerequisite for school learning. In D. Dickinson and S. Neuman (eds.), *Handbook of early literacy research*, Vol. 2. New York: Guilford.

Bishop, A. G. 2003. Prediction of first-grade reading achievement: A comparison of fall and winter kindergarten screenings. *Learning Disability Quarterly*, 26(3), pp. 189–200.

Carver, R. P. 2003. The highly lawful relationships among pseudoword decoding, word identification, spelling, listening, and reading. *Scientific Studies of Reading* 7, pp. 127–154.

Ehri, L. C., S. R. Nunes, D. M. Willows, B. V. Schuster, Z. Yaghoub-Zadeh, and T. Shanahan. 2001. Phonemic awareness instruction helps children learn to read: Evidence from the National Reading Panel's meta-analysis. *Reading Research Quarterly* 36, pp. 250–287.

Gillon, G. T. 2004. *Phonological awareness: From research to practice.* New York: Guilford.

Hudson, R. F., H. B. Lane, and P. C. Pullen. 2005. Reading fluency assessment and instruction: What, why, and how. *The Reading Teacher* 58(8), pp. 702–714.

Nagy, W. E. 2005. Why vocabulary instruction needs to be long-term and comprehensive. In E. H. Hiebert and M. L. Kamil (eds.), *Teaching and learning vocabulary: Bringing research to practice.* Mahwah, NJ: Erlbaum.

Rasinski, T. 2004. *Assessing reading fluency.* Honolulu: Pacific Resources for Education and Learning.

Share, D., and K. E. Stanovich. 1995b. Cognitive processes in early reading development: Accommodating individual differences into a mode of acquisition. *Issues in Education: Contributions for Educational Psychology* 1, pp. 1–57.

Thorndike, R. L. 1973. *Reading comprehension education in fifteen countries: An empirical study.* New York: Wiley.

Torgesen, J. K. 2002. The prevention of reading difficulties. *Journal of School Psychology* 40, p. 6.

Zeno, S. M., S. H. Ivens, R. T. Millard, and R. Duvvuri. 1995. *The educator's word frequency guide.* Brewster, NY: TASA.

## Assessment Sequence for Primary Grade Students (Grades K–3)

*See Diagnostic Plan for Grades 2–3 on page 14.*

| | Kindergarten<br>Early Mid. Late | Grade 1<br>Early Mid. Late | Grade 2<br>Early Mid. Late | Grade 3<br>Early Mid. Late |
|---|---|---|---|---|
| Choose 1 of the following:<br>▶ **CORE Phoneme Deletion Test**<br>▶ **CORE Phonological Segmentation Test**<br>▶ **CORE Spanish Phonemic Awareness Test** | | | Only if indicated | Only if indicated |
| ▶ **CORE Phoneme Segmentation Test** | | | Only if indicated | Only if indicated |
| ▶ **CORE Phonics Survey**<br>▶ **CORE Spanish Phonics Survey** | | Every 4–6 weeks until mastery; more frequently for at risk | Every 4–6 weeks until mastery; more frequently for at risk | Only if indicated |
| ▶ **CORE Spanish Spelling Inventory** | Late | 3 times a year | 3 times a year | 3 times a year |
| ▶ **CORE Graded High Frequency Word Survey** | Middle | Every 4–6 weeks until mastery | Every 4–6 weeks until mastery | Every 4–6 weeks until mastery |
| ▶ **San Diego Quick Assessment of Reading Ability** | | | If desired | If desired |
| ▶ **Critchlow Spanish Verbal Language Scales** | | Every 4–6 weeks until mastery | Every 4–6 weeks until mastery | Every 4–6 weeks until mastery |
| ▶ **CORE Vocabulary Screening** | | 2 times a year | 3 times a year | 3 times a year |
| ▶ **MASI-R Oral Reading Fluency Measure** | | Winter and Spring; at least 2 times per month for at risk | 3 times a year; at least 2 times per month for at risk | 3 times a year; at least 2 times per month for at risk |
| ▶ **CORE Reading Maze Comprehension** | n/a | n/a | 3 times a year | 3 times a year |

## Assessment Sequence for Upper Grade Students (Grades 4–12)

*See Diagnostic Plan for upper grades on page 15.*

| | Grade 4–6<br>Early Mid. Late | Grade 7–8<br>Early Mid. Late | Grade 9–12<br>Early Mid. Late |
|---|---|---|---|
| ▸ **CORE Reading Maze Comprehension** | 3 times a year | As indicated, or to screen | As indicated, or to screen |
| ▸ **MASI-R Oral Reading Fluency Measure** | Only if indicated | n/a | n/a |
| ▸ **CORE Vocabulary Screening** | 3 times a year | Only if indicated by low Maze or other comprehension scores | Only if indicated by low Maze or other comprehension scores |
| ▸ **Critchlow Spanish Verbal Language Scales** | Only if indicated | Only if indicated | Only if indicated |
| ▸ **San Diego Quick Assessment of Reading Ability** | Only if indicated | Only if indicated | Only if indicated |
| ▸ **CORE Graded High-Frequency Word Survey** | Only if indicated | Only if indicated | Only if indicated |
| ▸ **CORE Spanish Spelling Inventory** | Only if indicated | Only if indicated | Only if indicated |
| ▸ **CORE Phonics Survey** | Only if indicated | Only if indicated | Only if indicated |
| ▸ **CORE Phoneme Segmentation Test** | Only if indicated | Only if indicated | Only if indicated |

## Diagnostic Plan for Primary Grade Students (Grades 2–3)

*For Grades K and 1, follow the assessment sequence for primary grade students on page 12. For Grades 2 and 3, use the following diagnostic plan.*

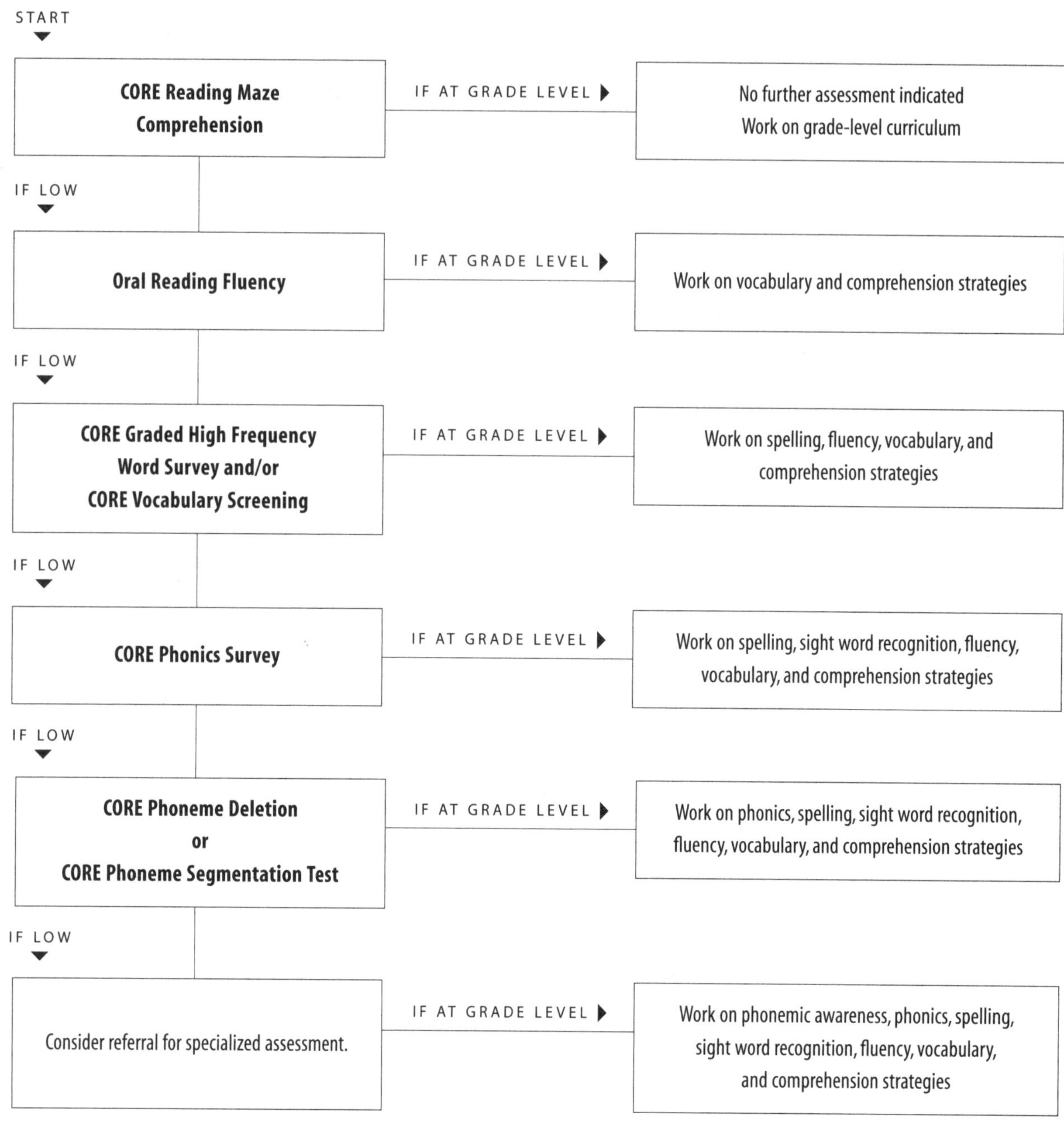


**NOTE:** Although it is not included in this Diagnostic Plan, the *San Diego Quick Assessment of Reading Ability* is also available as a measure of out-of-context word recognition.

## Diagnostic Plan for Upper Grade Students (Grades 4–12)

*For Grades 4 through 12, use the following diagnostic plan.*

**NOTE:** Although it is not included in this Diagnostic Plan, the *San Diego Quick Assessment of Reading Ability* is also available as a measure of out-of-context word recognition.

# Multiple Measures

SECOND EDITION

# CORE Phoneme Deletion Test

**SKILL ASSESSED**

## Phoneme Deletion

**Grade Level**

K–3

**Language**

English

**Grouping**

Individual

**Approximate Testing Time**

10–15 Minutes

**Materials**

Record Form (p. 24)

**Author**

Orna Lenchner, Ph.D.

**WHAT** This assessment includes four phoneme deletion tasks arranged in order of difficulty. The first task assesses the student's ability to delete initial phonemes. For example, the examiner may say the word cat and ask the student to say cat without the initial /k/ sound. The remaining tasks assess the student's ability to delete final phonemes, such as /t/ in the word seat; initial phonemes in blends, such as /s/ in the word slip; and phonemes embedded in blends, such as /l/ in the word play.

The *CORE Phoneme Deletion Test* can be used as a screening measure, a progress monitoring measure, and a diagnostic measure. The assessment contains tasks that are expected to be mastered in Grades K–3, but it can also be used for older students.

**WHY** These tasks may help to determine whether deficits in phonemic, or sound, awareness account for the student's reading or spelling delays. According to research, the lack of phonemic awareness is the most powerful determinant of the likelihood of a student's failure to learn to read.

**HOW** Before administering each task, administer the Practice Items. Use the Practice Items to teach the task. When teaching the task using the Practice Items, praise the student for even close approximations of the correct answer. However, when administering the Test Items, give only general feedback. Do not correct errors; instead encourage students by praising their willingness to participate.

For all students, begin with the tasks in Part A of the test. Assess as far as the student can go, regardless of his or her grade placement. Remember that this is an auditory assessment—students do not see the items on the test. The Correct Response column tells how the student's answer should sound, not how it should be spelled.

---

PART A

## Initial Sound (Late Kindergarten and Grade 1)

Begin by saying to the student: *We are going to play a word game. This game will give me information to help teach you better.* Then administer the following two Practice Items.

**Practice Item 1**

TEACHER: Say *cat.*
STUDENT: *cat*
TEACHER: Now say it without the /k/.
STUDENT: *at*

If the student responds incorrectly say: *Let's try that again.* For example, if the student says *kit,* model the correct response by emphasizing the /k/ and artificially separating it from the *at.* Help the student to give the correct response by saying each sound slowly. Repeat the Practice Item until the student gives the correct response—even if the student does not seem to understand the task. After the student repeats the correct response, proceed to Practice Item 2.

**Practice Item 2**

TEACHER: Say *table.*
STUDENT: *table*
TEACHER: Now say it without the /t/.
STUDENT: *able*

If the student responds incorrectly say: *Let's try that again.* For example, if the student says *bull,* model the correct response by emphasizing the /t/ and artificially separating it from *able.* Encourage the student to repeat the correct response.

If the student can correctly respond to these two Practice Items, proceed to the Test Items. If the student cannot correctly respond to these Practice Items, skip Part A and proceed to the Practice Item for Part B. Some students may be able to delete a final sound, but not an initial sound.

---

## PART B

### Final Sound (Grade 1)

Say to the student: *We are going to play another word game. The rules of this game are a little different. Pay close attention.* Then administer the following Practice Item.

**Practice Item**

TEACHER: Say *seat.*
STUDENT: *seat*
TEACHER: Now say it without the /t/.
STUDENT: *sea*

If the student responds incorrectly say: *Let's try that again.* For example, if the student says *seat,* model the correct response by elongating *sea* and artificially separating it from the /t/. Then say: *Seat without the /t/ is sea.* Encourage the student to repeat the correct response.

If the student can correctly respond to the Practice Item, proceed to the Test Items. If a student cannot correctly respond to any of the Part A or B Practice Items, discontinue the assessment.

---

## PART C

### First Sound of a Consonant Blend (Grade 2)

Say to the student: *We are going to do something different now. Pay close attention.* Then administer the following Practice Item.

**Practice Item**

TEACHER: Say *slip.*
STUDENT: *slip*
TEACHER: Now say it without the /s/.
STUDENT: *lip*

If the student responds incorrectly say: *Let's try that again.* For example, if the student deletes the entire /sl/ blend and says *ip,* model a correct response by emphasizing the /s/ and separating it from *lip*. Say: *Be careful, you're taking off too much. Try to say it without the /s/.* If necessary, help the student to repeat the correct response.

If the student can correctly respond to, or repeat, the Practice Item, proceed to the Test Items. If a student can respond correctly to at least two of the Test Items, proceed to Part D; otherwise, discontinue the assessment.

---

PART D

## Embedded Sound of a Consonant Blend (Grade 3)

Say to the student: *We are going to play another word game. The rules of this game are a little different.* Then administer the following Practice Item.

**Practice Item**

TEACHER: Say *play*.
STUDENT: *play*
TEACHER: Now say it without the /l/.
STUDENT: *pay*

If the student responds incorrectly say: *Let's try that again.* For example, if the student deletes the entire blend and says *ay*, say: *You are taking off too much. I just wanted you to say it without the /l/.* Model a correct response by separating all three sounds of the word: /p/ /l/ /ay/, and say: *Without the /l/ it is just /p/ /ay/—pay. So, what is play without the /l/? Yes, it is pay.* If necessary, help the student to repeat the correct response.

If the student can correctly respond to, or repeat, the Practice Item, proceed to the Test Items.

▶ **WHAT IT MEANS** Use the following guidelines to determine the student's performance level. Scores shown are expected end-of-year scores for each grade.

| Ending Grade Level Expectations | | | | |
|---|---|---|---|---|
| | **Ending Grade K** | **Ending Grade 1** | **Ending Grade 2** | **Ending Grade 3+** |
| **Part A: Initial Sounds** | | | | |
| Benchmark | 5 | 5 | 5 | 5 |
| Strategic | 4 | 4 | n/a | n/a |
| Intensive | 0–3 | 0–3 | 0–4 | 0–4 |
| **Part B: Final Sounds** | | | | |
| Benchmark | 5 | 5 | 5 | 5 |
| Strategic | 4 | 4 | n/a | n/a |
| Intensive | 0–3 | 0–3 | 0–4 | 0–4 |
| **Part C: First Sound, Blend** | | | | |
| Benchmark | n/a | 5 | 5 | 5 |
| Strategic | n/a | 4 | 4 | n/a |
| Intensive | n/a | 0–3 | 0–3 | 0–4 |
| **Part D: Embedded Sound, Blend** | | | | |
| Benchmark | n/a | 3–5 | 4–5 | 5 |
| Strategic | n/a | 2 | 3 | 4 |
| Intensive | n/a | 0–1 | 0–2 | 0–3 |

**WHAT'S NEXT?** Students who score at Strategic or Intensive levels will benefit from targeted and intensified instruction and extensive practice in the phonemic awareness concepts indicated. The *CORE Phoneme Deletion Test* can be used to monitor student progress or to assess outcomes from instruction.

CORE's *Teaching Reading Sourcebook,* Second Edition

Model lessons for explicit instruction in introducing and practicing phoneme awareness can be found in the "How" section of Phonemic Awareness in the *Teaching Reading Sourcebook*. Suggested lessons include "Bridge Game," "Sound Match," and "Say-It-and-Move-It."

# CORE Phoneme Deletion Test

Name ______________________ Grade ________ Date __________

Directions: Follow the format used in the Practice Items to administer the items for each level. Mark "+" to indicate a correct response or "–" to indicate an incorrect response. Write down incorrect responses, but do not correct the student. If the student cannot complete any of the items in Parts A or B, discontinue testing. If the student cannot do at least two items in Part C, discontinue testing. Remember that this is an auditory assessment. Students do not see the items. The Correct Response column tells how the student's answer should sound, not how it should be spelled.

**Part A: Initial Sound (Late Kindergarten, Grade 1)**

Practice Items

Say *cat* . . . now say it without the /k/ ___(at)

Say *table* . . . now say it without the /t/ ___(able)

| TEST ITEM | CORRECT RESPONSE | |
|---|---|---|
| 1. (t)ower | our | (+) (–) ________ |
| 2. (c)old | old | (+) (–) ________ |
| 3. (b)ake | ache | (+) (–) ________ |
| 4. (s)ize | eyes | (+) (–) ________ |
| 5. (l)ow | owe | (+) (–) ________ |

**Part B: Final Sound (Grade 1)**

Practice Items

Say *seat* . . . now say it without the /t/ ___(sea)

Say *rake* . . . now say it without the /k/ ___(ray)

| TEST ITEM | CORRECT RESPONSE | |
|---|---|---|
| 6. to(n)e | toe | (+) (–) ________ |
| 7. droo(p) | drew | (+) (–) ________ |
| 8. ti(m)e | tie | (+) (–) ________ |
| 9. ro(d)e | row | (+) (–) ________ |
| 10. pla(c)e | play | (+) (–) ________ |

**Items Correct** ________ **Grade Level** ________

**Part C: First Sound of a Consonant Blend (Grade 2)**

Practice Items

Say *slip* . . . now say it without the /s/ ___(lip)

Say *cloud* . . . now say it without the /k/ ___(loud)

| TEST ITEM | CORRECT RESPONSE | |
|---|---|---|
| 11. (f)reight | rate | (+) (–) ________ |
| 12. (p)layed | laid | (+) (–) ________ |
| 13. (s)weet | wheat | (+) (–) ________ |
| 14. (b)reak | rake | (+) (–) ________ |
| 15. (s)pill | pill | (+) (–) ________ |

**Part D: Embedded Sound of a Consonant Blend (Grade 3)**

Practice Items

Say *slip* . . . now say it without the /l/ ___(sip)

Say *play* . . . now say it without the /l/ ___(pay)

| TEST ITEM | CORRECT RESPONSE | |
|---|---|---|
| 16. b(l)end | bend | (+) (–) ________ |
| 17. t(w)in | tin | (+) (–) ________ |
| 18. g(r)ow | go | (+) (–) ________ |
| 19. be(s)t | bet | (+) (–) ________ |
| 20. li(f)t | lit | (+) (–) ________ |

# CORE Phonological Segmentation Test

**SKILL ASSESSED**

Phonological Segmentation

**Grade Level**

K–1

**Language**

English

**Grouping**

Individual

**Approximate Testing Time**

5–10 Minutes

**Materials**

- Colored Blocks
- Record Form (p. 29)

**Author**

Orna Lenchner, Ph.D.

**WHAT** This Grades K–1 phonological segmentation assessment contains three parts: Part A: Sentences into Words; Part B: Words into Syllables; and Part C: Words into Phonemes.

The *CORE Phonological Segmentation Test* can be used as a screening measure, a progress monitoring measure, and a diagnostic measure. It can provide information about a student's response to instruction. The assessment contains tasks that are expected to be mastered in Grades K–1.

**WHY** These tasks may help to determine whether deficits in phonemic, or sound, awareness account for the student's reading or spelling delays. According to research, the lack of phonemic awareness is the most powerful determinant of the likelihood of a student's failure to learn to read.

**HOW** Begin by demonstrating each task using the Practice Items. Proceed to the Test Items only after the student demonstrates understanding of a task. The color of the blocks is not important. However, when demonstrating, use a different colored block for each word segment. Make sure to lay out the blocks in a horizontal line, from left to right. After the student completes an item, put the blocks back in the original pile. When teaching the task using Practice items, praise the student for even close approximations to a correct response and for how quickly he or she is learning the new task. When administering the Test Items, give only general feedback. Do not indicate whether an answer was correct or not.

CONTINUED ▷

## PART A

### Sentences into Words

Begin this part by administering the following Practice Item.

**Practice Item**

TEACHER: John, what is something you like to eat?
STUDENT: Pizza.
TEACHER: I am going to use these blocks to show "John likes pizza." (Teacher uses three colored blocks and says each of the words as he or she places each of the blocks on the table.)
TEACHER: (Teacher points to each of the blocks from left to right and asks:) What is this one? *(John)* And this? *(likes)* And this? *(pizza)*

If the student understands the task, ask him or her to do the task independently.

TEACHER: Use these blocks to show me . . .

Record any incorrect segmentations. Splitting a word into syllables is not considered an error. Proceed with testing when the student clearly understands the task. Discontinue testing if the student does not respond correctly to any of the first three items.

---

## PART B

### Words into Syllables

Begin this part by administering the following Practice Item.

**Practice Item**

TEACHER: Now we are going to break words into parts. I am going to use the blocks to show the word *cupcake.* (Say the word *cup* and place the first block on the table; say the word *cake* and place the second block to the right of the first one.)

TEACHER: Which one is *cup*?
STUDENT: The first block.
TEACHER: (Point to the second block.) What is this?
STUDENT: *cake*

If the student still does not understand, it may help to clap the syllables. Provide additional practice using words such as *superman, doorbell, butterfly.* Proceed with testing when the student clearly understands the task. Discontinue assessment after five items if the student can't segment any of the words into syllables.

## PART C

### Words into Phonemes

Begin this part by administering the following Practice Items.

**Practice Item 1**

TEACHER: Now we are going to use these blocks to show the sounds in a word. Let's say I wanted to show you the word *time*. That word has three sounds /t/ /ī/ /m/. (Put out one block for each of the sounds as you say them slowly in order.) Can you say the sounds?

STUDENT: /t/ /ī/ /m/

If the student says the names of letters rather than their sound, say:

TEACHER: Yes, that is how it is spelled. Now can you tell me the sound that the letters make?

If the student cannot independently say the sounds, repeat the sounds and ask:

TEACHER: Can you point to the /t/? And which one is /m/? And what is the sound in the middle? (/ī/)

**Practice Item 2**

TEACHER: Now you try one. If you wanted to show the word *shop,* how many sounds is that? Use the blocks to show me.

If the student cannot do the segmentation independently, model the complete segmentation.

TEACHER: The word *shop* has three sounds (lay down a block for each of the sounds as you say them, in left-to-right progression): /sh/ /o/ /p/.

To check the student's understanding, ask:

TEACHER: What are the three sounds?
STUDENT: /sh/ /o/ /p/
TEACHER: Which one is /sh/? Which one is /p/? What is the sound of the block in the middle? (/o/)

If the student puts down four blocks, he or she is probably trying to spell the word. Remind the student to pay attention to the sounds, not the letters. Once the student can at least point to the block that represents the correct sound, proceed to the Test Items. Record the student's responses. Do not correct any items. If the student cannot completely segment a word, ask for the first sound—and, when appropriate, the last sound, as well.

**WHAT IT MEANS** Use the following guidelines to determine the student's performance level. Scores shown are expected end-of-year scores for each grade.

| Ending Grade Level Expectations | Grade K | Grade 1 |
|---|---|---|
| **Part A: Sentences into Words** | | |
| Benchmark | 5 | 5 |
| Strategic | 4 | n/a |
| Intensive | 0–3 | 0–4 |
| **Part B: Words into Syllables** | | |
| Benchmark | 7–8 | 8 |
| Strategic | 5–6 | 7 |
| Intensive | 0–4 | 0–6 |
| **Part C: Words into Phonemes** | | |
| Benchmark | 5–10 | 9–10 |
| Strategic | 3–4 | 6–8 |
| Intensive | 0–2 | 0–5 |

**WHAT'S NEXT?** Students who score at Strategic or Intensive levels will benefit from targeted and intensified instruction and extensive practice in the phonemic and phonological awareness concepts indicated.

Model lessons for explicit instruction in introducing and practicing phonemic and phonological awareness can be found in the "How" section of Phonemic Awareness in the *Teaching Reading Sourcebook.* Suggested lessons include "Starfish," "Salad Toss," and "Elkonin Sound Boxes."

**CORE's *Teaching Reading Sourcebook,* Second Edition**

# CORE Phonological Segmentation Test

Name ______________________________ Grade ________ Date __________

Directions: Have students use different-colored blocks to show the number of words, syllables, or phonemes in the Practice Item for each part of this test. Then administer each part of the test. Mark "+" to indicate a correct response or "–" to indicate an incorrect response. Record students' exact responses on the blank lines.

**Part A: Sentences into Words**

Practice Item: John likes pizza.

1. Father called. (+) (–) ______________________
2. What time is it? (+) (–) ______________________
3. How much does an apple cost? (+) (–) ______________________
4. I have to go to sleep soon. (+) (–) ______________________
5. On Sunday I will go swimming. (+) (–) ______________________

**Part B: Words into Syllables**

Practice Items: cup-cake; su-per-man

6. cowboy (cow-boy) (+) (–) ______________________
7. rabbit (rab-bit) (+) (–) ______________________
8. yesterday (yes-ter-day) (+) (–) ______________________
9. party (par-ty) (+) (–) ______________________
10. helicopter (hel-i-cop-ter) (+) (–) ______________________
11. basketball (bas-ket-ball) (+) (–) ______________________
12. playground (play-ground) (+) (–) ______________________
13. caterpillar (cat-er-pil-lar) (+) (–) ______________________

**Part C: Words into Phonemes**

Practice Items: time (t-ī-m); shop (sh-o-p)

14. keep (k-ē-p) (+) (–) ______________________
15. bag (b-a-g) (+) (–) ______________________
16. thumb (th-u-m) (+) (–) ______________________
17. night (n-ī-t) (+) (–) ______________________
18. rock (r-o-k) (+) (–) ______________________
19. itch (i-tch) (+) (–) ______________________
20. head (h-e-d) (+) (–) ______________________
21. short (sh-or-t) (+) (–) ______________________
22. steak (s-t-ā-k) (+) (–) ______________________
23. clown (k-l-ou-n) (+) (–) ______________________

**Items Correct** ______________________

# CORE Phoneme Segmentation Test

**SKILL ASSESSED**

## Phoneme Segmentation

**Grade Level**

2–12

**Language**

English

**Grouping**

Individual

**Approximate Testing Time**

5–10 minutes

**Materials**

- Colored Blocks
- Record Form (p. 33)

**Author**

Orna Lenchner, Ph.D.

**WHAT** This measure for Grades 2–12 assesses the student's ability to break a word into its component phonemes, or sounds. For example, the word *sat* has three phonemes: /s/ /a/ /t/. The word *shoe,* although it has four letters, has only two phonemes: /sh/ /oo/.

The *CORE Phoneme Segmentation Test* can be used as a screening measure, a progress monitoring measure, and a specific skills measure. It can provide information about a student's response to instruction. Use this assessment with students in Grades 2–12 who are experiencing delays in reading and spelling that cannot be attributed to limited English or limited exposure to instruction. Administer this measure only after giving tests of comprehension, fluency, and phonics.

**WHY** Many older students who are significantly behind in reading or spelling may have underdeveloped phonemic awareness. Use this test to determine whether deficits in sound awareness may account for serious delays in reading or spelling.

**HOW** Proceed to the Test Items only after the student demonstrates understanding of the Practice Item tasks. When teaching the task using the Practice Items, praise the student for even close approximations of the correct answer. However, when administering the Test Items, give only general feedback. Do not correct errors or praise correct answers. Record the student's exact response on the blank line. Then after administering each item, circle whether the response was correct or incorrect. Ask for the "sound" if the student says the letter name. If the student cannot segment the entire word correctly, ask just for the first and last sound. Discontinue testing if the student misses five items in a row.

**Practice Item 1**

Lay out on the table about eight blocks of assorted colors. Make sure to lay out the blocks in a horizontal line, from left to right. The color of the blocks is not important. However, to demonstrate, use a different colored block for each of the different sounds in the word. After the student completes an item, put the blocks back in the pile.

TEACHER: We are going to use these blocks to show the sounds in a word. Let's say I wanted to show you *sit.* That word has three sounds /s/ /i/ /t/. (Put out one block for each of the sounds as you say them slowly in order). Can you point to the /s/? Which one is the /t/? What is the sound in this block (the middle /i/)?
STUDENT: /i/
TEACHER: Now, tell me the three sounds.
STUDENT: /s/ /i/ /t/
TEACHER: Very good! You got that the first time!

If the student gives the names of letters, rather than their sounds, say:

TEACHER: Yes, that is how it is spelled. Now can you tell me the sounds the letters make?

**Practice Item 2**

TEACHER: If you wanted to show *shop,* how many sounds is that? Use the blocks to show me.

If the student cannot do the segmentation independently, demonstrate the complete segmentation.

TEACHER: The word *shop* has three sounds (lay down a block for each of the sounds as you say them, in left-to-right progression): /sh/ /o/ /p/.

To check the student's understanding, ask:
TEACHER: What are the three sounds?
STUDENT: /sh/ /o/ /p/
TEACHER: Which one is /sh/? Which one is /p/? What is the sound of the block in the middle? (/o/)

If the student puts down four blocks, he or she is probably trying to spell the word. Remind the student to attend to sounds, rather than letters. Once the student can at least point to the block that represents the correct sound, proceed to the test items.

**▸ WHAT IT MEANS** Use the guidelines below to determine the student's performance level. The ability to segment a word fully into phonemes can be mastered as early as Grade 1, and should be mastered no later than ending Grade 2. Scores shown are end-of-year scores.

| Ending Grade Level Expectations | Grade 2 | Grade 3 and up |
|---|---|---|
| Benchmark | 12–15 | 14–15 |
| Strategic | 9–11 | 11–13 |
| Intensive | 0–8 | 0–10 |

**▸ WHAT'S NEXT?** Students who score at Strategic or Intensive levels will benefit from targeted and intensified instruction and extensive practice in phonemic awareness. *The Phonological Awareness Training Kit—Intermediate* (LinguiSystems, East Moline, IL) and the *Lindamood Phoneme Sequencing Program* (PRO-ED, Austin, TX) are both useful resources for this purpose. Encouraging these students to write regularly will also improve their phonemic awareness. The *CORE Phoneme Segmentation Test* can be used to monitor student progress or to assess outcomes from instruction.

CORE's *Teaching Reading Sourcebook,* Second Edition

The model lesson "Elkonin Sound Boxes," which provides explicit instruction in phoneme segmentation, can be useful with younger students. This lesson can be found in the "How" section of Phonemic Awareness in the *Teaching Reading Sourcebook.*

# CORE Phoneme Segmentation Test

Name_______________________________ Grade________ Date___________

Directions: Have students use different-colored blocks to show the number of phonemes in each of the Practice Items. Then administer the test. Mark "+" to indicate a correct response or "–" to indicate an incorrect response. Record students' exact responses on the blank lines.

Practice Items: sit (s-i-t); shop (sh-o-p)

1. thumb (th-u-m) (+) (–) ____________________
2. skate (s-k-ā-t) (+) (–) ____________________
3. shriek (sh-r-ē-k) (+) (–) ____________________
4. large (l-ar-j) (+) (–) ____________________
5. drop (d-r-o-p) (+) (–) ____________________
6. flew (f-l-oo) (+) (–) ____________________
7. chalk (ch-au-k) (+) (–) ____________________
8. germ (j-er-m) (+) (–) ____________________
9. spread (s-p-r-e-d) (+) (–) ____________________
10. train (t-r-ā-n) (+) (–) ____________________
11. stork (s-t-or-k) (+) (–) ____________________
12. bolt (b-ō-l-t) (+) (–) ____________________
13. glare (g-l-air) (+) (–) ____________________
14. crowd (k-r-ou-d) (+) (–) ____________________
15. point (p-oi-n-t) (+) (–) ____________________

**Items Correct**____________________

 

# CORE Spanish Phonemic Awareness Test

**SKILLS ASSESSED**

Phoneme Oddity
Phoneme Deletion

**Grade Level**

K–2

**Language**

Spanish

**Grouping**

Individual

**Approximate Testing Time**

5–10 Minutes

**Materials**

Record Forms (pp. 37–40)

**Author**

Jacalyn Mahler

**▸ WHAT** This test consists of two measures of phonemic awareness:

1. Phoneme Oddity
In these subtests the examiner says three or four words and then asks the student which word has a different beginning, ending, or middle sound than the other words.

2. Phoneme Deletion
The examiner says a word (e.g., *mala*) and asks the student to repeat the word without the initial or final sound (e.g., *ala*). Initial and final deletion of single consonants and initial deletion of consonant blends are assessed.

**▸ WHY** Students need to have a minimal level of phonemic awareness to benefit from direct phonics instructions. Phoneme oddity and deletion tasks offer an effective way to assess these skills. Performance on these tasks is highly correlated to reading.

CONTINUED ▷

## Phoneme Oddity

▶ **HOW** Use the three-choice format for Kindergarten students and the four-choice format for first and second graders. Testing may start in Kindergarten mid-year and also be given to first graders in the fall and second graders who do not yet read in the fall.

When you say the group of words out loud, try to pronounce each word with the same emphasis so the student is not given any additional cues as to the correct word. Also, cover your mouth with a piece of paper as you say the words so you do not provide a visual cue.

Before administering the test, check the student's memory for words by saying: *Voy a decir tres/cuatro palabras y voy a pedirte que las repitas. Di casa, correr, caballo, jugar.* Wait for the student to repeat the three or four words. If the student doesn't understand, try again. If the student cannot repeat the words, do not administer this part of the test.

Work with the student on understanding and hearing the different sounds of the words in the first example. You may give the answer on these practice trials. Even if the student does not understand or perform correctly on the practice trials, proceed with the task.

Go through the first section, which focuses on the initial sound, then alert the student that you will next focus on the final sound, and then on the sound in the middle.

Write the student's response on the line if it is incorrect. If it is correct, simply put a check on the line. Do not let the student see the form. After each response, simply say "okay" in a positive tone and move to the next item.

---

## Phoneme Deletion

▶ **HOW** Administer the Initial Sound section to Kindergarten and early first-grade students. Continue with the Final Sound section with students who have little trouble with the Initial Sound section. For students who perform well on the Final Sound section, administer the Initial Blend section of the test, which is the most challenging. Follow the general procedures outlined above for administration.

**WHAT IT MEANS** Evaluate performance on each section following the guidelines listed below.

| Phoneme Oddity Mastery Level (Maximum: 18–20) | | |
|---|---|---|
| | (18 Item) | (20 Item) |
| Benchmark | 14+ | 16+ |
| Strategic | 11–13 | 12–15 |
| Intensive | 0–10 | 0–11 |

| Phoneme Deletion Mastery Level (Maximum: 30) | |
|---|---|
| | (30 Item) |
| Benchmark | 24+ |
| Strategic | 12–23 |
| Intensive | 0–11 |

**WHAT'S NEXT?** Students who perform poorly will benefit from more intensive instruction in phonemic awareness. Encouraging students to write regularly will also strengthen their phonemic awareness.

# CORE Spanish Phonemic Awareness Test
# Phoneme Oddity, Kindergarten

Name________________________ Grade________ Date__________

Tell the student: *Quiero que prestes atención al primer sonido de cada palabra. El primer sonido de una palabra será diferente del primer sonido de las otras palabras. Dime qué palabra tiene el sonido diferente. Practicaremos juntos.* Follow the same procedure for final sound (*último sonido*) and middle sound (*sonido intermedio*).

**Initial Sound**

| | | | |
|---|---|---|---|
| P1 | dedo *cama* duro | (+) (–) | __________ |
| 1. | foca foto *pero* | (+) (–) | __________ |
| 2. | sol sal *por* | (+) (–) | __________ |
| 3. | caja *dulce* cada | (+) (–) | __________ |
| 4. | niño *mono* nido | (+) (–) | __________ |
| 5. | *leche* pera pasa | (+) (–) | __________ |
| 6. | miel *taza* mano | (+) (–) | __________ |
| 7. | *baño* salsa sofá | (+) (–) | __________ |

**Final Sound**

| | | | |
|---|---|---|---|
| P1 | con *mes* pan | (+) (–) | __________ |
| 8. | sal mal *más* | (+) (–) | __________ |
| 9. | *ven* por mar | (+) (–) | __________ |
| 10. | casa masa *vaso* | (+) (–) | __________ |
| 11. | rosal *salud* barril | (+) (–) | __________ |
| 12. | *boca* foco loco | (+) (–) | __________ |
| 13. | das les *dar* | (+) (–) | __________ |
| 14. | sé *mi* le | (+) (–) | __________ |

**Middle Sound**

| | | | |
|---|---|---|---|
| P1 | *ama* hacha ocho | (+) (–) | __________ |
| 15. | ala ola *oro* | (+) (–) | __________ |
| 16. | día *leo* río | (+) (–) | __________ |
| 17. | ojo *hace* hijo | (+) (–) | __________ |
| 18. | *dan* ven ten | (+) (–) | __________ |
| 19. | *mal* con los | (+) (–) | __________ |
| 20. | uña año *uso* | (+) (–) | __________ |

**Items Correct** __________

# CORE Spanish Phonemic Awareness Test
# Phoneme Oddity, Grades 1–2

Name____________________________ Grade_______ Date__________

Tell the student: *Quiero que prestes atención al primer sonido de cada palabra. El primer sonido de una palabra será diferente del primer sonido de las otras palabras. Dime qué palabra tiene el sonido diferente. Practicaremos juntos.* Follow the same procedure for final sound (*último sonido*) and middle sound (*sonido intermedio*).

**Initial Sound**

P1 fecha foto *pala* fino (+) (–) ____________________

1. malo mano miro *loco* (+) (–) ____________________
2. barco *tela* baja busca (+) (–) ____________________
3. niño *seco* nido noche (+) (–) ____________________
4. *lado* copa cuna casa (+) (–) ____________________
5. papa *foca* perro paro (+) (–) ____________________
6. *barco* sopa seca seis (+) (–) ____________________

**Final Sound**

P1 beso digo tomo *cine* (+) (–) ____________________

7. sal mal cal *más* (+) (–) ____________________
8. *ven* por mar ver (+) (–) ____________________
9. *vaso* casa masa pasa (+) (–) ____________________
10. rosal trigal barril *salud* (+) (–) ____________________
11. foco *boca* loco toco (+) (–) ____________________
12. mis les *dan* das (+) (–) ____________________

**Middle Sound**

P1 *oso* uva ave iba (+) (–) ____________________

13. ala ola hilo *oro* (+) (–) ____________________
14. día *leo* río mío (+) (–) ____________________
15. hijo *hace* ojo ajo (+) (–) ____________________
16. ven *dan* ten ver (+) (–) ____________________
17. *mal* sol los pon (+) (–) ____________________
18. hago higo *ocho* Hugo (+) (–) ____________________

**Items Correct** ____________

# CORE Spanish Phonemic Awareness Test
# Phoneme Deletion

Name______________________________ Grade________ Date___________

Directions: For each section, go through the three practice trials, helping the student with the answers. If the student does not provide an accurate response, continue with that section of the assessment and do not provide any further assistance—simply write down each response, say "okay," and move to the next item.

**Initial Sound**

Tell the student: *Vamos a hacer un juego. Te voy a decir algunas palabras y vamos a quitar el primer sonido de cada palabra. Si digo* ***mala****, quitarás el sonido /m/ y me dirás* ***ala****. Hacemos otro juntos. Si digo* ***gato****, quitarás el sonido /g/ y me dirás* ***ato****.*

| | | | |
|---|---|---|---|
| P1 | dama (ama) | (+) (–) | ______________________ |
| P2 | bola (ola) | (+) (–) | ______________________ |
| P3 | marco (arco) | (+) (–) | ______________________ |
| 1. | gata (ata) | (+) (–) | ______________________ |
| 2. | luna (una) | (+) (–) | ______________________ |
| 3. | boca (oca) | (+) (–) | ______________________ |
| 4. | rojo (ojo) | (+) (–) | ______________________ |
| 5. | nido (ido) | (+) (–) | ______________________ |
| 6. | baños (años) | (+) (–) | ______________________ |
| 7. | falta (alta) | (+) (–) | ______________________ |
| 8. | toro (oro) | (+) (–) | ______________________ |
| 9. | resto (esto) | (+) (–) | ______________________ |
| 10. | tabla (habla) | (+) (–) | ______________________ |

**Items Correct** ____________

**Final Sound**

Tell the student: *Vamos a hacer un juego. Te voy a decir algunas palabras y vamos a quitar el último sonido de cada palabra. Si digo* ***mala****, quitarás el sonido /a/ y me dirás* ***mal****. Hacemos otro juntos. Si digo* ***ven****, quitarás el sonido /n/ y me dirás* ***ve****.*

| | | | |
|---|---|---|---|
| P1 | los (lo) | (+) (–) | ______________ |
| P2 | sala (sal) | (+) (–) | ______________ |
| P3 | daban (daba) | (+) (–) | ______________ |
| 11. | pone (pon) | (+) (–) | ______________ |
| 12. | dices (dice) | (+) (–) | ______________ |
| 13. | barril (barrí) | (+) (–) | ______________ |
| 14. | mío (mi) | (+) (–) | ______________ |
| 15. | sin (sí) | (+) (–) | ______________ |
| 16. | masa (más) | (+) (–) | ______________ |
| 17. | vid (vi) | (+) (–) | ______________ |
| 18. | cine (sin) | (+) (–) | ______________ |
| 19. | comían (comía) | (+) (–) | ______________ |
| 20. | ten (te) | (+) (–) | ______________ |

**Items Correct** ______________

**Initial Blend**

Tell the student: *Vamos a hacer un juego. Te voy a decir algunas palabras y vamos a quitar el primer sonido de cada palabra. Si digo* ***frío****, quitarás el sonido /f/ y me dirás* ***río****. Hacemos otro juntos. Si digo* ***brama****, quitarás el sonido /b/ y me dirás* ***rama****.*

| | | | |
|---|---|---|---|
| P1 | flote (lote) | (+) (–) | ______________ |
| P2 | trampa (rampa) | (+) (–) | ______________ |
| P3 | brisa (risa) | (+) (–) | ______________ |
| 21. | plomo (lomo) | (+) (–) | ______________ |
| 22. | globo (lobo) | (+) (–) | ______________ |
| 23. | blinda (linda) | (+) (–) | ______________ |
| 24. | trompa (rompa) | (+) (–) | ______________ |
| 25. | freír (reír) | (+) (–) | ______________ |
| 26. | drama (rama) | (+) (–) | ______________ |
| 27. | grito (rito) | (+) (–) | ______________ |
| 28. | crema (rema) | (+) (–) | ______________ |
| 29. | broma (Roma) | (+) (–) | ______________ |
| 30. | fruta (ruta) | (+) (–) | ______________ |

**Items Correct** ______________

# CORE Phonics Surveys

**SKILL ASSESSED**

## Phonics

**Grade Level**

K–12

**Language**

- English
- Spanish

**Grouping**

Individual

**Approximate Testing Time**

10–15 Minutes

**Materials**

- Pencil
- Lined Paper
- English Record Form (pp. 44–48)
- English Student Material (pp. 49–52)
- Spanish Record Form (pp. 53–58)
- Spanish Student Material (pp. 59–62)

**Source**

Consortium On Reading Excellence (CORE)

**▸ WHAT** The *CORE Phonics Survey* and the *CORE Spanish Phonics Survey* assess the phonics and phonics-related skills that have a high rate of application in beginning reading. Each survey presents a number of lists of letters and words for the student to identify or decode. Pseudowords, or made-up words, are included since the student must use decoding skills to correctly pronounce these words and cannot have memorized them.

The *CORE Phonics Surveys* can be used as screening measures, and also as outcome measures, providing data about growth and mastery at the end of an instructional period. As diagnostics, they can indicate whether or not a student needs instruction in selected phonics concepts, or if further assessment is needed. They may also be used to track progress from earlier skills to grade level mastery. The *CORE Phonics Surveys* are not meant to replace screening and progress monitoring tests such as those from AIMSweb or DIBELS, or other CBM tests that may already be in place but can be used to augment such tests.

**▸ WHY** A student's ability to use knowledge of sound/letter correspondences (phonics) to decode words determines, in large measure, his or her ability to read individual words. A detailed assessment of a student's phonics skills points to areas in which the student is likely to benefit most from systematic, explicit phonics instruction. Also, knowing the skills that the student does possess will help in selecting reading tasks that offer the most effective reinforcement of those skills.

CONTINUED ▷

**HOW** Instructions for administering each part of the survey are included on the Record Form. Students read from the Student Material on the pages that follow the Record Form. To focus the student's attention on the part of the test being given, cover the other parts with a piece of paper. The Record Form shows the same material that appears on the Student Material, in a reduced size, so that you may easily record the student's responses.

Following administration, score each of the test parts, and transfer the results to the first page of the Record Form under Skills Summary. Retest parts not yet mastered according to schedules found on the Types and Frequency of Effective Assessment Systems chart, page 7, or the Assessment Sequence for Primary Grade Students or Assessment Sequence for Upper Grade Students charts, pages 12 and 13, or your school or district assessment plan. Be aware of the student's behavior during testing. If the student is tiring or making many consecutive errors, discontinue testing at that time.

## WHEN

| | Fall | Winter | Spring |
|---|---|---|---|
| **Kindergarten** | | | |
| Parts A & B | X | X | X |
| Parts C–E | | X | X |
| **Grade 1** | | | |
| Parts A–D | If indicated → | | |
| Part E | X | X | X |
| Parts F–K | | X | X |
| Part L | | | X |
| **Grade 2** | | | |
| Parts A–K | If indicated → | | |
| Part L | | X | X |
| **Grades 3 and up** | | | |
| Parts A–L | If indicated → | | |

CORE's *Teaching Reading Sourcebook,* Second Edition

**WHAT IT MEANS** This test is a mastery test. It is expected that students will ultimately get all items correct. Score each list completed by student as shown below.

**CORE Phonics Survey—English, Mastery**

| | (Letter Names/ Sounds) | (15 Item) | (24 Item) |
|---|---|---|---|
| Benchmark | 83 (all) | 14+ | 21+ |
| Strategic | 65–82 | 10–13 | 15–20 |
| Intensive | 0–64 | 0–9 | 0–14 |

**CORE Phonics Survey—Spanish, Mastery**

| | (Letter Names/ Sounds) | (5 Item) | (10 Item) | (24 Item) |
|---|---|---|---|---|
| Benchmark | 73 (all) | 4+ | 9+ | 21+ |
| Strategic | 58–72 | 3 | 6–8 | 15–20 |
| Intensive | 0–57 | 0–2 | 0–5 | 0–14 |

**WHAT'S NEXT?** Students who score at Strategic or Intensive levels will benefit from targeted and intensified instruction and extensive practice in the phonics concepts indicated. An analysis of individual errors can give more specific information about phonic elements that need instruction. Additionally, the *CORE Phoneme Segmentation Test* or other tests of phoneme awareness can be administered to isolate phoneme awareness as an underlying factor. Older struggling readers who score at Intensive levels will need basic phonics instruction, possibly including instruction in phonemic awareness and sound/spelling correspondences. Students at all levels need repeated opportunities to develop automaticity through practice in reading words in isolation and in appropriately decodable text.

Model lessons for explicit instruction in introducing and practicing sound/spellings, blending, and reading and writing words can be found in the *Teaching Reading Sourcebook.*

# CORE Phonics Survey—Record Form

Name______________________________ Grade________ Date___________

SKILLS SUMMARY

**Alphabet Skills and Letter Sounds**

_____/26 A. Letter names—uppercase
_____/26 B. Letter names—lowercase
_____/21 C. Consonant sounds
_____/5 D. Long vowel sounds
_____/5 Short vowel sounds

**Reading and Decoding Skills**

_____/15 E. Short vowels in CVC words
_____/15 F. Consonant blends with short vowels
_____/15 G. Short vowels, digraphs, and *-tch* trigraph
_____/15 H. *R*-controlled vowels
_____/15 I. Long vowel spellings
_____/15 J. Variant vowels
_____/15 K. Low frequency vowel and consonant spellings
_____/24 L. Multisyllabic words

Skills to review: ________________________________________

______________________________________________________

Skills to teach: _________________________________________

______________________________________________________

# Alphabet Skills and Letter Sounds

## PART A **Letter names—uppercase**

Say to the student: *Can you tell me the names of these letters?* If the student cannot name three or more consecutive letters, say: *Look at all of the letters and tell me which ones you do know.*

| | | | | | | | | |
|---|---|---|---|---|---|---|---|---|
| D | A | N | S | X | Z | J | L | H |
| T | Y | E | C | O | M | R | P | W |
| K | U | G | B | F | Q | V | I | |

___/26

## PART B **Letter names—lowercase**

Say to the student: *Can you tell me the names of these letters?* If the student cannot name three or more consecutive letters, say: *Look at all of the letters and tell me which ones you do know.*

| | | | | | | | | |
|---|---|---|---|---|---|---|---|---|
| d | a | n | s | x | z | j | l | h |
| t | y | e | c | o | m | r | p | w |
| k | u | g | b | f | q | v | i | |

___/26

## PART C **Consonant sounds**

Say to the student: *Look at these letters. Can you tell me the sound each letter makes?* Be sure to ask if he or she knows of another sound for the letters *g* and *c*. If the sound given is correct, do not mark the Record Form. If it is incorrect, write the sound the student gives above each letter. If no sound is given, circle the letter. If the student cannot say the sound for three or more consecutive letters, say: *Look at all of the letters and tell me which sounds you do know.*

| | | | | | | |
|---|---|---|---|---|---|---|
| d | l | n | s | x | z | j |
| t | y | p | c | h | m | r |
| k | w | g | b | f | q | v |

___/21



 

## PART D **Vowel sounds**

Ask the student: *Can you tell me the sounds of each letter?* If the student names the letter, count it as the long vowel sound. Then ask: *Can you tell me another sound for the letter?* The student should name the short vowel sound.

e __ __ i __ __ a __ __ o __ __ u __ __

l = long sound s = short sound

Record "l" on the first line for the long sound (letter name) and "s" for the short sound on the second line. If the student makes an error, record the error over the letter.

_____/5 Long vowel sounds (count the number of l's above)

_____/5 Short vowel sounds (count the number of s's above)

---

# Reading and Decoding

For Parts E through K students must read both real and pseudowords (made-up words). For the real word lines, tell the student: *I want you to read each line of words aloud.* If the student cannot read two or more of the real words in each line, do not administer the line of pseudowords; go to the next set of items. Before asking the student to read the line of pseudowords, say: *Now I want you to read some made-up words. Do not try to make them sound like real words.* When using this assessment as a specific skills test or screening measure, do not discontinue testing if a student does not do well on one of the items in Parts F through K. Instead, move to the next item and continue testing.

## PART E **Short vowels in CVC words**

| | | | | | | |
|---|---|---|---|---|---|---|
| _____/5 | sip | mat | let | bun | hog | (real) |
| _____/5 | rut | fit | bat | hot | set | (real) |
| _____/5 | nop | sut | dit | pem | fap | (pseudo) |

_____/15

---

## PART F **Consonant blends with short vowels**

| | | | | | | |
|---|---|---|---|---|---|---|
| _____/5 | stop | trap | quit | spell | plan | (real) |
| _____/5 | silk | fast | sank | lump | held | (real) |
| _____/5 | nask | dilt | qued | cang | dran | (pseudo) |

_____/15

## PART G Short vowels, digraphs, and -tch trigraph

| | | | | | | |
|---|---|---|---|---|---|---|
| _____/5 | when | chop | thin | shut | wick | (real) |
| _____/5 | dodge | rash | ring | then | match | (real) |
| _____/5 | chid | shom | dath | phid | futch | (pseudo) |

_____/15

---

## PART H R-controlled vowels

| | | | | | | |
|---|---|---|---|---|---|---|
| _____/5 | harm | dirt | form | fern | surf | (real) |
| _____/5 | worn | pert | bark | turn | bird | (real) |
| _____/5 | nerm | sirt | gorf | murd | carn | (pseudo) |

_____/15

---

## PART I Long vowel spellings

| | | | | | | |
|---|---|---|---|---|---|---|
| _____/5 | tape | key | toe | paid | feet | (real) |
| _____/5 | leap | boat | tie | ray | blow | (real) |
| _____/5 | loe | hine | beap | faim | soat | (pseudo) |

_____/15

---

## PART J Variant vowels

| | | | | | | |
|---|---|---|---|---|---|---|
| _____/5 | few | down | moon | hawk | coin | (real) |
| _____/5 | cue | loud | cook | haunt | toy | (real) |
| _____/5 | voot | rew | fout | zoy | bawk | (pseudo) |

_____/15

---

## PART K Low frequency vowel and consonant spellings

| | | | | | | |
|---|---|---|---|---|---|---|
| _____/5 | kneel | cent | type | ghost | wrist | (real) |
| _____/5 | giant | sweat | gnat | bomb | sigh | (real) |
| _____/5 | bice | knod | dimb | tigh | wrep | (pseudo) |

_____/15

## PART L **Multisyllabic words**

To administer, say to the student: *I want you to read aloud down the first column of words. Each of the real words in this column has two syllables.* Point to the first column. If the student can read at least five out of eight of the words in this column, point to the second column and say: *Now I want you to read aloud the next column of words.* If the student can read at least five of the words in the second column, point to the third column and say: *Now I want you to read some made-up words. Do not try to make them sound like real words.*

| | | | | | |
|---|---|---|---|---|---|
| | ____/3 | Closed-closed | unless | consent | timbut |
| | ____/3 | Closed-silent *e* | competes | admire | rompete |
| | ____/3 | Open/closed-other | depend | radishes | podated* |
| | ____/3 | Open or closed | zero | menu | gromu* |
| | ____/3 | Silent *e* | locate | inhaled | pentate |
| | ____/3 | Consonant -*le* | stable | dimple | morkle |
| | ____/3 | r-Controlled | further | bordered | darber |
| | ____/3 | Vowel team | railways | roaring | fauntoon |
| ____/24 | | | | | |

* The first syllable of these words can be either open or a closed (long or short vowel sound, respectively); the second syllable of podated can be either a closed (short vowel sound) or a silent -*e* (long vowel sound) syllable, due to the rules for adding -*ed*.)

# CORE Phonics Survey—Student Material
## Alphabet and Letter Sounds

PART A

| | | | | | | | | |
|---|---|---|---|---|---|---|---|---|
| D | A | N | S | X | Z | J | L | H |
| T | Y | E | C | O | M | R | P | W |
| K | U | G | B | F | Q | V | I | |

PART B

| | | | | | | | | |
|---|---|---|---|---|---|---|---|---|
| d | a | n | s | x | z | j | l | h |
| t | y | e | c | o | m | r | p | w |
| k | u | g | b | f | q | v | i | |

PART C

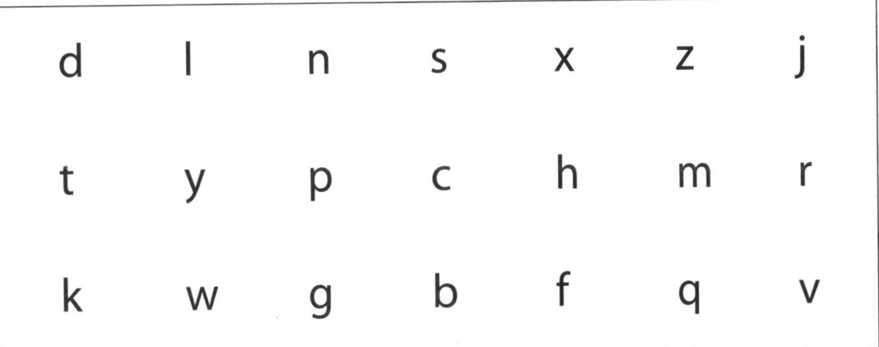

| | | | | | | |
|---|---|---|---|---|---|---|
| d | l | n | s | x | z | j |
| t | y | p | c | h | m | r |
| k | w | g | b | f | q | v |

PART D

| | | | | |
|---|---|---|---|---|
| e | i | a | o | u |

# CORE Phonics Survey—Student Material

## Reading and Decoding

PART E

| | | | | |
|---|---|---|---|---|
| sip | mat | let | bun | hog |
| rut | fit | bat | hot | set |
| nop | sut | dit | pem | fap |

PART F

| | | | | |
|---|---|---|---|---|
| stop | trap | quit | spell | plan |
| silk | fast | sank | lump | held |
| nask | dilt | qued | cang | dran |

PART G

| | | | | |
|---|---|---|---|---|
| when | chop | thin | shut | wick |
| dodge | rash | ring | then | match |
| chid | shom | dath | phid | futch |

## PART H

| | | | | |
|---|---|---|---|---|
| harm | dirt | form | fern | surf |
| worn | pert | bark | turn | bird |
| nerm | sirt | gorf | murd | carn |

## PART I

| | | | | |
|---|---|---|---|---|
| tape | key | toe | paid | feet |
| leap | boat | tie | ray | blow |
| loe | hine | beap | faim | soat |

## PART J

| | | | | |
|---|---|---|---|---|
| few | down | moon | hawk | coin |
| cue | loud | cook | haunt | toy |
| voot | rew | fout | zoy | bawk |

## PART K

| | | | | |
|---|---|---|---|---|
| kneel | cent | type | ghost | wrist |
| giant | sweat | gnat | bomb | sigh |
| bice | knod | dimb | tigh | wrep |

## PART L

| | | |
|---|---|---|
| unless | consent | timbut |
| competes | admire | rompete |
| depend | radishes | podated |
| zero | menu | gromu |
| locate | inhaled | pentate |
| stable | dimple | morkle |
| further | bordered | darber |
| railways | roaring | fauntoon |

# CORE Spanish Phonics Survey—Record Form

Name______________________________ Grade________ Date___________

SKILLS SUMMARY

**Alphabet Skills and Letter Sounds**

_____ /21 A. Consonant names—uppercase
_____ /21 B. Consonant names—lowercase
_____ /10 C. Vowel names and sounds—uppercase and lowercase
_____ /21 D. Consonant sounds

**Reading and Decoding Skills**

_____ /10 E. Open syllables, CV
_____ /10 F. Open syllables, V and CV
_____ /10 G. Closed syllables, CVC and VC
_____ /10 H. Open syllables with blends, CCV
_____ /10 I. Vowel combinations in open syllables
_____ /10 J. Diphthongs in closed syllables
_____ /24 K. Multisyllabic words

**Spelling Skills**

_____ /5 L. Initial sounds
_____ /5 M. Final sounds
_____ /10 N. Whole words

Spelling Skills Error Analysis

_____ /2 Consonant digraphs *leche, carro*
_____ /3 Phoneme /k/ *carro, cocina, parque*
_____ /2 Phoneme /rr/, spelled r and rr *carro, rompen*
_____ /1 Phoneme /x/, spelled j in *ja, jo, ju* *hijo*
_____ /2 Phoneme /s/, spelled s *triste, abuelos*
_____ /3 Phoneme /b/, spelled b and v *baño, voy, abuelos*
_____ /1 Phoneme /s/, spelled c in *ce, ci* *cocina*
_____ /4 Closed syllables *parque, rompen, triste, abuelos*
_____ /1 Blends *triste*
_____ /1 Silent h *hijo*
_____ /1 Words with m before p and b *rompen*
_____ /2 Diphthongs *voy, abuelos*

Skills to review:_______________________________________________

_______________________________________________________________

Skills to teach:________________________________________________

_______________________________________________________________

# Alphabet Skills and Letter Sounds

## PART A **Consonant names—uppercase**

Say to the student: *¿Puedes decirme los nombres de estas letras?* If the student cannot name three or more consecutive letters, say: *Mira todas las letras y dime si conoces alguna.*

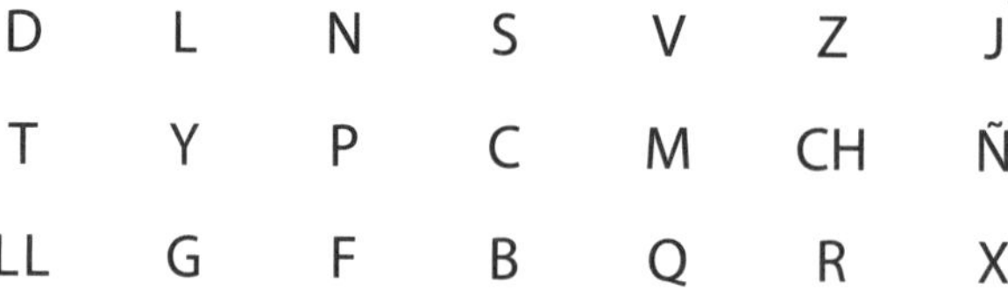

| | | | | | | |
|---|---|---|---|---|---|---|
| D | L | N | S | V | Z | J |
| T | Y | P | C | M | CH | Ñ |
| LL | G | F | B | Q | R | X |

___/21

---

## PART B **Consonant names—lowercase**

Say to the student: *¿Puedes decirme los nombres de estas letras?* If the student cannot name three or more consecutive letters, say: *Mira todas las letras y dime si conoces alguna.*

| | | | | | | |
|---|---|---|---|---|---|---|
| d | l | n | s | v | z | j |
| t | y | p | c | m | ch | ñ |
| ll | g | f | b | q | r | x |

___/21

---

## PART C **Vowel names and sounds**

Ask the student: *¿Puedes decirme cuáles son los sonidos de estas letras?* If the student names the letter, that is its sound. If the student makes an error, record the error over the letter.

___/5 O A I U E ___/5 o a i u e

___/10

## PART D **Consonant sounds**

Say to the student: *Mira estas letras. ¿Puedes decirme qué sonido tiene cada letra?* (The digraphs *ch* and *ll* are included here because they are usually taught as part of the Spanish alphabet.) Be sure to ask if he or she knows of another sound for the letters *c* and *g*. Do not expect the student to know more than one sound for *r* (either /r/ or /rr/ is acceptable). If the student gives the correct sound, do not mark the Record Form. If the sound given is incorrect, write the sound the student gives above each letter. If no sound is given, circle the letter. If the student cannot say the sound for three or more consecutive letters say: *Mira todas las letras y dime qué sonidos conoces.*

| | | | | | | |
|---|---|---|---|---|---|---|
| d | l | n | s | v | z | j |
| t | y | p | c | m | ch | ñ |
| ll | g | f | b | q | r | x |

___/21

---

# Reading and Decoding

For parts E through J, students must read both real and pseudowords (made-up words). For the first line of real words, tell the student: *Quiero que leas estas palabras.* If the student cannot read two or more of the real words, do not administer the line of pseudowords. Go to the next set of items. Before asking the student to read the line of pseudowords, say: *Ahora voy a pedirte que leas algunas palabras inventadas. No intentes leerlas como palabras reales que ya conoces.*

## PART E **Open syllables, CV**

| | | | | | |
|---|---|---|---|---|---|
| _____/5 | su | yo | luna | techo | jefe |
| _____/5 | ne | cu | mepa | sila | rago |

___/10

---

## PART F **Open syllables, V and CV**

| | | | | | |
|---|---|---|---|---|---|
| _____/5 | año | iba | oro | ella | ocho |
| _____/5 | oba | udo | eca | alle | imo |

___/10

## PART G Closed syllables, CVC and VC

| | | | | | |
|---|---|---|---|---|---|
| _____/5 | sol | pan | tambor | juntos | artes |
| _____/5 | jez | dor | cambal | portir | entad |

___/10

## PART H Open syllables with blends, CCV

| | | | | | |
|---|---|---|---|---|---|
| _____/5 | brazo | grillo | clase | pluma | globo |
| _____/5 | flece | crima | bruco | clopo | pleso |

___/10

## PART I Vowel combinations in open syllables

| | | | | | |
|---|---|---|---|---|---|
| _____/5 | cae | lee | hoy | ruido | quiere |
| _____/5 | cheo | moa | ray | yugia | vaida |

___/10

## PART J Diphthongs in closed syllables

| | | | | | |
|---|---|---|---|---|---|
| _____/5 | puerta | siempre | treinta | cuando | viento |
| _____/5 | pueste | guanto | tiemba | reinda | fianco |

___/10

## PART K **Multisyllabic words**

Administer this item if the student is able to read most of the single-syllable real and pseudowords in the previous items. Say to the student: *Ahora quiero que leas algunas palabras que tienen tres o cuatro sílabas. Empieza con la primera palabra de cada columna y lee todas las palabras de esa columna.* Point to the first column. If the student can read at least three out of eight of the words in this column, say: *Ahora las palabras serán inventadas. No intentes leerlas como palabras reales que ya conoces.* Point to the second column. Repeat the same procedure for the third column.

| | | | | |
|---|---|---|---|---|
| _____/3 | Open CV (4 SYLLABLES) | carretera | calabaje | taregudo |
| _____/3 | Closed CVC (3 SYLLABLES) | compartes | rescardan | zarcambol |
| _____/3 | Variable Letter/Sound (3 SYLLABLES) | gigante | caroce | giloga |
| _____/3 | Blends (3 SYLLABLES) | problema | frascura | tropazo |
| _____/3 | Hiatos (4 SYLLABLES) | soleado | paonante | nealtura |
| _____/3 | Diphthongs (3 SYLLABLES) | ciudades | jeralio | laicando |
| _____/3 | Diphthongs (4 SYLLABLES) | bailaremos | gilacioso | pauladista |
| _____/3 | Prefixes (4 SYLLABLES) | descompuesto | remolante | excavario |

___/24

# Spelling

## PART L **Initial sounds**

Give the student a pencil and a sheet of lined paper. Tell the student: *Escucha las palabras que te voy a leer y escribe **el primer** sonido que oigas.* Write the student's responses over the words.

| ____/5 | mal | pon | tus | leo | iba |
|---|---|---|---|---|---|

## PART M **Final sounds**

Tell the student: *Escucha las palabras que te voy a leer y escribe **el último** sonido que oigas.*

| ____/5 | sin | mes | por | uva | hace |
|---|---|---|---|---|---|

## PART N **Whole words**

Tell the student: *Escucha las palabras que te voy a leer y escribe **la palabra entera**.*

| ____/5 | leche | baño | carro | hijo | cocina |
|---|---|---|---|---|---|
| ____/5 | parque | rompen | triste | voy | abuelos |

____/10

# CORE Spanish Phonics Survey—Student Material

## Alphabet and Letter Sounds

PART A

| | | | | | | |
|---|---|---|---|---|---|---|
| D | L | N | S | V | Z | J |
| T | Y | P | C | M | CH | Ñ |
| LL | G | F | B | Q | R | X |

PART B

| | | | | | | |
|---|---|---|---|---|---|---|
| d | l | n | s | v | z | j |
| t | y | p | c | m | ch | ñ |
| ll | g | f | b | q | r | x |

PART C

| | | | | |
|---|---|---|---|---|
| O | A | I | U | E |
| o | a | i | u | e |

PART D

| | | | | | | |
|---|---|---|---|---|---|---|
| d | l | n | s | v | z | j |
| t | y | p | c | m | ch | ñ |
| ll | g | f | b | q | r | x |

CORE Spanish Phonics Survey—Student Material, Page 1

# CORE Spanish Phonics Survey—Student Material

## Reading and Decoding

PART E

| | | | | |
|---|---|---|---|---|
| su | yo | luna | techo | jefe |
| ne | cu | mepa | sila | rago |

PART F

| | | | | |
|---|---|---|---|---|
| año | iba | oro | ella | ocho |
| oba | udo | eca | alle | imo |

PART G

| | | | | |
|---|---|---|---|---|
| sol | pan | tambor | juntos | artes |
| jez | dor | cambal | portir | entad |

## PART H

| | | | | |
|---|---|---|---|---|
| brazo | grillo | clase | pluma | globo |
| flece | crima | bruco | clopo | pleso |

## PART I

| | | | | |
|---|---|---|---|---|
| cae | lee | hoy | ruido | quiere |
| cheo | moa | ray | yugia | vaida |

## PART J

| | | | | |
|---|---|---|---|---|
| puerta | siempre | treinta | cuando | viento |
| pueste | guanto | tiemba | reinda | fianco |

PART K

| | | |
|---|---|---|
| carretera | calabaje | taregudo |
| compartes | rescardan | zarcambol |
| gigante | caroce | giloga |
| problema | frascura | tropazo |
| soleado | paonante | nealtura |
| ciudades | jeralio | laicando |
| bailaremos | gilacioso | pauladista |
| descompuesto | remolante | excavario |

# CORE Graded High-Frequency Word Survey

**SKILL ASSESSED**

## High-Frequency Words

**Grade Level**

K–4, older struggling readers

**Language**

English

**Grouping**

Individual

**Approximate Testing Time**

5–7 Minutes

**Materials**

- Teacher Record Form (p. 65)
- Student Material (pp. 66–67)

**Source**

Consortium On Reading Excellence (CORE)

**WHAT** The *CORE Graded High-Frequency Word Survey* consists of five word lists that assess student recognition of words occurring very frequently in text at each of Grades K through 4. The lists take into account the changing frequency of particular words from grade to grade and reflect the high-frequency words encountered by students as they progress through the grades. Words that occur with high frequency at all grade levels (i.e. *the, and, is, you, was,* etc.) were included for consideration only in the grade where they first occur with very high frequency. All words are among the first 160 most frequent words in *The Educator's Word Frequency Guide* (Zeno et al. 1995) that students in the United States are likely to encounter in text from Grade 1 through college.

The *High-Frequency Word Survey* can be used as a screening measure, and also as an outcome measure, providing data about growth at the end of an instructional period. As a specific diagnostic skills test, it can indicate whether or not a student needs instruction in selected high-frequency words at his or her grade level, or if further assessment is needed. It may also be used to track progress from earlier level lists to grade level mastery. Testing students on lists beyond their grade level does not yield meaningful information because this measure is designed only to detect a lack of sufficient knowledge of high-frequency words typically included in a text at the specific grade level.

**WHY** High-frequency words are phonetically regular and irregular words that appear often in printed text and therefore are crucial for comprehension. Automatic recognition of these high-frequency words affects the flow and coherence of text and are therefore important contributors to reading fluency (Blevins 2006).

**HOW** For screening or specific skills use, administer the word list at the student's grade level and continue to monitor student progress to mastery. The grade level for each list corresponds to the Roman numeral on each; the Grade 3 list is List III, for example.

Place the Student Material word list in front of the student and ask the student to read the words out loud. Mark errors on the Record Form by crossing out missed words. If the student hesitates more than 3 seconds before saying a word, it is considered an error. If a student misses more than three words, more information about the student's ability can be gained by administering the word list for each preceding grade until reaching a list on which the student performs satisfactorily.

**WHAT IT MEANS** Score each list completed by student as shown below.

| CORE Graded High-Frequency Word Mastery Level | | |
|---|---|---|
| | List K (10 Item) | Lists I-IV (24 Item) |
| Benchmark | 9+ | 21+ |
| Strategic | 6–8 | 18–20 |
| Intensive | 0–5 | 0–17 |

**WHAT'S NEXT?** If students do poorly on this assessment, further assessment is necessary to indentify underlying causes. The *CORE Phonics Survey* will identify whether or not poor decoding skill knowledge is causing poor word recognition, and the *CORE Phonological Segmentation Test* or the *CORE Phoneme Segmentation Test* will isolate phoneme awareness as an underlying factor. However, since it is important that students master these words, explicit instruction and ample practice must be provided in them, particularly those that are irregular words. Methods for teaching irregular words include the *Sound-Out Strategy* and the *Spell-Out Strategy*, both of which can be found in the *Teaching Reading Sourcebook.*

# CORE Graded High-Frequency Word Survey–Record Form

Name ____________________ Grade ________ Date __________

| List K | List I | List II | List III | List IV |
|---|---|---|---|---|
| a | will | all | make | which |
| can | and | your | their | after |
| I | up | this | about | much |
| to | me | so | now | thought |
| in | are | how | an | each |
| the | was | as | who | years |
| is | then | were | other | also |
| on | of | out | been | long |
| you | she | be | things | another |
| it | said | could | by | first |
| | we | if | very | water |
| | at | from | day | never |
| | my | down | know | around |
| | what | when | or | than |
| | but | get | made | because |
| | do | had | over | only |
| | they | them | think | called |
| | for | him | many | may |
| | have | would | some | these |
| | that | just | time | before |
| | he | his | more | work |
| | not | like | way | even |
| | with | there | people | most |
| | her | one | too | through |
| **# correct** ______ | **# correct** ______ | **# correct** ______ | **# correct** ______ | **# correct** ______ |
| **Benchmark** ❑ | **Benchmark** ❑ | **Benchmark** ❑ | **Benchmark** ❑ | **Benchmark** ❑ |
| **Strategic** ❑ | **Strategic** ❑ | **Strategic** ❑ | **Strategic** ❑ | **Strategic** ❑ |
| **Intensive** ❑ | **Intensive** ❑ | **Intensive** ❑ | **Intensive** ❑ | **Intensive** ❑ |

**Observations**:

______________________________________________________________

______________________________________________________________

# CORE Graded High-Frequency Word Survey—Student Material

| List K | List I | List II |
|---|---|---|
| a | will | all |
| can | and | your |
| I | up | this |
| to | me | so |
| in | are | how |
| the | was | as |
| is | then | were |
| on | of | out |
| you | she | be |
| it | said | could |
| | we | if |
| | at | from |
| | my | down |
| | what | when |
| | but | get |
| | do | had |
| | they | them |
| | for | him |
| | have | would |
| | that | just |
| | he | his |
| | not | like |
| | with | there |
| | her | one |

| List III | List IV |
|---|---|
| make | which |
| their | after |
| about | much |
| now | thought |
| an | each |
| who | years |
| other | also |
| been | long |
| things | another |
| by | first |
| very | water |
| day | never |
| know | around |
| or | than |
| made | because |
| over | only |
| think | called |
| many | may |
| some | these |
| time | before |
| more | work |
| way | even |
| people | most |
| too | through |

# San Diego Quick Assessment of Reading Ability

**SKILL ASSESSED**

Word Recognition

**Grade Level**

K–11

**Language**

English

**Grouping**

Individual

**Approximate Testing Time**

10 Minutes

**Materials**

- Record Form (p. 70)
- Student Material (pp. 71–72)

**Source**

From "The Graded Word List: Quick Gauge of Reading Ability" by Margaret La Pray et al.

**WHAT** This test measures the recognition of words out of context. Generally, proficient readers read as accurately both in and out of context. The test consists of 13 graded word lists from preprimer to eleventh grade. The words within each list are of about equal difficulty.

**WHY** Weak readers overrely on context and recognize words in context more easily than out of context.

**HOW** Students will read word lists of increasing difficulty until they reach a "frustration" level (three or more errors in one list). Start with a list that is two or three grade levels below the student's current placement. Give the student the test sheet and say: *There are a number of short word lists on this page.* (Point to the list you are starting with.) *Start with this list and read each word aloud. Even if you're not sure what a word is, try it anyway. Ready? Start now.* If the student pauses before attempting to pronounce a word, encourage them to try, but after five seconds tell the student to move on to the next word.

If the student finishes the starting list with fewer than three errors, say: *Good. Now try the next list.* (Point to the next list.) Have student continue reading successive lists until student makes three or more errors in one list. Stop testing when student completes that list by saying: *Good. You can stop now.*

CONTINUED ▷

**WHAT IT MEANS** Each list completed by the student can be scored as shown below.

| Errors/List | Reading Level |
|---|---|
| 1 Error | Independent Level |
| 2 Errors | Instructional Level |
| 3 Errors | Frustration Level |

**Student Reading Level**

The student's reading level is the last grade-level word list in which the student reads eight or more words correctly.

CORE's *Teaching Reading Sourcebook,* Second Edition

**WHAT'S NEXT?** If students do poorly on this assessment, further assessment is necessary to identify underlying causes. The *CORE Phonics Survey* will identify whether or not poor decoding skill knowledge is causing poor word recognition, and the *CORE Phonological Segmentation Test* or the *CORE Phoneme Segmentation Test* will isolate phoneme awareness as an underlying factor.

# San Diego Quick Assessment—Record Form

Name________________________ Grade________ Date__________

Directions: Begin with a list that is at least two or three sets below the student's grade level. Have the student read each word aloud in that list. Continue until the student makes three or more errors in a list.

Reading Levels: One error, independent level; two errors, instructional level; three errors, frustration level. When testing is completed, record the highest grade level in each of these categories in the spaces below.

**Independent**__________ **Instructional** 2 **Frustration**__________

| Preprimer | Primer | Grade 1 | Grade 2 | Grade 3 |
|---|---|---|---|---|
| see | you | road | our | city |
| play | come | live | please place | middle |
| me | not | thank think | myself | moment |
| at | with | when win | town | frightened |
| run | jump | bigger | early | exclaimed |
| go | help | how | send | several |
| and | is | always | wide wind | lonely |
| look | work | night | believe | drew |
| can | are | spring | quietly quickly | since |
| here | this | today | carefully carfully | straight |
| **# of errors** | **# of errors** | **# of errors** 2 | **# of errors** 6 | **# of errors** |

| Grade 4 | Grade 5 | Grade 6 | Grade 7 |
|---|---|---|---|
| decided | scanty | bridge | amber |
| served | business | commercial | dominion |
| amazed | develop | abolish | sundry |
| silent | considered | trucker | capillary |
| wrecked | discussed | apparatus | impetuous |
| improved | behaved | elementary | blight |
| certainly | splendid | comment | wrest |
| entered | acquainted | necessity | enumerate |
| realized | escaped | gallery | daunted |
| interrupted | grim | relativity | condescend |
| **# of errors** | **# of errors** | **# of errors** | **# of errors** |

| Grade 8 | Grade 9 | Grade 10 | Grade 11 |
|---|---|---|---|
| capacious | conscientious | zany | galore |
| limitation | isolation | jerkin | rotunda |
| pretext | molecule | nausea | capitalism |
| intrigue | ritual | gratuitous | prevaricate |
| delusion | momentous | linear | visible |
| immaculate | vulnerable | inept | exonerate |
| ascent | kinship | legality | superannuate |
| acrid | conservatism | aspen | luxuriate |
| binocular | jaunty | amnesty | piebald |
| embankment | inventive | barometer | crunch |
| **# of errors** | **# of errors** | **# of errors** | **# of errors** |

# San Diego Quick Assessment—Student Material

| | | | | |
|---|---|---|---|---|
| see | you | road | our | city |
| play | come | live | please | middle |
| me | not | thank | myself | moment |
| at | with | when | town | frightened |
| run | jump | bigger | early | exclaimed |
| go | help | how | send | several |
| and | is | always | wide | lonely |
| look | work | night | believe | drew |
| can | are | spring | quietly | since |
| here | this | today | carefully | straight |

---

| | | | |
|---|---|---|---|
| decided | scanty | bridge | amber |
| served | business | commercial | dominion |
| amazed | develop | abolish | sundry |
| silent | considered | trucker | capillary |
| wrecked | discussed | apparatus | impetuous |
| improved | behaved | elementary | blight |
| certainly | splendid | comment | wrest |
| entered | acquainted | necessity | enumerate |
| realized | escaped | gallery | daunted |
| interrupted | grim | relativity | condescend |

San Diego Quick Assessment of Reading Ability—Student Material, Page 1

# San Diego Quick Assessment—Student Material

| | | | |
|---|---|---|---|
| capacious | conscientious | zany | galore |
| limitation | isolation | jerkin | rotunda |
| pretext | molecule | nausea | capitalism |
| intrigue | ritual | gratuitous | prevaricate |
| delusion | momentous | linear | visible |
| immaculate | vulnerable | inept | exonerate |
| ascent | kinship | legality | superannuate |
| acrid | conservatism | aspen | luxuriate |
| binocular | jaunty | amnesty | piebald |
| embankment | inventive | barometer | crunch |

# CORE Spanish Spelling Inventory

**SKILL ASSESSED**

Spelling

**Grade Level**

K–6

**Language**

Spanish

**Grouping**

Group/Individual

**Approximate Testing Time**

10–15 Minutes

**Materials**

- Pencil or pen
- Lined paper
- Spelling Skills Summary (p. 76)

**Author**

Jacalyn Mahler

**WHAT** The *CORE Spanish Spelling Inventory* consists of a single list of 20 Spanish words. The word list is administered in the same way as a standard spelling test. The words in the list represent a wide range of important phonetic concepts, sequenced to represent simple to more complex word structure and orthographic features. Following administration of the inventory, the student's application of specific spelling skills is summarized.

**WHY** Examination of a student's spelling shows the extent of the student's orthographic knowledge. The *CORE Spanish Spelling Inventory* shows how well the student is able to apply rules of phoneme/grapheme correspondence and accentuation. It also measures a student's spelling knowledge of high-utility words that do not follow predictable spelling patterns. Spelling skills are intimately tied to skills used in reading. Identifying the range of the student's skills assists in planning appropriate spelling and reading instruction.

**HOW** Each student should have a pencil or pen and a sheet of writing paper. Instructions for administering each inventory are included with the word list. Group size for young students should not exceed six. For students, such as those in second grade and above, who are capable of attending to a task in a large group setting, the inventory can be administered quickly and easily to the entire class.

Before beginning the inventory, it is important to let the students know that they will not be graded on their performance and that the reason for administering the inventory is to help plan instruction.

After administering each set of five words, inspect the students' papers. If the majority of students have misspelled three out of five words, stop testing. Otherwise continue with the next set of words. Others who have yet to reach the three-out-of-five criterion can complete the remaining sections as a separate group.

**WHAT IT MEANS** There are three steps to evaluating a student's spelling once administration is complete:

1. Score the student's paper for number correct. Words with letter reversals, but otherwise spelled correctly, should be counted correct. Although individual students' spelling development and instructional sequences vary, the following can be used as general grade-level expectations of performance:

| Grade | Number Correct |
|---|---|
| K | 1 – 2 |
| 1 | 3 – 5 |
| 2 | 7 – 10 |
| 3 | 12 – 15 |

| Grade | Number Correct |
|---|---|
| 4 | 15 – 18 |
| 5 | 20 |
| 6 | 20 |
| | |

2. Make a copy of the Spelling Skills Summary for each student. There are 17 skills listed on the summary, followed by the words from the inventory that measure those particular spelling skills. Locate on the summary each word the student misspelled and write the invented spelling above it. (Note that since many of the words from the inventory measure more than one spelling skill, they are repeated.) For the first five skills, award the student one point for correctly using the phonetic element, even if the word is otherwise misspelled.

3. Use the skill groupings on the summary to determine if there is a pattern to the student's misspellings. For example, a student may always use *s* to represent the phoneme /s/ or consistently omit the final consonant in closed syllables. Completion of the Spelling Skills Summary will show what the student knows as well as the elements that require further review and instruction.

CORE's *Teaching Reading Sourcebook,* Second Edition

**WHAT'S NEXT?** Based on the results, the teacher can use this information to design word lists and sorting activities that will match each student's development.

# CORE Spanish Spelling Inventory

This is a short spelling inventory to help you learn about your students' orthographic knowledge. The results of the spelling inventory will have implications for reading, writing, vocabulary, and spelling instruction.

Instructions: Let the students know that you are administering this inventory to learn about how they spell. Let them know that this is not a test, but that they will be helping you be a better teacher by doing their best.

Possible script: *Voy a pedirles que deletreen algunas palabras. Traten de escribirlas lo mejor que puedan. Algunas palabras serán fáciles; otras serán más difíciles. Si no saben cómo deletrear alguna palabra, escríbanla lo mejor que puedan. Escriban todos los sonidos que sientan y oigan.*

Say the word once, read the sentence, and then say the word again. Work with groups of five words. You may want to stop testing when students miss three out of five words. See the text for further instructions on administration and interpretation.

Have the students check their papers for their names and date.

**Set One**

| | | |
|---|---|---|
| 1. noche | Por la *noche*, duermo en mi cama. | noche |
| 2. corre | Estela *corre* a su casa porque tiene prisa. | corre |
| 3. pequeño | Tenemos un gatito *pequeño*. | pequeño |
| 4. jugo | ¿Te gusta el *jugo* de naranja? | jugo |
| 5. sigue | Su perrito le *sigue* a todas partes. | sigue |

**Set Two**

| | | |
|---|---|---|
| 6. vecino | Desde mi ventana se ve el jardín de mi *vecino*. | vecino |
| 7. ayuda | Necesito *ayuda* para mover la mesa. | ayuda |
| 8. cerca | La escuela queda *cerca* de mi casa. | cerca |
| 9. gigante | Leí un cuento sobre un *gigante* más alto que una torre. | gigante |
| 10. buscan | Las palomas *buscan* comida en el parque. | buscan |

**Set Three**

| | | |
|---|---|---|
| 11. triste | Carlos se puso *triste* cuando su amigo se fue. | triste |
| 12. hablaba | Mi abuelo siempre *hablaba* de cuando él era joven. | hablaba |
| 13. estoy | *Estoy* muy contenta porque es mi cumpleaños. | estoy |
| 14. hueso | Ese perro escondió el *hueso*. | hueso |
| 15. ciudad | Los Ángeles es una *ciudad* muy grande. | ciudad |

**Set Four**

| | | |
|---|---|---|
| 16. avión | Fuimos en *avión* a Venezuela. | avión |
| 17. lápiz | Me gusta escribir con *lápiz* porque se puede borrar. | lápiz |
| 18. llovía | *Llovía* tanto que el garaje se llenó de agua. | llovía |
| 19. lámpara | La *lámpara* de mi cuarto da mucha luz. | lámpara |
| 20. desayuno | Mamá prepara el *desayuno* a las siete de la mañana. | desayuno |

# CORE Spanish Spelling Inventory
# Spelling Skills Summary

Name______________________________ Grade________ Date__________

_____/3 consonant digraphs *noche, corre, llovía*

_____/4 phoneme /k/ *corre, pequeño, cerca, buscan*

_____/1 phoneme /rr/ *corre*

_____/3 phoneme /g/ *jugo, sigue, gigante*

_____/1 phoneme /x/, spelled j in *ja, jo, ju jugo*

_____/6 phoneme /s/, spelled s *sigue, buscan, triste, estoy, hueso, desayuno*

_____/5 phoneme /b/, spelled b and v *vecino, buscan, hablaba, avión, llovía*

_____/1 phoneme /x/, spelled g in *ge, gi gigante*

_____/3 phoneme /y/, spelled ll* and y *ayuda, llovía, desayuno*

_____/4 phoneme /s/, spelled c in *ce, ci* and z *vecino, cerca, ciudad, lápiz*

_____/9 closed syllables *cerca, gigante, buscan, triste, estoy, ciudad, avión, lápiz, lámpara*

_____/2 blends *triste, hablaba*

_____/2 silent h *hablaba, hueso*

_____/1 words with m before p and b *lámpara*

_____/3 diphthongs *estoy, hueso, ciudad*

_____/4 words requiring written accent mark

- aguda ending in n *avión*
- llana ending in a consonant other than n or s *lápiz*
- esdrújula *lámpara*
- dissolved diphthong *avión, llovía*

_____/1 words with prefix *desayuno*

*Although *ll* and *y* represent two distinct phonemes, most Spanish-speakers pronounce both as /y/.

# MASI-R Oral Reading Fluency Measures

**SKILL ASSESSED**

## Oral Reading Fluency

**Grade Level**

1–6

**Language**

English

**Grouping**

Individual

**Approximate Testing Time**

10–15 Minutes

**Materials**

- Three Teacher Passages per grade-level (pp. 83-100)
- Three Student Passages per grade-level (pp. 102-119)
- Timer or stopwatch

**Source**

MASI-R: Multi-Level Academic Skills Inventory – Revised © Kenneth W. Howell, Michelle K. Hosp, John L. Hosp & Mada Kay Morehead (Original Edition: Kenneth W. Howell, Stanley H. Zucker & Mada Kay Morehead)
For information:
MASI@comcast.net
www.cbEval.org

**WHAT** The *MASI-R Oral Reading Fluency Measures* represent a portion of the Multi-Level Academic Skills Inventory, Revised (MASI-R) by Howell, et al. The measures consist of Student and Teacher record versions of three oral reading fluency (ORF) curriculum-based measures (CBM) at each of Grades 1–6. These CBM measures are designed to sample a student's oral reading fluency and may be used up to three times a year. The results of the screening can help determine if there is reason to further explore student educational needs or to adjust curriculum or instruction.

**WHY** The literature documenting the relationship between reading fluency and reading comprehension is extensive, and indicates a linkage that is both causal and reciprocal. Oral reading fluency is a general outcome measure. It makes use of the complex and interactive tasks at the upper levels of reading skill sequences, tasks that depend on the use of many lower-level and prerequisite skills. Success on a general outcome measure suggests success on the prerequisites, making ORF a proxy for multiple reading skills and processes. When students read passages accurately and fluently, it can be assumed that they have mastered the lower-level skills and processes that are required, but are not explicitly observed, during passage reading.

**HOW** There are three Student Passages and three Teacher Passage and Direction pages for each of grade levels 1–6. Each Student Passage and Teacher Passage is on a separate page. Each Teacher Passage has a code identifying the passage, which should match the one on the Student Passage. Each also has a place for recording information about the student, conditions of assessment and results. Administer all three passages in one session and then calculate the median score. Types of errors are noted on page 79.

The directions to be read to the student are given on each Teacher Passage and Direction page. The directions are the same for each passage, but are to be read every time a passage is administered. The directions are:

1. Place the copy of the student passage in front of the student.

2. Place the teacher/examiner copy on clipboard so the student can not see it.

3. Say: *When I say* begin *start reading aloud at the top of the page. Read across the page* (point to the first line of the passage). *Begin.* (Trigger stopwatch or timer for one minute)

4. Follow along on the teacher/examiner copy as the student reads and put a slash (/) through any incorrect words.

5. At the end of one minute, say: *Thank You.* Mark the last word read with a bracket.

Note that if a student hesitates to correctly pronounce a word, after three seconds the student is told the word and an error is scored. Note also that the directions say *Begin* to start and *Thank you* to finish. Do not substitute language that might suggest the fluency assessment is a race, such as *Ready, get set, GO!* or *Stop!*

Be sure you are familiar with the timer and have a way to mark errors out of range of the student's vision (e.g., behind a clipboard or sitting to the side).

There are three calculations necessary to determine student results for each passage: **rate correct per minute (wcpm), rate incorrect per minute (wepm), and accuracy.**

Calculate a student's rate correct, or fluency, on each passage by subtracting the number of errors from the total number of words read in one minute. Enter that number in the box labeled **rate correct** on the Teacher Passage and Direction page. Enter the number of errors in one minute in the space labeled **rate incorrect.** Determine accuracy by counting the number of errors prior to the 100th word mark ▲ and subtracting this number from 100. Enter this in the space labeled **accuracy**. The 100th word mark ▲ appears only on the Teacher Passage and Direction page. For reporting purposes,on the forms in the Appendix, use the **median score** for each parameter from the scores on all three passages. The median score is the middle (**not average**) score.

The MASI-R passages provided here have not been explicitly aligned with any particular published instructional program, nor does their inclusion in this publication constitute an endorsement of other tests or measures in this publication.

| An error is marked for each of the following: |
|---|
| • Word is skipped |
| • Word is not pronounced correctly within 3 seconds |
| • Word is mispronounced |
| • Word is repeatedly mispronounced later in text, each instance |
| **The following is not marked as an error:** |
| • Student self-corrects word within 3 seconds |
| • Variations in pronunciation due to dialect |
| • Insertions/added words |

**WHAT IT MEANS** Refer to the Hasbrouck, & Tindal 2005 Oral Reading Fluency Norms on page 80 to determine the percentile rank of individual student scores for each grade level. For a discussion of performance criteria for fluency and fluency scores, see pages A18-A21 in the Appendix.

**WHAT'S NEXT?** Refer to the Diagnostic Plan for each grade level, on pages 14 to 15, to determine appropriate instruction or further diagnostic measures. Also, see pages A18–A21 for further discussion of problem solving student educational needs. Students with performance on the MASI-R Measures falling below the 50th percentile of the Hasbrouck & Tindal 2005 Oral Reading Norms may need this attention.

## Oral Reading Fluency Norms Grades 1–8 2005

Compiled by Jan Hasbrouck, Ph. D. & Gerald Tindal, Ph.D.

Raw scores are shown in the "Fall," "Winter" and "Spring" columns; corresponding Percentile ranks are shown in the "Percentile" column.

| GRADE | PERCENTILE | FALL WCPM* | WINTER WCPM* | SPRING WCPM* |
|---|---|---|---|---|
| 1 | 90 | | 81 | 111 |
| | 75 | | 47 | 82 |
| | 50 | | 23 | 53 |
| | 25 | | 12 | 27 |
| | 10 | | 6 | 15 |
| 2 | 90 | 106 | 125 | 142 |
| | 75 | 79 | 100 | 117 |
| | 50 | 51 | 72 | 89 |
| | 25 | 25 | 42 | 61 |
| | 10 | 11 | 18 | 31 |
| 3 | 90 | 128 | 146 | 162 |
| | 75 | 99 | 120 | 137 |
| | 50 | 71 | 92 | 107 |
| | 25 | 44 | 62 | 78 |
| | 10 | 21 | 36 | 48 |
| 4 | 90 | 145 | 166 | 180 |
| | 75 | 119 | 139 | 152 |
| | 50 | 94 | 112 | 123 |
| | 25 | 68 | 87 | 98 |
| | 10 | 45 | 61 | 72 |
| 5 | 90 | 166 | 182 | 194 |
| | 75 | 139 | 156 | 168 |
| | 50 | 110 | 127 | 139 |
| | 25 | 85 | 99 | 109 |
| | 10 | 61 | 74 | 83 |
| 6 | 90 | 177 | 195 | 204 |
| | 75 | 153 | 167 | 177 |
| | 50 | 127 | 140 | 150 |
| | 25 | 98 | 111 | 122 |
| | 10 | 68 | 82 | 93 |
| 7 | 90 | 180 | 192 | 202 |
| | 75 | 156 | 165 | 177 |
| | 50 | 128 | 136 | 150 |
| | 25 | 102 | 109 | 123 |
| | 10 | 79 | 88 | 98 |
| 8 | 90 | 185 | 199 | 199 |
| | 75 | 161 | 173 | 177 |
| | 50 | 133 | 146 | 151 |
| | 25 | 106 | 115 | 124 |
| | 10 | 77 | 84 | 97 |

***WCPM: Words correct per minute.**

Table adapted and summarized from Behavioral Research & Teaching (2005, January). Oral Reading Fluency: 90 Years of Assessment (BRT Technical Report No. 33), Eugene, OR: Author
www.brtprojects.org/techreports/ORF_90yrs_Intro_TechRpt33.pdf
See also: Hasbrouck, J & Tindal, G. (2006). Oral Reading Fluency Norms, *The Reading Teacher*, 59(7), 636-644.

# MASI–R

# ORAL READING FLUENCY MEASURES

## TEACHER PASSAGES AND DIRECTIONS

MAKE A COPY OF THE APPROPRIATE PAGE

FOR EACH STUDENT YOU ARE TESTING.

| Student: | Grade: | Rate correct: (words correct in 1 minute) | Rate incorrect: (words incorrect in 1 minute) |
|---|---|---|---|
| Examiner: | Date: | Accuracy (words correct in the first 100 words = ▲) | |

## Teacher Passage & Directions: 1-A

1) Place the copy of the student passage in front of the student.
2) Place the teacher/examiner copy on clipboard so the student cannot see it.
3) Say: *When I say* begin *start reading aloud at the top of the page. Read across the page* (point to the first line of the passage). ***Begin.*** (Trigger stopwatch or timer for 1 minute.)
4) Follow along on the teacher/examiner copy as the student reads and put a slash (/) through any incorrect words.
5) At the end of one minute, say: *Thank You*. Mark the last word read with a bracket (]).

**NOTE:** If a student hesitates to correctly pronounce a word within **three seconds**, the student is told the word and an error is scored.

Part of the park is for play. Some parts are not for 12
play. Cars drive down the street. Don't play there. People 22
walk on the sidewalks. Don't play there. 29

Pick a part of the park for play. There are many pretty 41
places. People play ball. Some people just sit. Some people 51
read books. Dogs run after birds. There are green trees. 61
Pick a part like that. 66

Do you need help? There are signs to help you. They 77
say where to play. No cars are there. There are just boys 89
and girls. They run and jump. They play with each other. ▲ 100
There is room for fun. 105

| Student: | Grade: | Rate correct: (words correct in 1 minute) | Rate incorrect: (words incorrect in 1 minute) |
|---|---|---|---|
| Examiner: | Date: | Accuracy (words correct in the first 100 words = ▲) | |

## Teacher Passage & Directions: 1-B

1) Place the copy of the student passage in front of the student.
2) Place the teacher/examiner copy on clipboard so the student cannot see it.
3) Say: *When I say* begin *start reading aloud at the top of the page. Read across the page* (point to the first line of the passage). *Begin.* (Trigger stopwatch or timer for 1 minute.)
4) Follow along on the teacher/examiner copy as the student reads and put a slash (/) through any incorrect words.
5) At the end of one minute, say: *Thank You*. Mark the last word read with a bracket (]).

**NOTE:** If a student hesitates to correctly pronounce a word within **three seconds**, the student is told the word and an error is scored.

One day a mouse came to our house. She was in a box. 13
That box was her home. She ate there and went to sleep 25
there. She was a little mouse with a little house. 35
A cat lives at our house too. The cat saw the mouse. 47
He sat still. He did not move. The mouse did not run. The 60
cat looked hard at the mouse. "I will eat you, mouse," the 72
cat was thinking. 75
The mouse was thinking too. "I see you, cat, and you 86
are bad news!" 89
I took the mouse to my room. No more cats for ▲ this 101
mouse! 102

| Student: | Grade: | Rate correct: (words correct in 1 minute) | Rate incorrect: (words incorrect in 1 minute) |
|---|---|---|---|
| Examiner: | Date: | Accuracy (words correct in the first 100 words = ▲) | |

# Teacher Passage & Directions: 1-C

1) Place the copy of the student passage in front of the student.
2) Place the teacher/examiner copy on clipboard so the student cannot see it.
3) Say: *When I say* begin *start reading aloud at the top of the page. Read across the page* (point to the first line of the passage). *Begin.* (Trigger stopwatch or timer for 1 minute.)
4) Follow along on the teacher/examiner copy as the student reads and put a slash (/) through any incorrect words.
5) At the end of one minute, say: *Thank You*. Mark the last word read with a bracket (]).

**NOTE**: If a student hesitates to correctly pronounce a word within **three seconds**, the student is told the word and an error is scored.

My dog waits by the door. He waits for me to let him 13
out. He wants to go out and play. 21
I look outside. It is fall. Some trees are yellow and 32
some trees are red. Some trees are still green. We will go 44
out and play. We like to play by the trees. 54
My dog runs by the big trees. He is happy and I am 67
happy too. We run and run. Then we rest. I tell him things. 80
He must not run into the street. There may be cars. He 92
listens to me and he stays with me. ▲He is my dog. 104

| Student: | Grade: | Rate correct: (words correct in 1 minute) | Rate incorrect: (words incorrect in 1 minute) |
|---|---|---|---|
| Examiner: | Date: | Accuracy (words correct in the first 100 words = ▲) | |

## Teacher Passage & Directions: 2-A

1) Place the copy of the student passage in front of the student.
2) Place the teacher/examiner copy on clipboard so the student cannot see it.
3) Say: *When I say* begin *start reading aloud at the top of the page. Read across the page* (point to the first line of the passage). ***Begin.*** (Trigger stopwatch or timer for 1 minute.)
4) Follow along on the teacher/examiner copy as the student reads and put a slash (/) through any incorrect words.
5) At the end of one minute, say: *Thank You*. Mark the last word read with a bracket (]).

**NOTE:** If a student hesitates to correctly pronounce a word within **three seconds**, the student is told the word and an error is scored.

Mr. Lee sometimes acts funny. The thing to remember 9
is this. It's almost always just an act. He seems like a silly 22
bear. But he can be a real friend. I found that out last 35
summer. 36

Jim and I had decided to clean up tree branches. There 47
had been a big storm the night before. Little branches were 58
all over the grass and sidewalks. 64

We would knock on someone's door. Then we would ask 74
them about cleaning up their yard. Most people asked about 84
our rates. Most of the time, we would let them decide. Most 96
people were fair. No ▲ one tried to cheat us. 105

We had just finished cleaning up one yard. But the owner 116
wouldn't pay us and wouldn't tell us what we did wrong. 127
"It wasn't worth it," he said. 133

Mr. Lee was walking by and heard the man. His face 144
got silly. His eyes popped out and his cheeks got red. He 156
marched right up to the man's door and knocked hard. When the 168
man saw him he started to laugh. "That was worth it!" he 180
said. Mr. Lee made him laugh and we got paid. 190

Mr. Lee's funny act really helped us out that time! 200

| Student: | Grade: | Rate correct: (words correct in 1 minute) | Rate incorrect: (words incorrect in 1 minute) |
| --- | --- | --- | --- |
| Examiner: | Date: | Accuracy (words correct in the first 100 words = ▲) | |

## Teacher Passage & Directions: 2-B

1) Place the copy of the student passage in front of the student.
2) Place the teacher/examiner copy on clipboard so the student cannot see it.
3) Say: *When I say* begin *start reading aloud at the top of the page. Read across the page* (point to the first line of the passage). ***Begin.*** (Trigger stopwatch or timer for 1 minute.)
4) Follow along on the teacher/examiner copy as the student reads and put a slash (/) through any incorrect words.
5) At the end of one minute, say: *Thank You*. Mark the last word read with a bracket (]).

**NOTE:** If a student hesitates to correctly pronounce a word within **three seconds**, the student is told the word and an error is scored.

| Passage | Words |
| --- | --- |
| Last Sunday afternoon, there was a party for Ben. | 9 |
| First, Mom baked a big cake. She fixed something for us to | 21 |
| drink and we put the food in a pretty basket. We put in | 34 |
| some balloons too. Ben likes balloons. Then I got Ben and | 45 |
| we were ready to go! | 50 |
| We walked to a place with big trees all around. It was | 62 |
| a forest, I think. We looked and looked. At last, we found | 74 |
| a nice spot with green grass. Ben rested and we fixed a | 86 |
| place for the party. | 90 |
| Mom poured some milk for me. I blew up a ▲ big red | 102 |
| balloon for Ben. We sang "Happy Birthday" with loud, funny | 112 |
| voices. We ate white cake with dark icing and it was good! | 124 |
| Then Mom asked some crazy riddles. I told her some riddles | 135 |
| from school. We laughed and played some more games. | 144 |
| Then it was time for Ben's presents. Mom gave him a | 155 |
| new blanket with soft insides. I gave him a new blue hat | 167 |
| and lots of balloons. We both gave him birthday hugs. | 177 |
| We walked home happy. Ben was happy too, but he was | 188 |
| tired. I put him on the bed upstairs. That bear had some | 200 |
| birthday! | 201 |

| Student: | Grade: | Rate correct: (words correct in 1 minute) | Rate incorrect: (words incorrect in 1 minute) |
| --- | --- | --- | --- |
| Examiner: | Date: | Accuracy (words correct in the first 100 words = ▲) | |

## Teacher Passage & Directions: 2-C

1) Place the copy of the student passage in front of the student.
2) Place the teacher/examiner copy on clipboard so the student cannot see it.
3) Say: *When I say* begin *start reading aloud at the top of the page. Read across the page* (point to the first line of the passage). *Begin.* (Trigger stopwatch or timer for 1 minute.)
4) Follow along on the teacher/examiner copy as the student reads and put a slash (/) through any incorrect words.
5) At the end of one minute, say: *Thank You*. Mark the last word read with a bracket (]).

**NOTE:** If a student hesitates to correctly pronounce a word within **three seconds**, the student is told the word and an error is scored.

"Don't be afraid," Sue said. She had already started 9
up the mountain. Bill looked up. The moon was shining down. 20
The mountain seemed dark and scary. But he was not afraid. 31
"I feel fine," he said bravely. His voice sounded 40
little in the big night. He put his foot carefully on the 52
first rock. He pulled on the rope that was tied around his 64
waist. The other end of the rope was around Sue. 74
"Are you ready?" Sue asked. 79
"Ready," he said. One foot at a time, he started up 90
the mountain. 92
Somehow he and Sue had gotten lost. There ▲ was still 102
time to find the others. They would have to hurry. Morning 113
would come very soon now. 118
A rock slipped under his foot and fell below. 127
"Watch where you're going," Sue yelled. 133
"Sorry," he yelled back. His legs were starting to 142
hurt. There would be no stopping for rest on this climb. 153
They had to catch up with the others by daybreak. They 164
could not spend another day lost and without food. They 174
would have to keep climbing. 179
At last they reached the top. 185
"Look," Sue said quietly. There were the others, 193
asleep in their sleeping bags. 198
"We made it," Bill yelled. And he gave Sue a great 209
big hug! 211

| Student: | Grade: | Rate correct: (words correct in 1 minute) | Rate incorrect: (words incorrect in 1 minute) |
|---|---|---|---|
| Examiner: | Date: | Accuracy (words correct in the first 100 words = ▲) | |

## Teacher Passage & Directions: 3-A

1) Place the copy of the student passage in front of the student.
2) Place the teacher/examiner copy on clipboard so the student cannot see it.
3) Say: *When I say* begin *start reading aloud at the top of the page. Read across the page* (point to the first line of the passage). *Begin.* (Trigger stopwatch or timer for 1 minute.)
4) Follow along on the teacher/examiner copy as the student reads and put a slash (/) through any incorrect words.
5) At the end of one minute, say: *Thank You*. Mark the last word read with a bracket (]).

**NOTE:** If a student hesitates to correctly pronounce a word within **three seconds**, the student is told the word and an error is scored.

Ann read the words in the newspaper twice. 8
"Must Sell Motorcycle," she read. Ann had wanted 16
a motorcycle for a long time. 22

All the money she had was upstairs, all fifty 31
dollars of it. That would never be enough. But the owner 42
of this cycle had written, "Will consider trade." Ann knew 52
she was a good trader. So, she carefully punched in the 63
number from the ad. 67

"Oh, you need to talk to John," the woman who 77
answered said. "He's at city hospital in room 203." 86

Ann took the bus to the hospital that day. The door 97
to room 203 ▲ was half-open, so she knocked gently and 108
went in. "How did you break both arms?" she asked 118
when she saw the casts on the man. 126

"It wasn't easy," he laughed. "And I know your 135
next question," he added. "No, this didn't happen on the 145
motorcycle. I'm a very careful rider." 151

Then he jerked his arms and wiggled. "It's this 160
itching under the casts, "he explained. "It's driving me crazy!" 170

"Just a minute, I'll be right back," Ann said. 179

When she returned, she had a back-scratcher 187
from the gift shop. "Now, about that trade," she joked. 197

"That's not a bad idea," John said. Noting her 206
surprised look he explained "Seriously, I need some help. 215
If you help me, I'll trade for some lessons on the cycle." 227

"Great!" Ann said as she grinned from ear to ear. 237
"I guess I'm a better trader than I thought!" 246

| Student: | Grade: | Rate correct: (words correct in 1 minute) | Rate incorrect: (words incorrect in 1 minute) |
|---|---|---|---|
| Examiner: | Date: | Accuracy (words correct in the first 100 words = ▲) | |

## Teacher Passage & Directions: 3-B

1) Place the copy of the student passage in front of the student.
2) Place the teacher/examiner copy on clipboard so the student cannot see it.
3) Say: *When I say* begin *start reading aloud at the top of the page. Read across the page* (point to the first line of the passage). *Begin.* (Trigger stopwatch or timer for 1 minute.)
4) Follow along on the teacher/examiner copy as the student reads and put a slash (/) through any incorrect words.
5) At the end of one minute, say: *Thank You*. Mark the last word read with a bracket (]).

**NOTE:** If a student hesitates to correctly pronounce a word within **three seconds**, the student is told the word and an error is scored.

Yesterday, we had just settled down to a good game of 11
checkers. Then Pete said he was hungry for cookies. "Not 21
just any cookies, good cookies," he said. 28
So there we were. I was just getting ready to do my 40
famous triple jump and this guy gets hungry for cookies. 50
"Okay," I said, "let's go look." 56
Looking for something to eat with Pete is an 65
experience. You would normally look in a cookie jar or in a 77
cupboard for cookies, right? Pete looks in the freezer 86
first. I guess it makes sense. I mean, people usually 96
freeze things in quantity. ▲ And Pete is a quantity eater. 106
Next, we looked in the oven. Pete always hopes that 116
something will be left in the oven. I suggested that we might 128
take a look in the cupboard. If there's a pack of graham 140
crackers or a box of sugar cookies to be had, it's usually 152
in the cupboard. A careful search revealed no cookies. 161
My family does not own a cookie jar, so that left us 173
with no place to search next. Pete had that look in his 185
eye. He was getting ready to say, "I'm going home to get 197
something to eat." I could see my chance at a triple jump 209
was ready to walk out the door. 216
"Wait," I yelled. Pete froze in his tracks. "Have you 226
ever heard of applesauce wonders?" I asked. "They're just 235
delicious!" 236
I ignored his funny look and grabbed the jar of 246
applesauce. 247
"Makes my mouth water just to think about them," I 257
said. I spread the applesauce on a handy soda cracker. I 268
pushed a marshmallow on top of the whole thing and shoved 279
it into Pete's mouth. Now Pete asks for "applesauce 288
wonders" every time he comes to my house. 296

| Student: | Grade: | Rate correct: (words correct in 1 minute) | Rate incorrect: (words incorrect in 1 minute) |
|---|---|---|---|
| Examiner: | Date: | Accuracy (words correct in the first 100 words = ▲) | |

## Teacher Passage & Directions: 3-C

1) Place the copy of the student passage in front of the student.
2) Place the teacher/examiner copy on clipboard so the student cannot see it.
3) Say: *When I say* begin *start reading aloud at the top of the page. Read across the page* (point to the first line of the passage). *Begin.* (Trigger stopwatch or timer for 1 minute.)
4) Follow along on the teacher/examiner copy as the student reads and put a slash (/) through any incorrect words.
5) At the end of one minute, say: *Thank You*. Mark the last word read with a bracket (]).

**NOTE:** If a student hesitates to correctly pronounce a word within **three seconds**, the student is told the word and an error is scored.

It was shiny, silver, and beautiful. Kris had never seen 10
such a trumpet before. She rubbed her eyes, but it was 21
still there. It rested in its deep blue case like the treasure 33
of a king. 36

Kris picked it up and fingered the keys. The action 46
was perfect. She could imagine the sounds that would 55
flow from that instrument! 59

"It's beautiful, isn't it?" the shopkeeper said, peering 67
over her shoulder. "You know, that horn belongs in the 77
hands of a talented young person like you," he added. 87

Kris frowned slightly and put the trumpet back in its 97
case. "Thank you,"▲ she said softly. "Do you have any used 108
trumpets?" she asked, remembering the purpose of her trip. 117

"Come right this way," the shopkeeper said. He 125
motioned toward the rear of the small store. "These are my 136
nearly new models," he joked. 141

Kris looked at the three battered trumpets in the display 151
case. "Let me try that one," she said. She shuddered as she 163
played the scale. She tried the second, then the third. Each 174
horn was all right, she thought. It was just that she would not 187
be proud to play any of them in front of an audience. 199

"They're nothing like the silver one, are they?" the 208
shopkeeper said gently. "Is there any chance you could pay 218
for the silver one over time?" he asked. 226

Kris thought awhile, then shook her head. There really 235
wasn't a chance. She knew that. There was only so much 246
money for extras at her house. The trumpet was an extra. 257
She was lucky to have the money to get a horn at all. She 271
began to pull the money out of her back pocket. 281

"No," the shopkeeper said firmly. "I can't sell you 290
something you don't want. But I can sell you something you 301
do want," he added. "I will sell you the silver horn. Then you 314
can work here after school to pay for it. Is it a deal?" 327

| Student: | Grade: | Rate correct: (words correct in 1 minute) | Rate incorrect: (words incorrect in 1 minute) |
|---|---|---|---|
| Examiner: | Date: | Accuracy (words correct in the first 100 words = ▲) | |

## Teacher Passage & Directions: 4-A

1) Place the copy of the student passage in front of the student.
2) Place the teacher/examiner copy on clipboard so the student cannot see it.
3) Say: *When I say* begin *start reading aloud at the top of the page. Read across the page* (point to the first line of the passage). ***Begin.*** (Trigger stopwatch or timer for 1 minute.)
4) Follow along on the teacher/examiner copy as the student reads and put a slash (/) through any incorrect words.
5) At the end of one minute, say: *Thank You*. Mark the last word read with a bracket (]).

**NOTE:** If a student hesitates to correctly pronounce a word within **three seconds**, the student is told the word and an error is scored.

Chess was first played in Asia and India. When armies 10
moved in and out of these countries the soldiers learned the game 22
of chess. They then brought the game with them wherever their 33
battles took them. Many hundreds of years ago, as the armies 44
moved west, the pieces were given the names we know today. 55
The knight, the bishop, the king, the queen, and the rook 66
(or castle) were all part of life at that time. 76

Chess is played on a chess board which is set up in 88
squares of two colors. Each piece is only allowed to move a ▲ 100
certain way. Some pieces can only move forward. Some pieces 110
can only move diagonally. Like most games, the object of 120
chess is to win by beating the person you are playing against. 132
All pieces are used to protect the king. If a player loses the 145
king, he or she loses the game. 152

During the game pieces are moved in order to capture 162
the other player's pieces. Or they can be used to protect a more 175
valuable piece, like the king. Each player has a full set of pieces. 188
One player has the white pieces. One player has the black pieces. 200
It doesn't matter how many pieces are captured. What matters is 211
whether the king is lost. 216

Thinking ahead is the key to playing good chess. Each 226
player must study the way the other player moves. Then, if that 238
player makes a mistake, the first player can move on the other's 250
king! 251

| Student: | Grade: | Rate correct: (words correct in 1 minute) | Rate incorrect: (words incorrect in 1 minute) |
|---|---|---|---|
| Examiner: | Date: | Accuracy (words correct in the first 100 words = ▲) | |

# Teacher Passage & Directions: 4-B

1) Place the copy of the student passage in front of the student.
2) Place the teacher/examiner copy on clipboard so the student cannot see it.
3) Say: *When I say* begin *start reading aloud at the top of the page. Read across the page* (point to the first line of the passage). *Begin.* (Trigger stopwatch or timer for 1 minute.)
4) Follow along on the teacher/examiner copy as the student reads and put a slash (/) through any incorrect words.
5) At the end of one minute, say: *Thank You*. Mark the last word read with a bracket (]).

**NOTE:** If a student hesitates to correctly pronounce a word within **three seconds**, the student is told the word and an error is scored.

There is a special desert plant that has long, spiny 10
leaves. Once a year, it bears beautiful white flowers. The 20
flowers bloom only at night or on a very dark day. The 32
flowers produce seeds to grow more plants. 39

The plant could not produce seeds without its partner, 48
the green moth. The green moth has only one goal in life. 60
Its goal is to find a safe place to lay eggs. The green plant 74
and the green moth have become partners because each 83
has something needed by the other. 89

There are many parts of any desert flower. In order to ▲ 100
produce seeds, yellow pollen dust from one part of the 110
flower must move to another. But the plant can't do this 121
alone. 122

When the flowers bloom, the green moth starts working. 131
The moth goes onto each flower and gathers the yellow 141
pollen in a ball. Then the moth pushes the ball of pollen 153
down into the flower to reach the right part of the plant. 165

Next the moth makes her own way down into the 175
bottom of the flower. She lays eggs there so that, when the 187
eggs hatch, they can eat food from the seeds of the plant. 199
But there will be enough seeds left over for new plants. 210

The moth would not have a safe place for her eggs 221
without the green plant. The green plant would have no way 232
to get pollen for seeds without the moth. This is a good 244
example of plant and animal partnership! 250

| Student: | Grade: | Rate correct: (words correct in 1 minute) | Rate incorrect: (words incorrect in 1 minute) |
|---|---|---|---|
| Examiner: | Date: | Accuracy (words correct in the first 100 words = ▲) | |

## Teacher Passage & Directions: 4-C

1) Place the copy of the student passage in front of the student.
2) Place the teacher/examiner copy on clipboard so the student cannot see it.
3) Say: *When I say* begin *start reading aloud at the top of the page. Read across the page* (point to the first line of the passage). *Begin.* (Trigger stopwatch or timer for 1 minute.)
4) Follow along on the teacher/examiner copy as the student reads and put a slash (/) through any incorrect words.
5) At the end of one minute, say: *Thank You*. Mark the last word read with a bracket (]).

**NOTE:** If a student hesitates to correctly pronounce a word within **three seconds**, the student is told the word and an error is scored.

There is a lot of sugar in candy and pop. And you 12
probably know it isn't good to have a can of pop and a 25
candy bar for lunch! But that is often what many of us 37
do eat. However, that doesn't mean they are good for us. 48
Actually, we know they are bad if we have them all of 60
the time. And they are worse if we have them at the 72
wrong time. These things are very high in sugar. 81

Your body needs to have sugar to work. So, why 91
shouldn't you eat a lot of sugar? A little ▲ sugar goes a long 104
way. You can give your body more sugar than it can use. 116
This will make you feel very tired later. A good lunch will 128
have some protein, fresh fruit, fresh vegetables and bread. 137
The protein is good because it needs a long time to take in. 150
That means energy from it will be there in the afternoon 161
when you need to burn it. You can get protein from cheese, 173
eggs, beans, and nuts. You can also get it from peanut butter. 185

As for fruits and vegetables, fresh is better than frozen 195
or canned. It has more fiber and the vitamins haven't been 206
lost in cooking. If you're tired of apples and carrots, try grapes 218
or small tomatoes. Your body quickly breaks these down. 227
This gives you the quick energy needed until the protein kicks in. 239
If a healthy lunch sounds too boring you can always try adding 251
sliced bananas to your peanut butter! 257

| Student: | Grade: | Rate correct: (words correct in 1 minute) | Rate incorrect: (words incorrect in 1 minute) |
|---|---|---|---|
| Examiner: | Date: | Accuracy (words correct in the first 100 words = ▲) | |

## Teacher Passage & Directions: 5-A

1) Place the copy of the student passage in front of the student.
2) Place the teacher/examiner copy on clipboard so the student cannot see it.
3) Say: *When I say* begin *start reading aloud at the top of the page. Read across the page* (point to the first line of the passage). *Begin.* (Trigger stopwatch or timer for 1 minute.)
4) Follow along on the teacher/examiner copy as the student reads and put a slash (/) through any incorrect words.
5) At the end of one minute, say: *Thank You*. Mark the last word read with a bracket (]).

**NOTE:** If a student hesitates to correctly pronounce a word within **three seconds**, the student is told the word and an error is scored.

Sugar is used with all types of foods. It is found naturally 12
in many fruits and vegetables. Do you know how sugar is made? 24
It is made different ways depending on the type of sugar. Pure 36
sugar crystals are usually made from maple sap, sugar cane, or 47
sugar beets. Maple sugar is brown and is made from the sweet 59
tree sap. Pails are hung on the trees and the sap drips into them. 73
Then the sap is cooked until the syrup or sugar is ready. 85

Cane sugar comes from the stalk of the sugar cane plant. 96
To make cane sugar ▲ juice is taken from the stalks and refined 108
into sugar crystals. Beet sugar comes from part of the root of the 121
sugar beet plant. The beets form under the ground and are then 133
pulled up, and hauled way to the refinery. There they are washed 145
several times and cut into pieces which are then soaked in water 157
to obtain the sweet juice. This is then cooked to thicken the 169
juice before it is dried. As it dries the sugar crystals form. 181

Molasses usually collects on sugar crystals. But if they are 191
spun around quickly in a big vat, the molasses will spin away. 203
What's left is the white sugar often used at home. However, these 215
boxes of white granulated sugar were not always around. Years 225
ago sugar was bought in cone-shaped loaves. Each loaf weighed 236
about three pounds. The loaf was broken into pieces to use. Many 248
bakers claimed their secret of success was to grind the sugar into a 261
fine powder. 263

| Student: | Grade: | Rate correct: (words correct in 1 minute) | Rate incorrect: (words incorrect in 1 minute) |
|---|---|---|---|
| Examiner: | Date: | Accuracy (words correct in the first 100 words = ▲) | |

## Teacher Passage & Directions: 5-B

1) Place the copy of the student passage in front of the student.
2) Place the teacher/examiner copy on clipboard so the student cannot see it.
3) Say: *When I say* begin *start reading aloud at the top of the page. Read across the page* (point to the first line of the passage). *Begin.* (Trigger stopwatch or timer for 1 minute.)
4) Follow along on the teacher/examiner copy as the student reads and put a slash (/) through any incorrect words.
5) At the end of one minute, say: *Thank You*. Mark the last word read with a bracket (]).

**NOTE:** If a student hesitates to correctly pronounce a word within **three seconds**, the student is told the word and an error is scored.

In ancient times, the Greeks held a series of games 10
every four years. These games tested athletic skill. They 19
also provided a chance for people to meet and share ideas 30
about art and the world. 35

These games became an important part of life in 44
those times. The Greeks said they wanted "a healthy mind 54
in a healthy body." 58

Today these games attract athletes from all over the 67
world. Having modern versions of the games was the idea 77
of a French nobleman who worked hard to establish the 87
four-year international competitions in modern times. 94

The site of the ancient games ▲ was discovered when 103
the French man was young. It must have given him an idea 115
that stayed with him for a long time. He traveled all over the 128
world. He noticed that young athletes were alike no matter 138
what country they were from. So, in 1892, he presented a 149
plan for the modern Olympic games to the Athletic Sports 159
Union of France. 162

The idea was not accepted at first. But he did not give 174
up. He wrote letters. He began to prepare for the International 185
Athletic Congress meeting in 1894. He got countries like the 195
United States and England and Sweden to back his plan. 205
When it came time to hold the meeting, he was ready. 216

His plan was accepted. The first modern world games 225
were planned for 1896. The idea of "A healthy mind in a 237
healthy body" is now a goal for athletes all over the world. 249

| Student: | Grade: | Rate correct:<br>(words correct in 1 minute) | Rate incorrect:<br>(words incorrect in 1 minute) |
|---|---|---|---|
| Examiner: | Date: | Accuracy<br>(words correct in the first 100 words = ▲) | |

## Teacher Passage & Directions: 5-C

1) Place the copy of the student passage in front of the student.
2) Place the teacher/examiner copy on clipboard so the student cannot see it.
3) Say: *When I say* begin *start reading aloud at the top of the page. Read across the page* (point to the first line of the passage). *Begin.* (Trigger stopwatch or timer for 1 minute.)
4) Follow along on the teacher/examiner copy as the student reads and put a slash (/) through any incorrect words.
5) At the end of one minute, say: *Thank You*. Mark the last word read with a bracket (]).

**NOTE:** If a student hesitates to correctly pronounce a word within **three seconds**, the student is told the word and an error is scored.

Toads and frogs are both amphibians, which means they 9
spend part of their lives in the water and part on land. Both of 24
them start out as tadpoles and both are cold-blooded. But there 36
are differences too. A toad's skin is rough and bumpy, while a 48
frog's skin is smooth. The toad's bumpy skin has led some people 60
to believe that they cause warts. However, that isn't true. The bumps 72
are really small poison glands. The poison is harmless to humans. 83
But if a dog picks a toad up in his mouth, he'll drop the toad in a ▲ 100
hurry because it tastes so bad. This added protection is a good thing. 113

Toads cannot leap away from trouble as well as frogs. 123
Some toads can blend in with the things around them and others 135
will flatten and lie very still until danger passes. They usually burrow 147
out of sight during the day. In the late afternoon and early evening, 160
they come out and eat large numbers of insects. Someone once 171
estimated that one toad could eat almost ten thousand insects in three 183
months. They catch their meals with their sticky tongues. 192

When autumn comes, the toad's activities slow down. It's time 202
to burrow deep in the earth and hibernate. He backs into his burrow, 215
letting the earth seal him inside. When the spring sun returns to warm 228
the earth, he will awaken for another busy year. 237

| Student: | Grade: | Rate correct: (words correct in 1 minute) | Rate incorrect: (words incorrect in 1 minute) |
|---|---|---|---|
| Examiner: | Date: | Accuracy (words correct in the first 100 words = ▲) | |

## Teacher Passage & Directions: 6-A

1) Place the copy of the student passage in front of the student.
2) Place the teacher/examiner copy on clipboard so the student cannot see it.
3) Say: *When I say* begin *start reading aloud at the top of the page. Read across the page* (point to the first line of the passage). ***Begin.*** (Trigger stopwatch or timer for 1 minute.)
4) Follow along on the teacher/examiner copy as the student reads and put a slash (/) through any incorrect words.
5) At the end of one minute, say: *Thank You*. Mark the last word read with a bracket (]).

**NOTE:** If a student hesitates to correctly pronounce a word within **three seconds**, the student is told the word and an error is scored.

Most farmers dislike groundhogs because the groundhogs 7
have only one purpose in life: to dig. The groundhog digs 18
everywhere – under trees, barns, and even houses. Everywhere he 27
digs, he leaves holes that tell of his passing. There are many 39
"tall tales" about farm buildings, equipment, and even families 48
disappearing into huge holes dug by groundhogs. 55

Of course, those are just stories and the facts about the 66
groundhog are different. Groundhogs are active during the daytime. 75
They eat mostly grains and grasses, and are strict vegetarians. 85
They can be found in many parts of the United States and 97
throughout Canada. You ▲ can sometimes see one sitting 105
erect on a mound of earth outside the entrance to its burrow. 117

The groundhog is one of the few mammals who is a true 129
hibernator. This means that the groundhog is in a kind of deep 141
sleep all through the winter months. During this sleep, his body 152
temperature drops from about 97 degrees Fahrenheit to about 161
37 degrees. His heartbeat slows from a normal rate of about 80 beats 174
per minute to about four beats per minute. 182

The reason for his winter hibernation is a simple one. 192
If the groundhog was awake during the winter, he would 202
certainly starve to death. The groundhog eats well before he 212
hibernates and then his stored body fat is used very slowly 223
while he sleeps. 226

Groundhog Day, February 2, is thought of as the day 236
the groundhog wakes. A fable states that if he sees his shadow, 248
winter will last another six weeks and he will go back into his 261
hole to hibernate. If he does not see his shadow, spring is on 274
its way. 276

| Student: | Grade: | Rate correct: (words correct in 1 minute) | Rate incorrect: (words incorrect in 1 minute) |
|---|---|---|---|
| Examiner: | Date: | Accuracy (words correct in the first 100 words = ▲) | |

# Teacher Passage & Directions: 6-B

1) Place the copy of the student passage in front of the student.
2) Place the teacher/examiner copy on clipboard so the student cannot see it.
3) Say: *When I say* begin *start reading aloud at the top of the page. Read across the page* (point to the first line of the passage). *Begin.* (Trigger stopwatch or timer for 1 minute.)
4) Follow along on the teacher/examiner copy as the student reads and put a slash (/) through any incorrect words.
5) At the end of one minute, say: *Thank You*. Mark the last word read with a bracket (]).

**NOTE:** If a student hesitates to correctly pronounce a word within **three seconds**, the student is told the word and an error is scored.

The praying mantis is an extremely strange insect; 8
in fact, some people say it looks frightening or weird, while 19
others regard it as a terrifying monster because it is so unusual. 31
A full-grown mantis is almost as big as your hand and looks 44
like a pale green stick with goggle eyes. It can swivel its head 57
when watching something. That *something* is usually the 65
other insect it's about to eat. 71

The praying mantis eats other insects; but they will also 81
occasionally eat others of their own kind. In fact, they have 92
actually been known to eat them! This habit ▲ of eating 102
everything in sight is another reason they are sometimes 111
referred to as monsters. However, like all insects, the praying 121
mantis has three pairs of legs. The two rear pairs are used only 134
for walking while the front legs are also used to hunt. These are 147
equipped with razor-sharp spines and have hooks on them. 157

This insect is a great hunter. It attaches itself to a blade 169
of grass or a twig and then it waits patiently for some other insect 183
to come into view. The mantis cannot hear and has no voice, but 196
it has exceptional eyesight. Once it sees its prey, it inches slowly 208
toward its victim and then it rears up on its hind legs and seizes 222
the victim with its front legs. After eating the catch (often alive), 234
the master hunter neatly wipes its claws and uses them to clean 246
its face. 248

| Student: | Grade: | Rate correct: (words correct in 1 minute) | Rate incorrect: (words incorrect in 1 minute) |
|---|---|---|---|
| Examiner: | Date: | Accuracy (words correct in the first 100 words = ▲) | |

## Teacher Passage & Directions: 6-C

1) Place the copy of the student passage in front of the student.
2) Place the teacher/examiner copy on clipboard so the student cannot see it.
3) Say: *When I say* begin *start reading aloud at the top of the page. Read across the page* (point to the first line of the passage). ***Begin.*** (Trigger stopwatch or timer for 1 minute.)
4) Follow along on the teacher/examiner copy as the student reads and put a slash (/) through any incorrect words.
5) At the end of one minute, say: *Thank You*. Mark the last word read with a bracket (]).

**NOTE:** If a student hesitates to correctly pronounce a word within **three seconds**, the student is told the word and an error is scored.

There are three basic types of snowflakes. The first 9
type is called “stellar,” and is the one most people 19
remember. Stellar flakes are feathery with small centers. 27
They form when it’s not extremely cold and when the clouds are 39
low and wet. Because they cling together when falling, it 49
sometimes appears as if they are descending in great, downy 59
clumps. The second variety of snowflake is called a “plate” 69
snowflake and this formation appears almost rock-solid in compact 79
configurations with six clearly seen outer edges. They form 88
when it’s exceptionally cold and when clouds are elevated and 98
almost dry. ▲ The final type of snowflake is a combination of the 110
other two. It has a plate-like center with feathering arms. 121

Even though there are these three types, each individual 130
snowflake is truly unique in its configuration because each snowflake 140
is actually the combination of thousands of ice crystals. In a cloud, 152
water droplets are attracted to frozen particles. They crystallize on that 163
core. The snowflake develops, crystal by crystal, until it is heavy 174
enough to fall to the earth as snow. 182

Snow does not seem very heavy when it falls. But don’t let 194
that fool you! If you have to shovel snow after a blizzard, you may lift a 210
great deal of snow. If the snow is 15 inches deep, you might lift half a 226
ton before clearing your walk. And that doesn’t count the weight of 238
the shovel you’re using! 242

# MASI–R

# ORAL READING FLUENCY MEASURES

## PASSAGES FOR STUDENTS

MAKE A COPY OF THE APPROPRIATE PAGE

FOR EACH STUDENT YOU ARE TESTING.

Part of the park is for play. Some parts are not for play. Cars drive down the street. Don't play there. People walk on the sidewalks. Don't play there.

Pick a part of the park for play. There are many pretty places. People play ball. Some people just sit. Some people read books. Dogs run after birds. There are green trees. Pick a part like that.

Do you need help? There are signs to help you. They say where to play. No cars are there. There are just boys and girls. They run and jump. They play with each other. There is room for fun.

One day a mouse came to our house. She was in a box. That box was her home. She ate there and went to sleep there. She was a little mouse with a little house.

A cat lives at our house too. The cat saw the mouse. He sat still. He did not move. The mouse did not run. The cat looked hard at the mouse. "I will eat you, mouse," the cat was thinking.

The mouse was thinking too. "I see you, cat, and you are bad news!"

I took the mouse to my room. No more cats for this mouse!

My dog waits by the door. He waits for me to let him out. He wants to go out and play.

I look outside. It is fall. Some trees are yellow and some trees are red. Some trees are still green. We will go out and play. We like to play by the trees.

My dog runs by the big trees. He is happy and I am happy too. We run and run. Then we rest. I tell him things. He must not run into the street. There may be cars. He listens to me and he stays with me. He is my dog.

Mr. Lee sometimes acts funny. The thing to remember is this. It's almost always just an act. He seems like a silly bear. But he can be a real friend. I found that out last summer.

Jim and I had decided to clean up tree branches. There had been a big storm the night before. Little branches were all over the grass and sidewalks.

We would knock on someone's door. Then we would ask them about cleaning up their yard. Most people asked about our rates. Most of the time, we would let them decide. Most people were fair. No one tried to cheat us.

We had just finished cleaning up one yard. But the owner wouldn't pay us and wouldn't tell us what we did wrong. "It wasn't worth it," he said.

Mr. Lee was walking by and heard the man. His face got silly. His eyes popped out and his cheeks got red. He marched right up to the man's door and knocked hard. When the man saw him he started to laugh. "That was worth it!" he said. Mr. Lee made him laugh and we got paid.

Mr. Lee's funny act really helped us out that time!

Last Sunday afternoon, there was a party for Ben. First, Mom baked a big cake. She fixed something for us to drink and we put the food in a pretty basket. We put in some balloons too. Ben likes balloons. Then I got Ben and we were ready to go!

We walked to a place with big trees all around. It was a forest, I think. We looked and looked. At last, we found a nice spot with green grass. Ben rested and we fixed a place for the party.

Mom poured some milk for me. I blew up a big red balloon for Ben. We sang "Happy Birthday" with loud, funny voices. We ate white cake with dark icing and it was good! Then Mom asked some crazy riddles. I told her some riddles from school. We laughed and played some more games.

Then it was time for Ben's presents. Mom gave him a new blanket with soft insides. I gave him a new blue hat and lots of balloons. We both gave him birthday hugs.

We walked home happy. Ben was happy too, but he was tired. I put him on the bed upstairs. That bear had some birthday!

"Don't be afraid," Sue said. She had already started up the mountain. Bill looked up. The moon was shining down. The mountain seemed dark and scary. But he was not afraid.

"I feel fine," he said bravely. His voice sounded little in the big night. He put his foot carefully on the first rock. He pulled on the rope that was tied around his waist. The other end of the rope was around Sue.

"Are you ready?" Sue asked.

"Ready," he said. One foot at a time, he started up the mountain.

Somehow he and Sue had gotten lost. There was still time to find the others. They would have to hurry. Morning would come very soon now.

A rock slipped under his foot and fell below.

"Watch where you're going," Sue yelled.

"Sorry," he yelled back. His legs were starting to hurt. There would be no stopping for rest on this climb. They had to catch up with the others by daybreak. They could not spend another day lost and without food. They would have to keep climbing.

At last they reached the top.

"Look," Sue said quietly. There were the others, asleep in their sleeping bags.

"We made it," Bill yelled. And he gave Sue a great big hug!

Ann read the words in the newspaper twice. "Must Sell Motorcycle," she read. Ann had wanted a motorcycle for a long time.

All the money she had was upstairs, all fifty dollars of it. That would never be enough. But the owner of this cycle had written, "Will consider trade." Ann knew she was a good trader. So, she carefully punched in the number from the ad.

"Oh, you need to talk to John," the woman who answered said. "He's at city hospital in room 203."

Ann took the bus to the hospital that day. The door to room 203 was half-open, so she knocked gently and went in. "How did you break both arms?" she asked when she saw the casts on the man.

"It wasn't easy," he laughed. "And I know your next question," he added. "No, this didn't happen on the motorcycle. I'm a very careful rider."

Then he jerked his arms and wiggled. "It's this itching under the casts," he explained. "It's driving me crazy!"

"Just a minute, I'll be right back," Ann said.

When she returned, she had a back-scratcher from the gift shop. "Now, about that trade," she joked.

"That's not a bad idea," John said. Noting her surprised look he explained, "Seriously, I need some help. If you help me, I'll trade for some lessons on the cycle."

"Great!" Ann said as she grinned from ear to ear. "I guess I'm a better trader than I thought!"

## 3-B

Yesterday, we had just settled down to a good game of checkers. Then Pete said he was hungry for cookies. "Not just any cookies, good cookies," he said.

So there we were. I was just getting ready to do my famous triple jump and this guy gets hungry for cookies. "Okay," I said, "let's go look."

Looking for something to eat with Pete is an experience. You would normally look in a cookie jar or in a cupboard for cookies, right? Pete looks in the freezer first. I guess it makes sense. I mean, people usually freeze things in quantity. And Pete is a quantity eater.

Next, we looked in the oven. Pete always hopes that something will be left in the oven. I suggested that we might take a look in the cupboard. If there's a pack of graham crackers or a box of sugar cookies to be had, it's usually in the cupboard. A careful search revealed no cookies.

My family does not own a cookie jar, so that left us with no place to search next. Pete had that look in his eye. He was getting ready to say, "I'm going home to get something to eat." I could see my chance at a triple jump was ready to walk out the door.

"Wait," I yelled. Pete froze in his tracks. "Have you ever heard of applesauce wonders?" I asked. "They're just delicious!"

I ignored his funny look and grabbed the jar of applesauce.

"Makes my mouth water just to think about them," I said. I spread the applesauce on a handy soda cracker. I pushed a marshmallow on top of the whole thing and shoved it into Pete's mouth. Now Pete asks for "applesauce wonders" every time he comes to my house.

It was shiny, silver and beautiful. Kris had never seen such a trumpet before. She rubbed her eyes, but it was still there. It rested in its deep blue case like the treasure of a king.

Kris picked it up and fingered the keys. The action was perfect. She could imagine the sounds that would flow from that instrument!

"It's beautiful, isn't it?" the shopkeeper said, peering over her shoulder. "You know, that horn belongs in the hands of a talented young person like you," he added.

Kris frowned slightly and put the trumpet back in its case. "Thank you," she said softly. "Do you have any used trumpets?" she asked, remembering the purpose of her trip.

"Come right this way," the shopkeeper said. He motioned toward the rear of the small store. "These are my nearly new models," he joked.

Kris looked at the three battered trumpets in the display case. "Let me try that one," she said. She shuddered as she played the scale. She tried the second, then the third. Each horn was all right, she thought. It was just that she would not be proud to play any of them in front of an audience.

"They're nothing like the silver one, are they?" the shopkeeper said gently. "Is there any chance you could pay for the silver one over time?" he asked.

Kris thought awhile, then shook her head. There really wasn't a chance. She knew that. There was only so much money for extras at her house. The trumpet was an extra. She was lucky to have the money to get a horn at all. She began to pull the money out of her back pocket.

"No," the shopkeeper said firmly. "I can't sell you something you don't want. But I can sell you something you do want," he added. "I will sell you the silver horn. Then you can work here after school to pay for it. Is it a deal?"

## 4-A

Chess was first played in Asia and India. When armies moved in and out of these countries the soldiers learned the game of chess. They then brought the game with them wherever their battles took them. Many hundreds of years ago, as the armies moved west, the pieces were given the names we know today. The knight, the bishop, the king, the queen, and the rook (or castle) were all part of life at that time.

Chess is played on a chess board which is set up in squares of two colors. Each piece is only allowed to move a certain way. Some pieces can only move forward. Some pieces can only move diagonally. Like most games, the object of chess is to win by beating the person you are playing against. All pieces are used to protect the king. If a player loses the king, he or she loses the game.

During the game pieces are moved in order to capture the other player's pieces. Or they can be used to protect a more valuable piece, like the king. Each player has a full set of pieces. One player has the white pieces. One player has the black pieces. It doesn't matter how many pieces are captured. What matters is whether the king is lost.

Thinking ahead is the key to playing good chess. Each player must study the way the other player moves. Then, if that player makes a mistake, the first player can move on the other's king!

There is a special desert plant that has long, spiny leaves. Once a year, it bears beautiful white flowers. The flowers bloom only at night or on a very dark day. The flowers produce seeds to grow more plants.

The plant could not produce seeds without its partner, the green moth. The green moth has only one goal in life. Its goal is to find a safe place to lay eggs. The green plant and the green moth have become partners because each has something needed by the other.

There are many parts of any desert flower. In order to produce seeds, yellow pollen dust from one part of the flower must move to another. But the plant can't do this alone.

When the flowers bloom, the green moth starts working. The moth goes onto each flower and gathers the yellow pollen in a ball. Then the moth pushes the ball of pollen down into the flower to reach the right part of the plant.

Next the moth makes her own way down into the bottom of the flower. She lays eggs there so that, when the eggs hatch, they can eat food from the seeds of the plant. But there will be enough seeds left over for new plants.

The moth would not have a safe place for her eggs without the green plant. The green plant would have no way to get pollen for seeds without the moth. This is a good example of plant and animal partnership!

4-C

There is a lot of sugar in candy and pop. And you probably know it isn't good to have a can of pop and a candy bar for lunch! But that is often what many of us do eat. However, that doesn't mean they are good for us. Actually, we know they are bad if we have them all of the time. And they are worse if we have them at the wrong time. These things are very high in sugar.

Your body needs to have sugar to work. So, why shouldn't you eat a lot of sugar? A little sugar goes a long way. You can give your body more sugar than it can use. This will make you feel very tired later. A good lunch will have some protein, fresh fruit, fresh vegetables and bread. The protein is good because it needs a long time to take in. That means energy from it will be there in the afternoon when you need to burn it. You can get protein from cheese, eggs, beans, and nuts. You can also get it from peanut butter.

As for fruits and vegetables, fresh is better than frozen or canned. It has more fiber and the vitamins haven't been lost in cooking. If you're tired of apples and carrots, try grapes or small tomatoes. Your body quickly breaks these down. This gives you the quick energy needed until the protein kicks in. If a healthy lunch sounds too boring, you can always try adding sliced bananas to your peanut butter!

## 5-A

Sugar is used with all types of foods. It is found naturally in many fruits and vegetables. Do you know how sugar is made? It is made different ways depending on the type of sugar. Pure sugar crystals are usually made from maple sap, sugar cane, or sugar beets. Maple sugar is brown and is made from the sweet tree sap. Pails are hung on the trees and the sap drips into them. Then the sap is cooked until the syrup or sugar is ready.

Cane sugar comes from the stalk of the sugar cane plant. To make cane sugar juice is taken from the stalks and refined into sugar crystals. Beet sugar comes from part of the root of the sugar beet plant. The beets form under the ground and are then pulled up, and hauled way to the refinery. There they are washed several times and cut into pieces which are then soaked in water to obtain the sweet juice. This is then cooked to thicken the juice before it is dried. As it dries the sugar crystals form.

Molasses usually collects on sugar crystals. But if they are spun around quickly in a big vat, the molasses will spin away. What's left is the white sugar often used at home. However, these boxes of white granulated sugar were not always around. Years ago sugar was bought in cone shaped loaves. Each loaf weighed about three pounds. The loaf was broken into pieces to use. Many bakers claimed their secret of success was to grind the sugar into a fine powder.

5-B

In ancient times, the Greeks held a series of games every four years. These games tested athletic skill. They also provided a chance for people to meet and share ideas about art and the world.

These games became an important part of life in those times. The Greeks said they wanted "a healthy mind in a healthy body."

Today these games attract athletes from all over the world. Having modern versions of the games was the idea of a French nobleman who worked hard to establish the four-year international competitions in modern times.

The site of the ancient games was discovered when the French man was young. It must have given him an idea that stayed with him for a long time. He traveled all over the world. He noticed that young athletes were alike no matter what country they were from. So, in 1892, he presented a plan for the modern Olympic games to the Athletic Sports Union of France.

The idea was not accepted at first. But he did not give up. He wrote letters. He began to prepare for the International Athletic Congress meeting in 1894. He got countries like the United States and England and Sweden to back his plan. When it came time to hold the meeting, he was ready.

His plan was accepted. The first modern world games were planned for 1896. The idea of "a healthy mind in a healthy body" is now a goal for athletes all over the world.

**5-C**

Toads and frogs are both amphibians, which means they spend part of their lives in the water and part on land. Both of them start out as tadpoles and both are cold-blooded. But there are differences too. A toad's skin is rough and bumpy, while a frog's skin is smooth. The toad's bumpy skin has led some people to believe that they cause warts. However, that isn't true. The bumps are really small poison glands. The poison is harmless to humans. But if a dog picks a toad up in his mouth, he'll drop the toad in a hurry because it tastes so bad. This added protection is a good thing.

Toads cannot leap away from trouble as well as frogs. Some toads can blend in with the things around them and others will flatten and lie very still until danger passes. They usually burrow out of sight during the day. In the late afternoon and early evening, they come out and eat large numbers of insects. Someone once estimated that one toad could eat almost ten thousand insects in three months. They catch their meals with their sticky tongues.

When autumn comes, the toad's activities slow down. It's time to burrow deep in the earth and hibernate. He backs into his burrow, letting the earth seal him inside. When the spring sun returns to warm the earth, he will awaken for another busy year.

6-A

Most farmers dislike groundhogs because the groundhogs have only one purpose in life: to dig. The groundhog digs everywhere – under trees, barns, and even houses. Everywhere he digs, he leaves holes that tell of his passing. There are many "tall tales" about farm buildings, equipment, and even families disappearing into huge holes dug by groundhogs.

Of course, those are just stories and the facts about the groundhog are different. Groundhogs are active during the daytime. They eat mostly grains and grasses, and are strict vegetarians. They can be found in many parts of the United States and throughout Canada. You can sometimes see one sitting erect on a mound of earth outside the entrance to its burrow.

The groundhog is one of the few mammals who is a true hibernator. This means that the groundhog is in a kind of deep sleep all through the winter months. During this sleep, his body temperature drops from about 97 degrees Fahrenheit to about 37 degrees. His heartbeat slows from a normal rate of about 80 beats per minute to about four beats per minute.

The reason for his winter hibernation is a simple one. If the groundhog was awake during the winter, he would certainly starve to death. The groundhog eats well before he hibernates and then his stored body fat is used very slowly while he sleeps.

Groundhog Day, February 2, is thought of as the day the groundhog wakes. A fable states that if he sees his shadow, winter will last another six weeks and he will go back into his hole to hibernate. If he does not see his shadow, spring is on its way.

## 6-B

The praying mantis is an extremely strange insect; in fact, some people say it looks frightening or weird, while others regard it as a terrifying monster because it is so unusual. A full-grown mantis is almost as big as your hand and looks like a pale green stick with goggle eyes. It can swivel its head when watching something. That something is usually the other insect it's about to eat.

The praying mantis eats other insects; but they will also occasionally eat others of their own kind. In fact, they have actually been known to eat them! This habit of eating everything in sight is another reason they are sometimes referred to as monsters. However, like all insects, the praying mantis has three pairs of legs. The two rear pairs are used only for walking while the front legs are also used to hunt. These are equipped with razor-sharp spines and have hooks on them.

This insect is a great hunter. It attaches itself to a blade of grass or a twig and then it waits patiently for some other insect to come into view. The mantis cannot hear and has no voice, but it has exceptional eyesight. Once it sees its prey, it inches slowly toward its victim and then it rears up on its hind legs and seizes the victim with its front legs. After eating the catch (often alive), the master hunter neatly wipes its claws and uses them to clean its face.

6-C

There are three basic types of snowflakes. The first type is called "stellar," and is the one most people remember. Stellar flakes are feathery with small centers. They form when it's not extremely cold and when the clouds are low and wet. Because they cling together when falling, it sometimes appears as if they are descending in great, downy clumps. The second variety of snowflake is called a "plate" snowflake and this formation appears almost rock-solid in compact configurations with six clearly seen outer edges. They form when it's exceptionally cold and when clouds are elevated and almost dry. The final type of snowflake is a combination of the other two. It has a plate-like center with feathering arms.

Even though there are these three types, each individual snowflake is truly unique in its configuration because each snowflake is actually the combination of thousands of ice crystals. In a cloud, water droplets are attracted to frozen particles. They crystallize on that core. The snowflake develops, crystal by crystal, until it is heavy enough to fall to the earth as snow.

Snow does not seem very heavy when it falls. But don't let that fool you! If you have to shovel snow after a blizzard, you may lift a great deal of snow. If the snow is 15 inches deep, you might lift half a ton before clearing your walk. And that doesn't count the weight of the shovel you're using!

# CORE Vocabulary Screening

**SKILL ASSESSED**

## Reading Vocabulary

**Grade Level**

1–8

**Language**

English

**Grouping**

Group/Individual

**Approximate Testing Time**

10–20 Minutes

**Materials**

- Teacher Instructions (pp.120–122)
- Pencil
- Student Record Forms and Keys (pp.123–146)

**Author**

Michael Milone, Ph.D.

**▸ WHAT** The *CORE Vocabulary Screening* measures how well students know the meaning of grade-level words they read silently. The task involves reading a word in a box and choosing which of three answer choices means about the same as the word in the box. It is a pure measure of reading vocabulary in that there is no need to comprehend text in order to complete the task and there is no context to provide clues to the meaning of the word.

**▸ WHY** Vocabulary knowledge is critical to understanding grade-appropriate text. Even students who are good decoders will have difficulty comprehending what they read if they do not have adequate vocabulary knowledge. The *CORE Vocabulary Screening* can identify students whose vocabulary knowledge is significantly lower than that of their peers.

**▸ HOW** Students are tested in groups or individually; they read a word in a box and choose (by underlining) one of the three answer choices which means about the same as the word in the box. The words in the boxes were chosen because they typically appear in both literature and instructional text in a given grade. The correct answer is a synonym or near-synonym from a lower grade. Two forms, A and B, are provided for each grade level.

Make a copy of the assessment for each student. Be sure students have a pencil or pen to mark their answers. Have students write their names and the date at the top of the page.

Read these directions to the students: *This activity is about word meanings. You will read a word in a box and some other words in the same row. Underline the answer that means the same or about the same as the word in the box. We will begin with a sample item. Look at the sample at the top of the page. Read the word in the box and the other words in the row. Which answer means about the same as the word in the box?* (pause) *The word in the box is* scream. *The answer that means about the same as* scream *is* yell*; underline* yell. (Allow time for students to answer.)

*Now we will do more items like the sample. For each item, read the word in the box. Think about what it means and then read the other words in the row. You should choose the answer that means the same or about the same as the word in the box; underline the answer you think is correct. Do you have any questions?* (Answer any questions students have.) *You may begin now.*

Allow time for students to fill in their answers. If some students are lagging behind the others and need additional time, you may allow them to complete the assessment on their own at a different time.

The *CORE Vocabulary Screening Tests* for Grades 1–8 and the Answer Keys are on the following pages.

**WHAT IT MEANS** The results of the reading vocabulary assessment are reported as the number of words correct (see chart below). A student who scores at the Intensive level (49% or less correct) may be having significant difficulty with understanding grade-level material because of insufficient vocabulary knowledge. A student who scores at the Strategic level (between 50% and 74% correct) may be having some difficulty understanding grade-level material because of insufficient vocabulary knowledge. A student who scores at the Benchmark level (75% or more correct) has adequate vocabulary knowledge for typical reading.

**CORE Vocabulary Screening Scores**

| Performance Level | Proportion Correct | Words Correct |
|---|---|---|
| Benchmark | 75% or more | 23-30 |
| Strategic | between 50-74% | 15-22 |
| Intensive | 49% or less | 0-14 |

For progress monitoring purposes, the vocabulary assessment may be used more than once if the students receive no feedback about their responses. The two versions (A and B) of the assessment are approximately parallel forms and can be used for pre- and post-assessments or can be alternated for progress monitoring purposes.

It is important to keep in mind that progress monitoring for vocabulary is different from many other skill areas. Letter recognition, word decoding, and oral fluency skills reflect the application of a relatively small set of sound/spelling correspondences and are quickly responsive to direct instruction and meaningful practice. Vocabulary differs in that only a relatively small number of words are taught directly, and most vocabulary development occurs incidentally through oral interaction and reading. For these reasons, the *CORE Vocabulary Screening* is more useful for identifying students who have insufficient vocabulary knowledge than for monitoring student progress.

**WHAT'S NEXT?** Vocabulary development may be improved somewhat through direct instruction and practice, but the greatest gains will be the result of oral interaction and reading material with a rich vocabulary. Typical conversation does little to expand a student's vocabulary because the pool of everyday words is relatively small. Hearing grade-level or higher text read aloud, paired reading of grade level text, and independent reading contribute in a meaningful way to vocabulary acquisition, particularly when it is supported by feedback from peers and adults. In addition, students' ability to understand word meanings can be enhanced through instruction and practice in structural analysis and using context.

Name: ____________________ Date: __________

## CORE VOCABULARY SCREENING—FORM 1A

***Sample***

| | ***scream*** | ***want*** | ***yell*** | ***hope*** |
|---|---|---|---|---|
| A 1 | gift | hair | present | spring |
| A 2 | below | gone | without | under |
| A 3 | breeze | wind | house | letter |
| A 4 | rip | poke | rain | tear |
| A 5 | carpet | rug | toy | pony |
| A 6 | ocean | home | train | sea |
| A 7 | quit | stop | hold | wear |
| A 8 | jacket | prize | coat | aunt |
| A 9 | large | fun | big | neat |
| A 10 | noise | apple | toe | sound |
| A 11 | shop | buy | hike | saw |
| A 12 | feel | ride | nest | touch |
| A 13 | peek | step | look | grow |
| A 14 | enjoy | drive | play | like |
| A 15 | beat | hit | talk | met |

| | | | | |
|---|---|---|---|---|
| A 16 | clip | burn | cut | break |
| A 17 | afraid | scared | cold | dry |
| A 18 | listen | meet | miss | hear |
| A 19 | trail | barn | fence | path |
| A 20 | little | pretty | small | dusty |
| A 21 | suddenly | quickly | only | slowly |
| A 22 | unhappy | another | lazy | sad |
| A 23 | difficult | hard | tall | weak |
| A 24 | woman | picnic | lady | day |
| A 25 | merry | happy | leaky | busy |
| A 26 | sip | wait | drink | put |
| A 27 | napping | writing | fixing | sleeping |
| A 28 | trap | chew | catch | climb |
| A 29 | auto | car | baby | cookie |
| A 30 | hop | work | sing | jump |

# correct: ______
# incorrect: ______
# no response: ______

Name: ______________________ Date: ____________

## CORE VOCABULARY SCREENING—FORM 1B

***Sample***

| | | | | |
|---|---|---|---|---|
| | ***owns*** | ***pays*** | ***has*** | ***opens*** |
| B 1 | spin | add | show | turn |
| B 2 | hurry | rush | dive | cry |
| B 3 | careless | resting | sloppy | wild |
| B 4 | sleepy | brave | about | tired |
| B 5 | evening | night | shoe | hill |
| B 6 | drag | wish | pull | thank |
| B 7 | stone | animal | rock | tail |
| B 8 | begin | start | ask | chase |
| B 9 | wise | out | furry | smart |
| B 10 | blanket | cover | yard | pond |
| B 11 | quick | after | near | fast |
| B 12 | stir | sit | mix | bend |
| B 13 | angry | mad | around | but |
| B 14 | forest | spot | glove | woods |
| B 15 | piece | way | star | part |

| | | | | |
|---|---|---|---|---|
| B 16 | thoughts | races | ideas | doors |
| B 17 | ship | boat | sun | pup |
| B 18 | leaving | eating | dropping | going |
| B 19 | bake | see | cook | find |
| B 20 | wonderful | good | messy | strong |
| B 21 | road | bell | street | bark |
| B 22 | greater | bigger | warmer | better |
| B 23 | loud | late | stiff | noisy |
| B 24 | clean | run | wash | tell |
| B 25 | tricked | fooled | helped | watched |
| B 26 | town | water | city | brick |
| B 27 | shut | know | dance | close |
| B 28 | shove | push | keep | float |
| B 29 | over | soon | above | ready |
| B 30 | kind | back | wet | nice |

# correct: ______
# incorrect: ______
# no response: ______

# CORE VOCABULARY SCREENING KEY

## FORM 1A

***Sample***

| | *scream* | *yell* |
|---|---|---|
| A 1 | gift | present |
| A 2 | below | under |
| A 3 | breeze | wind |
| A 4 | rip | tear |
| A 5 | carpet | rug |
| A 6 | ocean | sea |
| A 7 | quit | stop |
| A 8 | jacket | coat |
| A 9 | large | big |
| A 10 | noise | sound |
| A 11 | shop | buy |
| A 12 | feel | touch |
| A 13 | peek | look |
| A 14 | enjoy | like |
| A 15 | beat | hit |
| A 16 | clip | cut |
| A 17 | afraid | scared |
| A 18 | listen | hear |
| A 19 | trail | path |
| A 20 | little | small |
| A 21 | suddenly | quickly |
| A 22 | unhappy | sad |
| A 23 | difficult | hard |
| A 24 | woman | lady |
| A 25 | merry | happy |
| A 26 | sip | drink |
| A 27 | napping | sleeping |
| A 28 | trap | catch |
| A 29 | auto | car |
| A 30 | hop | jump |

## FORM 1B

***Sample***

| | *owns* | *has* |
|---|---|---|
| B 1 | spin | turn |
| B 2 | hurry | rush |
| B 3 | careless | sloppy |
| B 4 | sleepy | tired |
| B 5 | evening | night |
| B 6 | drag | pull |
| B 7 | stone | rock |
| B 8 | begin | start |
| B 9 | wise | smart |
| B 10 | blanket | cover |
| B 11 | quick | fast |
| B 12 | stir | mix |
| B 13 | angry | mad |
| B 14 | forest | woods |
| B 15 | piece | part |
| B 16 | thoughts | ideas |
| B 17 | ship | boat |
| B 18 | leaving | going |
| B 19 | bake | cook |
| B 20 | wonderful | good |
| B 21 | road | street |
| B 22 | greater | bigger |
| B 23 | loud | noisy |
| B 24 | clean | wash |
| B 25 | tricked | fooled |
| B 26 | town | city |
| B 27 | shut | close |
| B 28 | shove | push |
| B 29 | over | above |
| B 30 | kind | nice |

Name: ______________________________ Date: ______________

## CORE VOCABULARY SCREENING—FORM 2A

***Sample***

| | | | | |
|---|---|---|---|---|
| | ***swift*** | ***must*** | ***into*** | ***fast*** |

| Item | Target | | | |
|---|---|---|---|---|
| A 1 | gather | light | believe | collect |
| A 2 | chunk | piece | dish | floor |
| A 3 | certain | only | sure | most |
| A 4 | greedy | selfish | baggy | always |
| A 5 | ache | bag | pain | street |
| A 6 | build | sleep | live | make |
| A 7 | gladly | happily | sadly | weakly |
| A 8 | dash | bark | lost | run |
| A 9 | place | put | scare | fill |
| A 10 | toss | hope | throw | sign |
| A 11 | pail | bucket | calf | trick |
| A 12 | foolish | real | hard | silly |
| A 13 | base | snow | bottom | money |
| A 14 | rescue | dress | start | save |
| A 15 | equal | same | next | mad |

| Item | Target | | | |
|---|---|---|---|---|
| A 16 | kettle | bear | pot | uncle |
| A 17 | spoiled | rocked | baked | ruined |
| A 18 | understand | know | rest | pass |
| A 19 | completed | hidden | finished | roared |
| A 20 | huge | red | proud | big |
| A 21 | lovely | away | pretty | small |
| A 22 | bright | long | very | shiny |
| A 23 | nearly | almost | quiet | safe |
| A 24 | terrible | other | awful | sorry |
| A 25 | harm | wave | follow | hurt |
| A 26 | attach | join | have | wash |
| A 27 | raise | lift | row | trip |
| A 28 | choose | land | pick | reach |
| A 29 | finish | belong | roll | end |
| A 30 | shout | catch | yell | take |

# correct: ______
# incorrect: ______
# no response: ______

Name: ______________________ Date: ______________

## CORE VOCABULARY SCREENING—FORM 2B

***Sample***

| | | | | |
|---|---|---|---|---|
| | ***village*** | ***town*** | ***cake*** | ***ring*** |
| B 1 | center | middle | story | school |
| B 2 | autumn | park | bee | fall |
| B 3 | grin | sock | smile | mat |
| B 4 | repair | fix | let | tag |
| B 5 | cheered | made | yelled | planted |
| B 6 | flaming | rubbing | burning | mooing |
| B 7 | speak | paint | need | talk |
| B 8 | stained | dirty | every | short |
| B 9 | gentle | soft | open | poor |
| B 10 | friendly | here | slow | nice |
| B 11 | jerk | hear | pull | mail |
| B 12 | slide | slip | cover | hunt |
| B 13 | plenty | first | secret | enough |
| B 14 | appear | play | seem | last |
| B 15 | freezing | cold | tiring | hungry |
| B 16 | leap | tie | bite | jump |
| B 17 | calm | still | best | just |
| B 18 | slope | bat | hill | truck |
| B 19 | fold | race | wag | bend |
| B 20 | brook | balloon | turtle | creek |
| B 21 | pitched | napped | guessed | threw |
| B 22 | sudden | quick | some | mean |
| B 23 | switch | bring | change | happen |
| B 24 | cattle | trees | shoes | cows |
| B 25 | chuckle | mother | laugh | river |
| B 26 | stare | look | splash | break |
| B 27 | patched | named | pushed | fixed |
| B 28 | discover | kick | sell | find |
| B 29 | notice | fly | see | draw |
| B 30 | bother | tease | walk | picture |

# correct: ______
# incorrect: ______
# no response: ______

# CORE VOCABULARY SCREENING KEY

## FORM 2A

***Sample***

| | *swift* | *fast* |
|---|---|---|
| A 1 | gather | collect |
| A 2 | chunk | piece |
| A 3 | certain | sure |
| A 4 | greedy | selfish |
| A 5 | ache | pain |
| A 6 | build | make |
| A 7 | gladly | happily |
| A 8 | dash | run |
| A 9 | place | put |
| A 10 | toss | throw |
| A 11 | pail | bucket |
| A 12 | foolish | silly |
| A 13 | base | bottom |
| A 14 | rescue | save |
| A 15 | equal | same |
| A 16 | kettle | pot |
| A 17 | spoiled | ruined |
| A 18 | understand | know |
| A 19 | completed | finished |
| A 20 | huge | big |
| A 21 | lovely | pretty |
| A 22 | bright | shiny |
| A 23 | nearly | almost |
| A 24 | terrible | awful |
| A 25 | harm | hurt |
| A 26 | attach | join |
| A 27 | raise | lift |
| A 28 | choose | pick |
| A 29 | finish | end |
| A 30 | shout | yell |

## FORM 2B

***Sample***

| | *village* | *town* |
|---|---|---|
| B 1 | center | middle |
| B 2 | autumn | fall |
| B 3 | grin | smile |
| B 4 | repair | fix |
| B 5 | cheered | yelled |
| B 6 | flaming | burning |
| B 7 | speak | talk |
| B 8 | stained | dirty |
| B 9 | gentle | soft |
| B 10 | friendly | nice |
| B 11 | jerk | pull |
| B 12 | slide | slip |
| B 13 | plenty | enough |
| B 14 | appear | seem |
| B 15 | freezing | cold |
| B 16 | leap | jump |
| B 17 | calm | still |
| B 18 | slope | hill |
| B 19 | fold | bend |
| B 20 | brook | creek |
| B 21 | pitched | threw |
| B 22 | sudden | quick |
| B 23 | switch | change |
| B 24 | cattle | cows |
| B 25 | chuckle | laugh |
| B 26 | stare | look |
| B 27 | patched | fixed |
| B 28 | discover | find |
| B 29 | notice | see |
| B 30 | bother | tease |

Name: ______________________ Date: __________

## CORE VOCABULARY SCREENING—FORM 3A

***Sample***

| | | | | |
|---|---|---|---|---|
| | ***soaked*** | ***wet*** | ***brave*** | ***rocky*** |
| A 1 | invite | sting | ask | melt |
| A 2 | battle | weather | highway | fight |
| A 3 | polite | nice | sure | blind |
| A 4 | silent | rough | scary | quiet |
| A 5 | character | jewel | person | needle |
| A 6 | select | choose | forget | expect |
| A 7 | starving | serious | thick | hungry |
| A 8 | tune | pillow | music | crash |
| A 9 | fearful | afraid | awake | delicious |
| A 10 | awkward | magic | round | clumsy |
| A 11 | curious | together | clear | strange |
| A 12 | removed | guarded | took | hung |
| A 13 | heap | throat | pile | motor |
| A 14 | flock | group | kite | voice |
| A 15 | stumble | hang | drip | fall |

| | | | | |
|---|---|---|---|---|
| A 16 | admire | boil | like | wander |
| A 17 | tug | pull | enter | sink |
| A 18 | flame | month | fire | herd |
| A 19 | rinse | trot | cost | wash |
| A 20 | dull | boring | fierce | hilly |
| A 21 | entire | lumpy | nearby | all |
| A 22 | glistening | shining | spinning | planning |
| A 23 | damage | pour | sail | break |
| A 24 | trim | wipe | cut | copy |
| A 25 | clump | bunch | feast | market |
| A 26 | pause | cross | wait | growl |
| A 27 | scent | smell | joke | block |
| A 28 | matching | juicy | alike | lazy |
| A 29 | thief | robber | cloth | stair |
| A 30 | distant | important | lively | far |

# correct: ______
# incorrect: ______
# no response: ______

Name: ______________________________ Date: ______________

## CORE VOCABULARY SCREENING—FORM 3B

***Sample***

| | | | | |
|---|---|---|---|---|
| | ***hoof*** | ***hose*** | ***foot*** | ***lean*** |
| B 1 | simple | tight | easy | wide |
| B 2 | hollow | rich | sandy | empty |
| B 3 | tremble | honk | shake | stand |
| B 4 | dawn | morning | breath | metal |
| B 5 | trust | freeze | swim | believe |
| B 6 | within | special | inside | welcome |
| B 7 | steal | take | leak | pitch |
| B 8 | filthy | dirty | warm | healthy |
| B 9 | waste | band | neck | trash |
| B 10 | roast | send | cook | pay |
| B 11 | replied | answered | tasted | flooded |
| B 12 | shift | comb | save | move |
| B 13 | basement | temper | cellar | excuse |
| B 14 | tender | rainy | worn | soft |
| B 15 | searched | looked | wrapped | enjoyed |
| B 16 | enormous | different | silly | large |
| B 17 | avenue | hunter | street | chimney |
| B 18 | boast | dive | wake | brag |
| B 19 | galloping | running | touching | winking |
| B 20 | remain | grab | stay | form |
| B 21 | giggled | stretched | laughed | poked |
| B 22 | creep | warn | study | crawl |
| B 23 | guide | lead | brush | paste |
| B 24 | evil | fancy | bad | possible |
| B 25 | journey | brick | meal | trip |
| B 26 | sob | hook | cry | roll |
| B 27 | disturb | bother | swallow | repeat |
| B 28 | chore | insect | knife | job |
| B 29 | meadow | idea | field | bucket |
| B 30 | plate | dish | key | berry |

# correct: ______
# incorrect: ______
# no response: ______

# CORE VOCABULARY SCREENING KEY

## FORM 3A

***Sample***

| | ***soaked*** | ***wet*** |
|---|---|---|
| A 1 | invite | ask |
| A 2 | battle | fight |
| A 3 | polite | nice |
| A 4 | silent | quiet |
| A 5 | character | person |
| A 6 | select | choose |
| A 7 | starving | hungry |
| A 8 | tune | music |
| A 9 | fearful | afraid |
| A 10 | awkward | clumsy |
| A 11 | curious | strange |
| A 12 | removed | took |
| A 13 | heap | pile |
| A 14 | flock | group |
| A 15 | stumble | fall |
| A 16 | admire | like |
| A 17 | tug | pull |
| A 18 | flame | fire |
| A 19 | rinse | wash |
| A 20 | dull | boring |
| A 21 | entire | all |
| A 22 | glistening | shining |
| A 23 | damage | break |
| A 24 | trim | cut |
| A 25 | clump | bunch |
| A 26 | pause | wait |
| A 27 | scent | smell |
| A 28 | matching | alike |
| A 29 | thief | robber |
| A 30 | distant | far |

## FORM 3B

***Sample***

| | ***hoof*** | ***foot*** |
|---|---|---|
| B 1 | simple | easy |
| B 2 | hollow | empty |
| B 3 | tremble | shake |
| B 4 | dawn | morning |
| B 5 | trust | believe |
| B 6 | within | inside |
| B 7 | steal | take |
| B 8 | filthy | dirty |
| B 9 | waste | trash |
| B 10 | roast | cook |
| B 11 | replied | answered |
| B 12 | shift | move |
| B 13 | basement | cellar |
| B 14 | tender | soft |
| B 15 | searched | looked |
| B 16 | enormous | large |
| B 17 | avenue | street |
| B 18 | boast | brag |
| B 19 | galloping | running |
| B 20 | remain | stay |
| B 21 | giggled | laughed |
| B 22 | creep | crawl |
| B 23 | guide | lead |
| B 24 | evil | bad |
| B 25 | journey | trip |
| B 26 | sob | cry |
| B 27 | disturb | bother |
| B 28 | chore | job |
| B 29 | meadow | field |
| B 30 | plate | dish |

Name: ______________________ Date: ______________

## CORE VOCABULARY SCREENING—FORM 4A

***Sample***

| | | | | |
|---|---|---|---|---|
| | ***mention*** | ***cheek*** | ***rise*** | ***say*** |

| Item | Target | | | |
|---|---|---|---|---|
| A 1 | roaming | dreaming | walking | spending |
| A 2 | wildlife | myth | paddle | animals |
| A 3 | locate | wound | find | sharpen |
| A 4 | gobble | eat | arrive | snap |
| A 5 | shiver | attack | handle | shake |
| A 6 | pebble | stone | warmth | shed |
| A 7 | cord | jelly | string | list |
| A 8 | trace | draw | fool | agree |
| A 9 | familiar | lonely | peaceful | known |
| A 10 | riddle | creature | puzzle | miner |
| A 11 | plunge | dive | flap | sigh |
| A 12 | capture | groan | soak | catch |
| A 13 | pleasant | nice | speedy | whole |
| A 14 | whirl | flow | spin | search |
| A 15 | necessary | faraway | level | needed |

| Item | Target | | | |
|---|---|---|---|---|
| A 16 | odd | strange | wavy | cruel |
| A 17 | sway | aim | bend | spoil |
| A 18 | canyon | valley | salad | barrel |
| A 19 | garbage | victory | trash | hoop |
| A 20 | flavor | result | adventure | taste |
| A 21 | slick | gloomy | slippery | kindly |
| A 22 | weep | dare | chop | cry |
| A 23 | bruised | hurt | wiggled | scooped |
| A 24 | command | cabin | health | order |
| A 25 | honest | weak | true | curly |
| A 26 | legend | rink | alarm | story |
| A 27 | view | see | jab | lend |
| A 28 | expensive | foggy | bony | costly |
| A 29 | ancient | hot | old | thin |
| A 30 | examine | check | rule | howl |

# correct: ______
# incorrect: ______
# no response: ______

Name: ______________________ Date: ____________

# CORE VOCABULARY SCREENING—FORM 4B

***Sample***

| | ***rim*** | ***yarn*** | ***edge*** | ***bead*** |
|---|---|---|---|---|

| Item | Target | | | |
|---|---|---|---|---|
| B 1 | several | few | instead | unusual |
| B 2 | nasty | plain | ripe | bad |
| B 3 | voyage | bargain | trip | giggle |
| B 4 | grasp | offer | scratch | hold |
| B 5 | fortunate | sour | lucky | twisted |
| B 6 | exchange | switch | drive | weave |
| B 7 | shriek | float | spray | yell |
| B 8 | gleam | shine | trudge | pack |
| B 9 | container | hawk | nation | box |
| B 10 | rage | pride | anger | beard |
| B 11 | weary | frozen | jealous | tired |
| B 12 | limb | apron | branch | crack |
| B 13 | object | thing | blink | reward |
| B 14 | vanish | glance | disappear | improve |
| B 15 | performers | closets | harbors | actors |

| Item | Target | | | |
|---|---|---|---|---|
| B 16 | final | last | phony | tough |
| B 17 | soil | hobby | dirt | baggage |
| B 18 | blend | mix | charge | greet |
| B 19 | mend | grip | rent | fix |
| B 20 | spare | famous | extra | bossy |
| B 21 | relax | skip | cure | rest |
| B 22 | cheerful | happy | untied | apart |
| B 23 | tow | dip | pull | fade |
| B 24 | dangled | waddled | ruined | hung |
| B 25 | transfer | change | lift | paint |
| B 26 | burst | unrolled | flew | broke |
| B 27 | pasture | field | chest | scene |
| B 28 | jog | rob | run | pump |
| B 29 | powerful | fuzzy | strong | alive |
| B 30 | burrow | horse | waist | hole |

# correct: ______
# incorrect: ______
# no response: ______

# CORE VOCABULARY SCREENING KEY

## FORM 4A

***Sample***

| | *mention* | *say* |
|---|---|---|
| A 1 | roaming | walking |
| A 2 | wildlife | animals |
| A 3 | locate | find |
| A 4 | gobble | eat |
| A 5 | shiver | shake |
| A 6 | pebble | stone |
| A 7 | cord | string |
| A 8 | trace | draw |
| A 9 | familiar | known |
| A 10 | riddle | puzzle |
| A 11 | plunge | dive |
| A 12 | capture | catch |
| A 13 | pleasant | nice |
| A 14 | whirl | spin |
| A 15 | necessary | needed |
| A 16 | odd | strange |
| A 17 | sway | bend |
| A 18 | canyon | valley |
| A 19 | garbage | trash |
| A 20 | flavor | taste |
| A 21 | slick | slippery |
| A 22 | weep | cry |
| A 23 | bruised | hurt |
| A 24 | command | order |
| A 25 | honest | true |
| A 26 | legend | story |
| A 27 | view | see |
| A 28 | expensive | costly |
| A 29 | ancient | old |
| A 30 | examine | check |

## FORM 4B

***Sample***

| | *rim* | *edge* |
|---|---|---|
| B 1 | several | few |
| B 2 | nasty | bad |
| B 3 | voyage | trip |
| B 4 | grasp | hold |
| B 5 | fortunate | lucky |
| B 6 | exchange | switch |
| B 7 | shriek | yell |
| B 8 | gleam | shine |
| B 9 | container | box |
| B 10 | rage | anger |
| B 11 | weary | tired |
| B 12 | limb | branch |
| B 13 | object | thing |
| B 14 | vanish | disappear |
| B 15 | performers | actors |
| B 16 | final | last |
| B 17 | soil | dirt |
| B 18 | blend | mix |
| B 19 | mend | fix |
| B 20 | spare | extra |
| B 21 | relax | rest |
| B 22 | cheerful | happy |
| B 23 | tow | pull |
| B 24 | dangled | hung |
| B 25 | transfer | change |
| B 26 | burst | broke |
| B 27 | pasture | field |
| B 28 | jog | run |
| B 29 | powerful | strong |
| B 30 | burrow | hole |

Name: ______________________ Date: ____________

# CORE VOCABULARY SCREENING—FORM 5A

***Sample***

| ***fling*** | ***accuse*** | ***demand*** | ***throw*** |
|---|---|---|---|

| | Target | | | |
|---|---|---|---|---|
| A 1 | splendid | moody | wonderful | private |
| A 2 | cowardly | afraid | thrifty | uneven |
| A 3 | shrub | buckle | favor | bush |
| A 4 | cling | topple | hold | prove |
| A 5 | hoisted | lifted | supplied | glued |
| A 6 | stroll | dislike | munch | walk |
| A 7 | delay | wait | succeed | prepare |
| A 8 | decision | statue | choice | uniform |
| A 9 | vibrate | shake | suggest | depend |
| A 10 | miserable | endless | absent | sad |
| A 11 | slice | heat | cut | doubt |
| A 12 | concerned | worried | tangled | included |
| A 13 | chant | vase | song | barge |
| A 14 | boulder | stitch | theater | rock |
| A 15 | attempt | try | respect | peel |

| | Target | | | |
|---|---|---|---|---|
| A 16 | uncommon | plump | shallow | rare |
| A 17 | district | strap | area | target |
| A 18 | glimpse | see | lose | halt |
| A 19 | convention | meeting | surface | telescope |
| A 20 | dense | direct | thick | stolen |
| A 21 | occasionally | terribly | anyhow | sometimes |
| A 22 | abandon | defend | leave | sweat |
| A 23 | scrub | clean | develop | hatch |
| A 24 | gulped | continued | swallowed | grazed |
| A 25 | drain | empty | rush | sniff |
| A 26 | gale | lamp | terror | storm |
| A 27 | bathed | pretended | refused | washed |
| A 28 | tremendous | helpless | powerful | royal |
| A 29 | symbol | sign | thunder | judge |
| A 30 | inspect | travel | harden | check |

# correct: ______
# incorrect: ______
# no response: ______

Name: ______________________ Date: __________

## CORE VOCABULARY SCREENING—FORM 5B

***Sample***

| | | | | |
|---|---|---|---|---|
| | ***value*** | ***worth*** | ***report*** | ***siren*** |

| Item | Word | | | |
|---|---|---|---|---|
| B 1 | witnessed | sneezed | felt | saw |
| B 2 | secure | safe | extra | flat |
| B 3 | crate | speck | box | treaty |
| B 4 | dread | mark | trade | fear |
| B 5 | permit | allow | scatter | declare |
| B 6 | alter | tickle | lean | change |
| B 7 | thaw | dump | melt | glide |
| B 8 | twirl | spin | flop | grip |
| B 9 | instruct | unfold | teach | adjust |
| B 10 | demonstrate | receive | sharpen | show |
| B 11 | risky | perfect | dangerous | crowded |
| B 12 | sturdy | strong | savage | shaggy |
| B 13 | squirm | affect | heal | wiggle |
| B 14 | gently | briefly | softly | deeply |
| B 15 | furious | dim | mighty | angry |
| B 16 | desire | want | reply | spill |
| B 17 | coarse | sticky | rough | torn |
| B 18 | dodge | sew | tape | move |
| B 19 | task | buggy | job | mist |
| B 20 | bloom | flower | accent | design |
| B 21 | initial | first | either | greedy |
| B 22 | defeat | load | rattle | beat |
| B 23 | hunch | broom | guess | lodge |
| B 24 | snatch | grab | behave | argue |
| B 25 | sketch | harvest | order | draw |
| B 26 | chilly | horrible | cool | sore |
| B 27 | courage | bravery | mixture | swamp |
| B 28 | chamber | accident | delivery | room |
| B 29 | connect | join | accept | serve |
| B 30 | drowsy | dusty | tired | firm |

# correct: ______
# incorrect: ______
# no response: ______

# CORE VOCABULARY SCREENING KEY

## FORM 5A

***Sample***

| | ***fling*** | ***throw*** |
|---|---|---|
| A 1 | splendid | wonderful |
| A 2 | cowardly | afraid |
| A 3 | shrub | bush |
| A 4 | cling | hold |
| A 5 | hoisted | lifted |
| A 6 | stroll | walk |
| A 7 | delay | wait |
| A 8 | decision | choice |
| A 9 | vibrate | shake |
| A 10 | miserable | sad |
| A 11 | slice | cut |
| A 12 | concerned | worried |
| A 13 | chant | song |
| A 14 | boulder | rock |
| A 15 | attempt | try |
| A 16 | uncommon | rare |
| A 17 | district | area |
| A 18 | glimpse | see |
| A 19 | convention | meeting |
| A 20 | dense | thick |
| A 21 | occasionally | sometimes |
| A 22 | abandon | leave |
| A 23 | scrub | clean |
| A 24 | gulped | swallowed |
| A 25 | drain | empty |
| A 26 | gale | storm |
| A 27 | bathed | washed |
| A 28 | tremendous | powerful |
| A 29 | symbol | sign |
| A 30 | inspect | check |

## FORM 5B

***Sample***

| | ***value*** | ***worth*** |
|---|---|---|
| B 1 | witnessed | saw |
| B 2 | secure | safe |
| B 3 | crate | box |
| B 4 | dread | fear |
| B 5 | permit | allow |
| B 6 | alter | change |
| B 7 | thaw | melt |
| B 8 | twirl | spin |
| B 9 | instruct | teach |
| B 10 | demonstrate | show |
| B 11 | risky | dangerous |
| B 12 | sturdy | strong |
| B 13 | squirm | wiggle |
| B 14 | gently | softly |
| B 15 | furious | angry |
| B 16 | desire | want |
| B 17 | coarse | rough |
| B 18 | dodge | move |
| B 19 | task | job |
| B 20 | bloom | flower |
| B 21 | initial | first |
| B 22 | defeat | beat |
| B 23 | hunch | guess |
| B 24 | snatch | grab |
| B 25 | sketch | draw |
| B 26 | chilly | cool |
| B 27 | courage | bravery |
| B 28 | chamber | room |
| B 29 | connect | join |
| B 30 | drowsy | tired |

Name: ____________________ Date: __________

## CORE VOCABULARY SCREENING—FORM 6A

***Sample***

| | ***gesture*** | ***entrance*** | ***towel*** | ***movement*** |
|---|---|---|---|---|

| Item | Target | | | |
|---|---|---|---|---|
| A 1 | display | plot | show | bend |
| A 2 | sentry | guard | blaze | habit |
| A 3 | physician | blade | gallon | doctor |
| A 4 | adore | cause | love | tap |
| A 5 | summit | top | flight | lane |
| A 6 | regulate | wrinkle | attend | control |
| A 7 | error | knight | mistake | chain |
| A 8 | conflict | battle | factory | marker |
| A 9 | conceal | chew | hide | lead |
| A 10 | applaud | stain | frown | clap |
| A 11 | memorize | remember | flutter | obey |
| A 12 | circular | least | steady | round |
| A 13 | resign | absorb | quit | imagine |
| A 14 | rapid | fast | inner | smoky |
| A 15 | restricted | hired | whined | limited |

| Item | Target | | | |
|---|---|---|---|---|
| A 16 | core | alley | center | marsh |
| A 17 | infant | baby | acorn | college |
| A 18 | gracious | hairy | kind | unclear |
| A 19 | absurd | fairly | glassy | silly |
| A 20 | local | nearby | natural | responsible |
| A 21 | odor | instant | smell | scenery |
| A 22 | drench | lace | stoop | wet |
| A 23 | decay | beg | rot | hug |
| A 24 | request | type | cheat | ask |
| A 25 | attire | clothing | drought | moth |
| A 26 | moist | hopeful | damp | known |
| A 27 | frequent | often | golden | halfway |
| A 28 | peddle | grind | sell | wobble |
| A 29 | terrifying | joyous | tilted | scary |
| A 30 | typical | normal | playful | salty |

# correct: ______
# incorrect: ______
# no response: ______

Name: ______________________ Date: ______________

# CORE VOCABULARY SCREENING—FORM 6B

***Sample***

| | | | | |
|---|---|---|---|---|
| | ***gorge*** | ***film*** | ***valley*** | ***hinge*** |
| B 1 | quantity | amount | freckle | clerk |
| B 2 | conclusion | actor | dusk | end |
| B 3 | method | way | bushel | vine |
| B 4 | required | grumbled | imitated | needed |
| B 5 | combine | seek | join | vote |
| B 6 | estimate | operate | proceed | guess |
| B 7 | annoy | hitch | bother | shrink |
| B 8 | devoured | ate | considered | brought |
| B 9 | courteous | hazy | polite | modern |
| B 10 | employee | accident | liquid | worker |
| B 11 | superb | general | wonderful | national |
| B 12 | respond | prevent | answer | scrape |
| B 13 | vacant | naughty | precious | empty |
| B 14 | major | important | ordinary | slippery |
| B 15 | image | hunger | picture | leash |

| | | | | |
|---|---|---|---|---|
| B 16 | lengthy | fond | muddy | long |
| B 17 | assistant | helper | cable | grill |
| B 18 | revolve | brag | turn | purr |
| B 19 | perspire | sweat | interrupt | arrange |
| B 20 | cautious | greasy | married | careful |
| B 21 | occur | blame | click | happen |
| B 22 | reduce | lessen | admit | purchase |
| B 23 | shatter | break | insist | steer |
| B 24 | parcel | ancestor | package | lantern |
| B 25 | twine | string | guest | hotel |
| B 26 | doze | glow | kneel | sleep |
| B 27 | remote | nervous | far | shady |
| B 28 | active | lively | especially | gradually |
| B 29 | genuine | husky | real | partly |
| B 30 | contribute | hesitate | wink | give |

# correct: ______
# incorrect: ______
# no response: ______

# CORE VOCABULARY SCREENING KEY

## FORM 6A

***Sample***

| | *gesture* | *movement* |
|---|---|---|
| A 1 | display | show |
| A 2 | sentry | guard |
| A 3 | physician | doctor |
| A 4 | adore | love |
| A 5 | summit | top |
| A 6 | regulate | control |
| A 7 | error | mistake |
| A 8 | conflict | battle |
| A 9 | conceal | hide |
| A 10 | applaud | clap |
| A 11 | memorize | remember |
| A 12 | circular | round |
| A 13 | resign | quit |
| A 14 | rapid | fast |
| A 15 | restricted | limited |
| A 16 | core | center |
| A 17 | infant | baby |
| A 18 | gracious | kind |
| A 19 | absurd | silly |
| A 20 | local | nearby |
| A 21 | odor | smell |
| A 22 | drench | wet |
| A 23 | decay | rot |
| A 24 | request | ask |
| A 25 | attire | clothing |
| A 26 | moist | damp |
| A 27 | frequent | often |
| A 28 | peddle | sell |
| A 29 | terrifying | scary |
| A 30 | typical | normal |

## FORM 6B

***Sample***

| | *gorge* | *valley* |
|---|---|---|
| B 1 | quantity | amount |
| B 2 | conclusion | end |
| B 3 | method | way |
| B 4 | required | needed |
| B 5 | combine | join |
| B 6 | estimate | guess |
| B 7 | annoy | bother |
| B 8 | devoured | ate |
| B 9 | courteous | polite |
| B 10 | employee | worker |
| B 11 | superb | wonderful |
| B 12 | respond | answer |
| B 13 | vacant | empty |
| B 14 | major | important |
| B 15 | image | picture |
| B 16 | lengthy | long |
| B 17 | assistant | helper |
| B 18 | revolve | turn |
| B 19 | perspire | sweat |
| B 20 | cautious | careful |
| B 21 | occur | happen |
| B 22 | reduce | lessen |
| B 23 | shatter | break |
| B 24 | parcel | package |
| B 25 | twine | string |
| B 26 | doze | sleep |
| B 27 | remote | far |
| B 28 | active | lively |
| B 29 | genuine | real |
| B 30 | contribute | give |

Name: ______________________ Date: ____________

# CORE VOCABULARY SCREENING—FORM 7A

***Sample***

| | | | | |
|---|---|---|---|---|
| | ***fabric*** | ***diamond*** | ***cloth*** | ***history*** |
| A 1 | recall | bounce | untie | remember |
| A 2 | reveal | show | act | tear |
| A 3 | incomplete | amazing | unfinished | shaky |
| A 4 | flaw | shirt | meeting | weakness |
| A 5 | ballad | garage | song | iron |
| A 6 | broth | cave | hero | soup |
| A 7 | donate | manage | give | sense |
| A 8 | originated | began | escaped | wrote |
| A 9 | humid | born | lousy | damp |
| A 10 | chasm | bench | gap | lump |
| A 11 | fragile | unkind | realistic | breakable |
| A 12 | amusement | fun | darkness | lumber |
| A 13 | utter | drop | say | break |
| A 14 | abrupt | certain | narrow | quick |
| A 15 | misery | difference | sadness | grain |

| | | | | |
|---|---|---|---|---|
| A 16 | crimson | red | beneath | giant |
| A 17 | confront | forgive | release | challenge |
| A 18 | regularly | finally | frequently | early |
| A 19 | depart | wind | seal | leave |
| A 20 | initiate | recognize | spread | start |
| A 21 | jubilant | tired | happy | tame |
| A 22 | notable | important | pleasant | ready |
| A 23 | overdue | broken | spotless | late |
| A 24 | massive | large | neat | careful |
| A 25 | persuasive | convincing | smelly | foolish |
| A 26 | haste | camera | package | speed |
| A 27 | commerce | message | business | palace |
| A 28 | detect | find | except | season |
| A 29 | tedious | boring | weak | frozen |
| A 30 | enthusiastic | hungry | excited | fresh |

# correct: ______
# incorrect: ______
# no response: ______

Name: ____________________ Date: ____________

## CORE VOCABULARY SCREENING—FORM 7B

***Sample***

| | | | | |
|---|---|---|---|---|
| | ***consumer*** | ***apartment*** | ***path*** | ***buyer*** |
| B 1 | wary | cautious | leaky | patient |
| B 2 | postpone | carve | delay | learn |
| B 3 | similar | bent | fair | alike |
| B 4 | pursue | chase | shout | throw |
| B 5 | bashful | aboard | thirsty | shy |
| B 6 | repeatedly | catchy | often | probably |
| B 7 | option | choice | beauty | force |
| B 8 | utilize | chew | use | call |
| B 9 | conceit | blast | party | pride |
| B 10 | cherish | love | visit | slide |
| B 11 | isolated | flattened | alone | sharp |
| B 12 | formerly | against | without | before |
| B 13 | hub | center | example | pole |
| B 14 | eternity | address | forever | hospital |
| B 15 | modify | harness | link | change |

| | | | | |
|---|---|---|---|---|
| B 16 | persist | continue | treat | gasp |
| B 17 | inactive | expensive | still | pretty |
| B 18 | fee | bubble | wall | price |
| B 19 | outcome | result | captain | stamp |
| B 20 | currently | really | now | tiny |
| B 21 | mimic | copy | pull | rush |
| B 22 | cavity | juice | hole | machine |
| B 23 | ajar | indeed | open | lower |
| B 24 | infinite | unlimited | practical | split |
| B 25 | dismayed | appeared | concerned | hurried |
| B 26 | desolate | hurt | tight | empty |
| B 27 | elevated | high | bundled | impossible |
| B 28 | frigid | heavy | odd | cold |
| B 29 | linger | wait | lick | startle |
| B 30 | approximately | slowly | loudly | nearly |

# correct: ______
# incorrect: ______
# no response: ______

# CORE VOCABULARY SCREENING KEY

## FORM 7A

***Sample***

| | *fabric* | *cloth* |
|---|---|---|
| A 1 | recall | remember |
| A 2 | reveal | show |
| A 3 | incomplete | unfinished |
| A 4 | flaw | weakness |
| A 5 | ballad | song |
| A 6 | broth | soup |
| A 7 | donate | give |
| A 8 | originated | began |
| A 9 | humid | damp |
| A 10 | chasm | gap |
| A 11 | fragile | breakable |
| A 12 | amusement | fun |
| A 13 | utter | say |
| A 14 | abrupt | quick |
| A 15 | misery | sadness |
| A 16 | crimson | red |
| A 17 | confront | challenge |
| A 18 | regularly | frequently |
| A 19 | depart | leave |
| A 20 | initiate | start |
| A 21 | jubilant | happy |
| A 22 | notable | important |
| A 23 | overdue | late |
| A 24 | massive | large |
| A 25 | persuasive | convincing |
| A 26 | haste | speed |
| A 27 | commerce | business |
| A 28 | detect | find |
| A 29 | tedious | boring |
| A 30 | enthusiastic | excited |

## FORM 7B

***Sample***

| | *consumer* | *buyer* |
|---|---|---|
| B 1 | wary | cautious |
| B 2 | postpone | delay |
| B 3 | similar | alike |
| B 4 | pursue | chase |
| B 5 | bashful | shy |
| B 6 | repeatedly | often |
| B 7 | option | choice |
| B 8 | utilize | use |
| B 9 | conceit | pride |
| B 10 | cherish | love |
| B 11 | isolated | alone |
| B 12 | formerly | before |
| B 13 | hub | center |
| B 14 | eternity | forever |
| B 15 | modify | change |
| B 16 | persist | continue |
| B 17 | inactive | still |
| B 18 | fee | price |
| B 19 | outcome | result |
| B 20 | currently | now |
| B 21 | mimic | copy |
| B 22 | cavity | hole |
| B 23 | ajar | open |
| B 24 | infinite | unlimited |
| B 25 | dismayed | concerned |
| B 26 | desolate | empty |
| B 27 | elevated | high |
| B 28 | frigid | cold |
| B 29 | linger | wait |
| B 30 | approximately | nearly |

Name: ______________________ Date: ____________

## CORE VOCABULARY SCREENING—FORM 8A

***Sample***

| | | | | |
|---|---|---|---|---|
| | ***loathe*** | ***rely*** | ***open*** | ***hate*** |
| A 1 | prosper | drill | succeed | volunteer |
| A 2 | intricate | elected | terrific | complex |
| A 3 | brawl | canal | fight | railing |
| A 4 | fortify | strengthen | imitate | remove |
| A 5 | revision | improvement | tournament | vibration |
| A 6 | implore | flip | risk | beg |
| A 7 | jovial | upset | cheerful | noble |
| A 8 | exterior | festival | outside | patience |
| A 9 | verdict | operator | decision | witness |
| A 10 | precise | exact | coastal | generous |
| A 11 | abode | interval | quality | house |
| A 12 | baffling | fleeing | puzzling | relaxing |
| A 13 | merge | shave | conduct | join |
| A 14 | pact | agreement | outfit | shack |
| A 15 | resume | design | continue | scribble |

| | | | | |
|---|---|---|---|---|
| A 16 | sequence | order | talent | badge |
| A 17 | evade | increase | deliver | avoid |
| A 18 | consequence | result | license | reservation |
| A 19 | hamper | nudge | limit | invent |
| A 20 | speculate | clamp | recommend | guess |
| A 21 | accumulate | review | gather | explore |
| A 22 | motive | concrete | liberty | reason |
| A 23 | deduct | subtract | obtain | control |
| A 24 | maneuver | ignore | move | replace |
| A 25 | situated | jagged | assembled | located |
| A 26 | uproar | noise | journal | arrival |
| A 27 | swindle | launch | cheat | attend |
| A 28 | hostage | captive | interference | furniture |
| A 29 | apparel | clothing | ability | machinery |
| A 30 | chime | prefer | sort | ring |

# correct: ______
# incorrect: ______
# no response: ______

Name: ____________________ Date: ____________

# CORE VOCABULARY SCREENING—FORM 8B

***Sample***

| | Target | | | |
|---|---|---|---|---|
| | ***occurrence*** | ***restaurant*** | ***happening*** | ***treasure*** |

| Item | Target | | | |
|---|---|---|---|---|
| B 1 | mishap | banquet | terrace | accident |
| B 2 | specific | humble | detailed | rotten |
| B 3 | hazard | danger | energy | platter |
| B 4 | procedure | ripple | salary | method |
| B 5 | significant | foreign | important | pure |
| B 6 | acceleration | speed | hail | parlor |
| B 7 | portrait | ditch | shield | picture |
| B 8 | genial | handy | selfish | friendly |
| B 9 | capsize | overturn | blush | separate |
| B 10 | inhale | gulp | hire | breathe |
| B 11 | frank | dreary | honest | magical |
| B 12 | gingerly | carefully | innocently | partially |
| B 13 | beverage | drink | occasion | remark |
| B 14 | adequate | loyal | enough | scarce |
| B 15 | ravine | fashion | bracelet | valley |

| Item | Target | | | |
|---|---|---|---|---|
| B 16 | convert | change | pledge | trample |
| B 17 | luster | benefit | saucer | shine |
| B 18 | irk | bother | produce | soften |
| B 19 | substantial | graceful | ridiculous | large |
| B 20 | maximum | glorious | most | official |
| B 21 | authentic | immense | real | obedient |
| B 22 | tremor | thorn | glacier | shaking |
| B 23 | valor | bravery | fern | wealth |
| B 24 | scorch | coil | oppose | burn |
| B 25 | reunion | glider | meeting | climate |
| B 26 | lapse | break | flake | pain |
| B 27 | wily | definite | clever | humorous |
| B 28 | diminish | lessen | graduate | introduce |
| B 29 | ignite | accompany | light | measure |
| B 30 | client | blunder | outline | customer |

# correct: ______
# incorrect: ______
# no response: ______

# CORE VOCABULARY SCREENING KEY

## FORM 8A

***Sample***

| | ***loathe*** | ***hate*** |
|---|---|---|
| A 1 | prosper | succeed |
| A 2 | intricate | complex |
| A 3 | brawl | fight |
| A 4 | fortify | strengthen |
| A 5 | revision | improvement |
| A 6 | implore | beg |
| A 7 | jovial | cheerful |
| A 8 | exterior | outside |
| A 9 | verdict | decision |
| A 10 | precise | exact |
| A 11 | abode | house |
| A 12 | baffling | puzzling |
| A 13 | merge | join |
| A 14 | pact | agreement |
| A 15 | resume | continue |
| A 16 | sequence | order |
| A 17 | evade | avoid |
| A 18 | consequence | result |
| A 19 | hamper | limit |
| A 20 | speculate | guess |
| A 21 | accumulate | gather |
| A 22 | motive | reason |
| A 23 | deduct | subtract |
| A 24 | maneuver | move |
| A 25 | situated | located |
| A 26 | uproar | noise |
| A 27 | swindle | cheat |
| A 28 | hostage | captive |
| A 29 | apparel | clothing |
| A 30 | chime | ring |

## FORM 8B

***Sample***

| | ***occurrence*** | ***happening*** |
|---|---|---|
| B 1 | mishap | accident |
| B 2 | specific | detailed |
| B 3 | hazard | danger |
| B 4 | procedure | method |
| B 5 | significant | important |
| B 6 | acceleration | speed |
| B 7 | portrait | picture |
| B 8 | genial | friendly |
| B 9 | capsize | overturn |
| B 10 | inhale | breathe |
| B 11 | frank | honest |
| B 12 | gingerly | carefully |
| B 13 | beverage | drink |
| B 14 | adequate | enough |
| B 15 | ravine | valley |
| B 16 | convert | change |
| B 17 | luster | shine |
| B 18 | irk | bother |
| B 19 | substantial | large |
| B 20 | maximum | most |
| B 21 | authentic | real |
| B 22 | tremor | shaking |
| B 23 | valor | bravery |
| B 24 | scorch | burn |
| B 25 | reunion | meeting |
| B 26 | lapse | break |
| B 27 | wily | clever |
| B 28 | diminish | lessen |
| B 29 | ignite | light |
| B 30 | client | customer |

# Critchlow Spanish Verbal Language Scale

**SKILL ASSESSED**

## Vocabulary

**Grade Level**

K–8

**Language**

Spanish

**Grouping**

Individual

**Approximate Testing Time**

15 Minutes

**Materials**

Spanish Record Form (p. 149)

**Source**

From *Dos Amigos Verbal Language Scales* by Donald E. Critchlow.

**WHAT** The *Critchlow Spanish Verbal Language Scale* measures one aspect of a student's vocabulary in Spanish. Vocabulary is assessed by asking a student to say the "opposite" of a series of words spoken by the examiner. The words on this assessment are arranged in increasing order of difficulty. The scale contains 75 Spanish stimulus words.

**WHY** As students progress through the grades, they build larger and larger vocabularies. A more advanced vocabulary enables students to better comprehend what they read and hear as well as to express their thoughts more clearly. Measuring vocabulary provides an index of what a student has learned and how well equipped the student is for future learning.

**HOW** Before beginning the test, determine that the student understands what an opposite is and can demonstrate this knowledge. For example say: *If it is not daytime, it is* _____ or say: *Children who are not boys are* ______ to help establish the concept of opposite.

Explain to the student that you are going to say a word and he or she is to respond with the opposite of that word. Begin with the first item for all students, and discontinue testing after the child misses five consecutive words or completes the scale. Do not give credit for a response that is not listed.

Note that alternatives are sometimes provided for a stimulus or acceptable response. For example, the first stimulus is *muchacho-niño.* In this case, give the student the first stimulus, *muchacho.* If the student does not give the correct response (*muchacha*), the stimulus *niño* should be given. If the student gives a correct response (*niña*), then he or she receives credit for that item.

**WHAT IT MEANS** Count the number correct and refer to the scoring criteria below to identify the approximate vocabulary grade level. For students who score below their current grade level, provide direct instruction in specific vocabulary needed for school success.

| Number Correct Spanish | Spanish Vocabulary Grade Level |
|---|---|
| 1–9 | Grade K and below |
| 10–13 | Grade 1 |
| 14–17 | Grade 2 |
| 18–20 | Grade 3 |
| 21–24 | Grade 4 |
| 25–28 | Grade 5 |
| 29–32 | Grade 6 |
| 33 and above | Grade 7 and above |

**CORE's *Teaching Reading Sourcebook*, Second Edition**

**WHAT'S NEXT?** For students with limited vocabulary, more intense support in developing other underlying reading skills may be warranted. Further assessment is necessary to determine if there are other underlying causes for a student's limited vocabulary development. The *CORE Spanish Phonics Survey* will identify whether or not poor decoding skill knowledge is causing poor word recognition, and the *CORE Spanish Phonemic Awareness Test* will isolate phoneme awareness as an underlying factor.

# Critchlow Spanish Verbal Language Scale

Name ______________________________ Grade ________ Date ___________

Directions: Tell the student: *Quiero que me digas lo contrario de cada palabra.* Discontinue testing after five consecutive errors.

| | | STIMULUS | RESPONSE |
|---|---|---|---|
| ______ | 1. | muchacho | muchacha |
| ______ | 2. | niño | niña |
| ______ | 3. | caliente | frío |
| ______ | 4. | sucio | limpio |
| ______ | 5. | enfrente | detrás |
| ______ | 6. | mojado | seco |
| ______ | 7. | hermano | hermana |
| ______ | 8. | cerrar | abrir |
| ______ | 9. | muerto | vivo |
| ______ | 10. | temprano | tarde |
| ______ | 11. | apagar | prender-encender |
| ______ | 12. | joven | viejo-anciano |
| ______ | 13. | hija | hijo |
| ______ | 14. | torcido | derecho-recto |
| ______ | 15. | cerca | lejos |
| ______ | 16. | perder | encontrar-hallar |
| ______ | 17. | ruidoso | quieto-callado |
| ______ | 18. | vacío | lleno |
| ______ | 19. | venir | ir |
| ______ | 20. | enfermo | sano |
| ______ | 21. | apretado | suelto |
| ______ | 22. | bonito | feo |
| ______ | 23. | agrio-ácido | dulce |
| ______ | 24. | norte | sur |
| ______ | 25. | reír | llorar |
| ______ | 26. | recordar | olvidar |
| ______ | 27. | pesado | ligero-liviano |
| ______ | 28. | enemigo | amigo |
| ______ | 29. | igual | diferente-distinto |
| ______ | 30. | falso | cierto |
| ______ | 31. | crudo | cocido |
| ______ | 32. | noche | día |
| ______ | 33. | después | antes |
| ______ | 34. | ausente | presente |
| ______ | 35. | angosto-estrecho | ancho |
| ______ | 36. | empezar | terminar |
| ______ | | comenzar | acabar |
| ______ | 37. | amor | odio |
| ______ | 38. | sumar | restar-quitar-substraer |

| | | STIMULUS | RESPONSE |
|---|---|---|---|
| ______ | 39. | multiplicar | dividir |
| ______ | 40. | entrada | salida |
| ______ | 41. | mentira-falsedad | verdad |
| ______ | 42. | difícil | fácil |
| ______ | 43. | liso | tosco-áspero |
| ______ | 44. | fuerte | débil |
| ______ | 45. | costoso | barato |
| ______ | 46. | encarcelado-aprisionado | libre |
| ______ | 47. | anterior | posterior |
| ______ | | primero | último |
| ______ | 48. | público | privado |
| ______ | 49. | ganancia | pérdida |
| ______ | 50. | salvaje | manso-doméstico |
| ______ | 51. | alargar | acortar |
| ______ | 52. | rancio | fresco |
| ______ | 53. | triunfo-victoria | derrota |
| ______ | 54. | complicado | simple-sencillo |
| ______ | 55. | tímido | valiente |
| ______ | 56. | unir | separar |
| ______ | 57. | peligroso | seguro |
| ______ | 58. | máximo | mínimo |
| ______ | 59. | éxito | fracaso |
| ______ | 60. | ventaja | desventaja |
| ______ | 61. | vertical | horizontal |
| ______ | 62. | bendecir | maldecir |
| ______ | 63. | crear | destruir |
| ______ | 64. | inferior | superior |
| ______ | 65. | ignorante | inteligente-sabio |
| ______ | 66. | disminuir | aumentar |
| ______ | 67. | convexo | cóncavo |
| ______ | 68. | ingenuo | sofisticado |
| ______ | 69. | pasivo | activo |
| ______ | 70. | autocracia | democracia |
| ______ | 71. | corpulento | delgado |
| ______ | 72. | amplificar | reducir |
| ______ | 73. | síntesis | análisis |
| ______ | 74. | intermitente | continuo |
| ______ | 75. | tentativo | permanente |

Score: ______ /75

# CORE Reading Maze Comprehension Test

**SKILL ASSESSED**

## Reading Comprehension

**Grade Level**

2–10

**Language**

English

**Grouping**

Individual/Group

**Approximate Testing Time**

3 Minutes

**Materials**

- a copy of the appropriate passage
- a stopwatch
- pencils

**Author**

Michael Milone, Ph.D.

**WHAT** A maze reading assessment is a task that measures how well students understand text they read silently. The maze task differs from traditional comprehension in that it is based completely on the text. After the first sentence, every seventh word in the passage is replaced with the correct word and two distracters. Students choose the word from among the three choices that fits best with the rest of the passage.

**WHY** Capable readers understand the syntax of what they read and the meanings of the words as they are used in the text. Some students with reading difficulties can't comprehend what they read well enough to choose words based on semantic and syntactic accuracy. A maze reading assessment can identify these students and measure changes in their reading behaviors as the result of instruction or practice.

**HOW** Students read one passage that has been modified in a specific way. The first sentence of the passage is left intact to provide a meaningful start to the reading. For the rest of the passage, every seventh word is replaced with parentheses in which are found the correct word from the passage and two distracters arranged randomly. The student circles one word within the parentheses that makes sense with the rest of the passage.

Neither of the distracters maintains the meaning of the passage. One is a near distracter that is the same part of speech or otherwise resembles the correct word. The other is a far distracter that is chosen randomly from a pool of words that are comparable to the words in the passage.

The length of the passages varies from around 150 to 400 words; the passage is chosen depending on the grade placement or reading ability of the student. The student has three minutes to complete the task (reading the passage). The student's score is the number of correct words circled in three minutes. The grade levels and titles of the passages are shown below. For each grade, two equivalent passages (A and B) are provided; these may be used for pre- / post-testing and/or progress monitoring. Passages are provided starting on page 158.

A Teaching Passage is also provided (on page 156) to use with students who may not understand the task initially; you may use that passage (and that passage only) to teach the task if necessary.

Administration instructions to be used with the teaching passage are on page 155.

| **List of Passages at each Grade Level** | | |
|---|---|---|
| **Grade** | **A** | **B** |
| 2 | A City Walk | Rabbits in the Garden |
| 3 | Their First Train Ride | The Fish Kite |
| 4 | Playing the Game | The Best Picture |
| 5 | The Big Move | A Great Day |
| 6 | Not So Boring | The Morning News |
| 7 | The People at the Top of the Hill | The Islanders |
| 8 | Basketball Saturday | The Perfect Trip |
| 9 | A Circle of Friends | A Strange Place to Practice |
| 10 | Their First Century | College Girl |

Give each student a copy of the appropriate maze passage. Be sure each student has a pencil. Have the students write their names and the date on the page. Ask the students to put the passage face-down on the desk. Read the directions below to the students.

Say: *For this activity, you will read a special kind of story. Some of the words in the story have been replaced with a group of three words. You are to decide which word in each group fits best in the story. You will circle the word you think is best.*

Be sure the students understand the task. (You may restate the directions, if necessary).

Say: *When I tell you to begin, read the story to yourself. When you come to each group of three words, circle the word that fits best with the rest of the story. Work quickly, but not so fast that you make mistakes. Think about the word in each group that is correct. Circle this word and continue working. If you see the words GO ON at the bottom of a page, go on to the next page.*

*You will have three minutes. After three minutes, I will say "Stop working." If you finish before the three minutes are up, you can check your work. Do you have any questions?* (Answer any questions the students have.) *Turn your papers over. You may begin.*

Start timing and allow three minutes. Check the students as they work to be sure the students understand the task, but do not help them choose any answers. For passages that are more than one page long, remind the students to go on to the next page when they see the words "GO ON".

When three minutes have elapsed, say: *Stop working now. Thank you for completing the activity.*

Collect the completed maze assessments.

## Scoring the Maze Reading Assessment

Compare the student's responses to the answer key (provided on pages 176-180) for the passage. Count any correct answer that is circled, underlined, or otherwise indicated. Put a check beside each correct response and a line through each incorrect response. Record the number of correct responses and number of errors on the corresponding lines at the bottom of the page.

For ninth and tenth grade students, use eighth grade scoring.

An example of a scored passage is provided on page 157.

| Grade | Performance | Fall | Winter | Spring |
|---|---|---|---|---|
| 2 | Benchmark | 4 | 10 | 13 |
| | Strategic | 2 | 6 | 9 |
| | Intensive | 1 | 3 | 5 |
| 3 | Benchmark | 11 | 13 | 15 |
| | Strategic | 8 | 9 | 10 |
| | Intensive | 5 | 6 | 7 |
| 4 | Benchmark | 13 | 16 | 19 |
| | Strategic | 10 | 12 | 14 |
| | Intensive | 5 | 8 | 9 |
| 5 | Benchmark | 15 | 17 | 20 |
| | Strategic | 12 | 15 | 18 |
| | Intensive | 8 | 10 | 12 |
| 6 | Benchmark | 16 | 18 | 21 |
| | Strategic | 10 | 13 | 14 |
| | Intensive | 7 | 9 | 10 |
| 7 | Benchmark | 17 | 19 | 22 |
| | Strategic | 13 | 14 | 15 |
| | Intensive | 9 | 10 | 12 |
| 8 | Benchmark | 18 | 20 | 22 |
| | Strategic | 14 | 15 | 17 |
| | Intensive | 10 | 11 | 13 |

**WHAT IT MEANS** The results of the maze assessment are reported as the number of correct replacements. This measure is consistent across assessment passages and grades, so a student's understanding of the text can be compared to prior or subsequent assessments and with other students in the same grade. A student with few correct responses may be experiencing reading difficulties, so the measure can be used for screening. Over time, the number of correct responses should increase as the student is able to read more text in the same period of time and understand it better.

The scoring table on p.153 shows typical grade-level expectations for the number of correct replacements in a maze assessment. If the assessment is used for screening purposes, a reasonable guideline is that students whose score is significantly lower than expected (about half of the values shown in the table), will probably be having reading difficulties. If scores fall between those shown on the scoring table, teachers should take into account other sources of information in order to make instructional decisions.

For progress monitoring purposes, the maze assessment may be used more than once if the students receive no feedback about their responses. Goal setting can be accomplished using the information in the table. Typical students will show a score increase from the beginning to the end of the school year.

**WHAT'S NEXT?** A useful strategy to improve students' understanding of text is to pair reading with comprehension checks through peer questions, summarization, or retelling. Another good strategy is to create practice maze passages or have the students create the passages. Have the students collaborate to read the passages and choose the correct words. Ask the students to explain to one another why the correct answer fits best with the rest of the selection. If capable cross-age or adult readers are available, they can discuss why certain words don't fit because they are the wrong part of speech and why others don't match the meaning of the text.

## Teaching Passage Administration (Optional)

Use this passage to teach the task to some younger students or older students with reading difficulties who may need a practice (teaching) activity before attempting the maze assessment. For these students, duplicate the teaching passage on page 156 and distribute it to the student/s. Be sure each student has a pencil. The directions are below.

Say: *For this activity, you will read a special kind of story. Some of the words in the story have been replaced with a group of three words. You are to decide which word in each group fits best in the story. You will circle the word you think is best.*

*We will begin with the practice story I gave you. Read the first sentence to yourself while I read it out loud.*

The bird landed on the ground.

*Now read the second sentence.*

It picked up a piece of (book, grass, tired) in its bill.

*The word* grass *fits best with the rest of the story. Draw a circle around the word* grass. (Check to be sure the students have circled the correct word.)

*Let's read the next sentence.*

The bird flew (back, when, shirt) to its nest.

*Which word fits best in the sentence?* (Encourage a volunteer to choose the correct answer.) *Yes, the word* back *is correct. Draw a circle around the word* back.

*For the last sentence, I want you to read it to yourself and circle the word that fits best in the sentence. Work quickly, but not so fast that you make mistakes. Now read the sentence and circle the word.* (Allow time for the students to read the sentence and circle the word.)

*The third word,* the, *is correct. If you circled another word, cross out your answer and circle* the *now.*

Check to be sure the students have circled the correct answer. It may be helpful to read the passage aloud with the correct words in place to ensure that the students understand the task.

**Teaching Passage**

The bird landed on the ground.

It picked up a piece of (**book, grass, tired**) in its bill.

The bird flew (**back, when, shirt**) to its nest with the grass.

(**Rug, So, The**) nest was in a tall pine tree.

**Example of a Scored Passage**

A City Walk

The light changed to green, and Ted and his mother walked across the street. They were on their way to (**for, the, met**) food store.

Ted liked walking to (**and, is, the**) store. The city was a busy (**place, hat, want**). He saw lots of different things. (**Them, He, Say**) also saw many of the people (**bad, fat, who**) worked near his house.

"Hello Ted, (**once, hello, you**) Mrs. Gomez," said Mr. Hill. He (**grow, happy, was**) standing outside his store. He sold (**books, name, stay**). On rainy days after school, Ted (**bark, would, cold**) visit the store. Mr. Hill would (**show, ride, frog**) him books that he thought Ted (**got, glad, would**) like.

A little bit later, the (**mat, two, soon**) of them reached the food store. (**Mrs., How, Noise**) King ran the store, and she (**but, truck, always**) had a special treat for Ted. (**Today, Little, Paint**), she gave him some fresh grapes. (**day, be, Ted**) thanked her and shared the grapes (**out, with, fish**) his mother. She said they were (**just, the, chair**) best grapes she had ever tasted. (**Ted, Girl, See**) thought they were really good, too. (**Let, Cry, Then**) Ted and his mother got a (**duck, cart, late**) and started their shopping.

Number Correct 11 Number of Errors 3

## CORE Reading Maze Comprehension 2-A

**Name**_____________________________ **Grade**_________ **Date**_____________________

A City Walk

The light changed to green, and Ted and his mother walked across the street. They were on their way to (**for, the, met**) food store.

Ted liked walking to (**and, is, the**) store. The city was a busy (**place, hat, want**). He saw lots of different things. (**Them, He, Say**) also saw many of the people (**bad, fat, who**) worked near his house.

"Hello Ted, (**once, hello, you**) Mrs. Gomez," said Mr. Hill. He (**grow, happy, was**) standing outside his store. He sold (**books, name, stay**). On rainy days after school, Ted (**bark, would, cold**) visit the store. Mr. Hill would (**show, ride, frog**) him books that he thought Ted (**got, glad, would**) like.

A little bit later, the (**mat, two, soon**) of them reached the food store. (**Mrs., How, Noise**) King ran the store, and she (**but, truck, always**) had a special treat for Ted. (**Today, Little, Paint**), she gave him some fresh grapes. (**Day, Be, Ted**) thanked her and shared the grapes (**out, with, fish**) his mother. She said they were (**just, the, chair**) best grapes she had ever tasted. (**Ted, Girl, See**) thought they were really good, too. (**Let, Cry, Then**) Ted and his mother got a (**duck, cart, late**) and started their shopping.

Number Correct __________ Number of Errors __________

## CORE Reading Maze Comprehension 2-B

**Name**__________________________ **Grade**________ **Date**____________________

### Rabbits in the Garden

The rabbit hopped across the lawn. It looked around carefully. Then it (**following, hopped, shorter**) to the garden.

Fred and his (**pen, full, mother**) sat on the porch. They didn't (**sent, quick, move**) at all. They were watching the (**rabbit, balloon, fight**).

"Won't the rabbit eat your plants?" (**drown, whispered, tricky**) Fred.

"Maybe," said Mother. "But I (**splash, nest, have**) lots of plants. I don't mind (**so, if, band**) the rabbit eats a few leaves."

(**By, At, Two**) now, the rabbit had reached the (**lunch, garden, seven**). It sniffed the air before hopping (**with, over, flied**) to a plant. The plant had (**pretty, glad, keep**) green leaves and purple flowers. The (**dinner, clip, rabbit**) nibbled some of the leaves.

Mother (**bought, tapped, thing**) Fred on the arm. She pointed (**to, until, duck**) the lawn. Two baby rabbits were (**thanked, hopping, book**) across the grass. Soon they reached (**the, shiny, mail**) garden and hurried over to the (**many, card, big**) rabbit. Each of the little rabbits (**whisper, sniffed, gold**) the big rabbit's nose.

"I'm glad (**them, duck, you**) didn't chase the big rabbit away," (**said, climb, truck**) Fred.

Number Correct __________ Number of Errors __________

## CORE Reading Maze Comprehension 3-A

**Name**________________________ **Grade**______ **Date**__________________

Their First Train Ride

The train made a lot of noise as it came to a stop at the station. Martha waited for a moment until (**it, in, her**) father held her hand. They walked (**onto, with, sad**) the train together. Her mother and (**afternoon, brother, finish**) walked behind them.

This was the (**first, hungry, seat**) train ride for Martha and her (**horse, brother, still**), Brian. They were going to ride (**close, farmer, the**) train to the city and visit (**he, rock, their**) grandparents. They usually went by car, (**but, if, street**) today, Mom and Dad said they (**shop, would, clock**) like to try something different.

The (**four, wild, truck**) of them walked to the middle (**until, clap, of**) the train car. They found some (**tent, seats, sorry**) together and sat down. In a (**few, father, pat**) minutes the train began to move. (**Grass, Camp, Martha**) and Brian felt a little nervous, (**what, but, guess**) their parents said they would enjoy (**the, right, sang**) ride.

"The train isn't as noisy (**how, as, mat**) I thought it would be," said (**Martha, bunny, bark**). "And I can stand up and (**walk, break, faster**) around. With all the windows, I (**believe, can, sweet**) see everything."

"I like it because (**pail, I, time**) can relax," said Dad.

Mom added, "(**I, hair, cup**) can talk to you two children (**under, road, without**) turning around to the back of (**how, the, hunt**) car."

"The train really goes fast," (**said, petted, four**) Brian. "I like that best of (**sad, all, pond**)."

Number Correct __________ Number of Errors __________

# CORE Reading Maze Comprehension 3-B

**Name**______________________________ **Grade**______ **Date**______________________

## The Fish Kite

The sky was filled with colorful kites. Laura had never seen so many (**kites, wood, pass**) in one place. "This is wonderful," (**their, she, burn**) said to her uncle, "almost like (**in, paw, a**) dream."

Aunt Marian handed Laura a (**wagon, kite, raced**) and some string. The kite had (**so, an, use**) unusual shape and looked like a (**fish, shoe, listen**).

"It looks like a fish, so (**them, wild, it**) is called a fish kite," said (**toast, Uncle, feel**) Juan. He held the kite and (**told, must, white**) Laura to walk backward into the (**bottle, wind, chase**). When she was about twenty yards (**with, hay, away**), he told Laura to stop.

Laura (**had, walk, bank**) seen her uncle fly a kite (**loud, before, pretty**), so she knew what to do. (**Bank, She, True**) waited until a breeze came along, (**while, peep, and**) then she asked Uncle Juan to (**rake, hold, brave**) the kite high and let go. (**Ride, Bear, When**) he did, she pulled on the (**string, people, empty**) a few times. In just a (**bush, wait, moment**), the kite was up in the (**face, air, over**). Laura let more string out, and (**the, none, mud**) kite climbed higher and higher.

"How (**high, new, wife**) do you think it can go?" (**cares, asked, quiet**) Laura.

"I'm not sure," answered Aunt (**butter, but, Marian**), "but I am sure of one (**board, thing, else**). You have the only fish kite (**unless, forest, in**), the sky today."

Number Correct __________ Number of Errors __________

## CORE Reading Maze Comprehension 4-A

**Name**__________________________ **Grade**_______ **Date**____________________

Playing the Game

Patrick put the game controller down and turned on the television. He clicked through the channels and (**cry, hurry, saw**) nothing interesting. He couldn't believe it, (**more, but, name**) he was bored with his games (**and, no, hunt**) television.

The voices and laughter from (**pie, thank, upstairs**) drifted down. The rest of the (**family, ladder, above**) was playing a board game. He (**landed, thought, bottle**) the game was silly, so he (**said, mail, thing**) he didn't want to play. Instead, (**their, have, he**) went down to the basement by himself (**enough, step, to**) play video games.

Taking a deep (**hall, breath, baby**), he decided he would go upstairs (**to, for, toast**) see what they were doing. Maybe (**yet, the, fan**) game wasn't as silly as he (**thought, shouted, lunch**).

When he reached the dining room, (**bowl, everybody, red**) stopped for a moment. Then Aunt (**pencil, Lydia, while**) pulled an empty chair to her (**edge, make, side**) and said, "Over here, Patrick. We (**want, drive, slow**) you on our team."

Before long, (**clown, Patrick, tomorrow**) understood why everyone was laughing. The (**game, money, teach**) was challenging and fun. He loved (**for, paint, the**) way everyone teased one another, and (**he, their, bone**) felt proud when he answered a (**radio, question, drove**) right and put his team ahead.

"(**Stone, Way, Patrick**), you are actually pretty good at (**this, when, candle**) game. Have you ever played it (**under, before, mean**)?" asked his father.

Blushing a little, (**Patrick, clothes, play**) admitted he had played it a (**loud, few, air**) times at school, but it was (**near, join, never**) this much fun. His aunt gave (**cake, him, scare**) a hug and said, "Well, we (**don't, using, bell**) care if you played before. We're (**rocky, track, happy**) you are on our team."

Number Correct __________ Number of Errors __________

# CORE Reading Maze Comprehension 4-B

**Name**____________________________ **Grade**_____ **Date**____________________

The Best Picture

The picture was really funny. Sheri was sitting on a pony (**earlier, outside, sweet**) her grandmother's house. It was taken (**when, those, shoe**) she was about a year old. (**Store, Bigger, Grandfather**) was holding her so she wouldn't (**answer, fall, hen**) out of the saddle. Grandmother was (**with, on, job**) the other side of the horse (**holding, suppose, never**) its bridle. It was Sheri's favorite (**step, stay, picture**).

"Do you remember when this picture (**was, help, dish**) taken, Dad?" she asked.

"Of course (**Them, I, Put**) do. I took the picture." Sheri's (**tree, drop, father**) walked over to look at it (**more, then, cold**) closely. "Your grandparents certainly look happy (**down, luck, in**) that picture, don't they?"

"Tell me (**over, about, glove**) that day again, Dad," asked Sheri. (**She, Their, Boat**) was too young to remember, but (**that, she, ride**) loved hearing about it.

"Yes," said (**it, sell, her**) little brother, "tell us about the (**hurt, pony, chase**) picture." Rodney liked the story as (**much, where, glass**) as Sheri did.

"Let me tell (**yet, the, lamb**) story," suggested Sheri's mother. "Your father (**always, soon, trick**) leaves out the good part."

Mother (**slept, leg, began**) telling the story as she always (**rest, did, skate**). They drove to the farm where (**Father, nail, pay**) grew up. They had a picnic (**since, coat, under**) the tree behind the house. Grandfather (**diving, brought, funny**) a pony over and put Sheri (**in, without, hear**) the saddle. He and Grandmother posed (**unless, with, push**) Sheri and the pony. Father took (**why, your, the**) picture. Then Father asked everyone to (**hold, climb, farm**) still. He backed up to take (**few, another, long**) picture. As he walked backward, he (**fell, have, mouth**) into the pond, dropping the camera (**early, old, just**) before he did. And as always, (**country, everyone, off**) laughed, even Father.

Number Correct __________ Number of Errors __________

## CORE Reading Maze Comprehension 5-A

**Name**_____________________________ **Grade**______ **Date**_____________________

The Big Move

It looked like a parade. People lined the streets, traffic was (**stopped, splash, storm**), and utility wires had been raised (**until, send, by**) supporting them with tall poles. Police (**waved, were, today**) stationed at every intersection, and news (**mountains, trucks, reached**) were parked beside the street. A (**reporter, cookie, wrong**) stood on the street beside the (**year, break, truck**), microphone in hand.

From far down (**Main, crawled, spoon**) Street came the sound of people (**saved, clapping, another**). It rolled up the street like (**a, so, eat**) wave, and soon everyone on the (**basket, sidewalks, chase**) could see the object of the (**football, clip, applause**). The applause wasn't for a parade, (**but, his, city**) for something much more exciting. The (**wonder, Torrey, gave**) House was being moved from its (**kind, paper, original**) site to a vacant lot in (**red, the, draw**) center of town.

Ken held his (**video, boat, around**) camera as high as he could (**over, after, take**) his head while Mona talked into (**why, an, for**) audio recorder. They were capturing the (**shady, came, big**) move for their school's digital yearbook.

"(**Pick, River, Do**) you really think you are getting (**young, good, carry**) pictures?" asked Mona. She had turned (**off, at, chip**) the recorder for a moment and (**joined, looked, window**) at Ken.

"I practiced this for (**berry, tease, weeks**)," answered Ken. "I took videos from (**where, girl, this**) spot twice a week for a (**river, month, please**). I even marked the sidewalk with (**shout, about, chalk**) so I'd be standing in the (**same, both, weigh**) spot. After I took the video, (**of, I, sit**) looked it over to be sure (**I, by, so**) got the best angle. Don't worry, (**her, bed, it**) will be okay."

Mona rolled her (**rope, eyes, high**), turned on the recorder, and started (**find, talking, horse**). Ken was right, of course. He (**use, mop, had**) planned their event for months, and (**she, their, sea**) was sure he knew what he (**call, was, ride**) doing. She smiled as she spoke, (**walk, fair, knowing**) they were recording one of the (**most, young, toy**) important events in the history of (**hard, give, their**) town.

Number Correct __________ Number of Errors __________

# CORE Reading Maze Comprehension 5-B

**Name**____________________________ **Grade**______ **Date**____________________

A Great Day

The snow couldn't have been better. Peter stepped into the front binding (**up, of, tag**) his snowboard and fastened the toe (**pail, write, strap**). Standing up, he pushed off with (**his, sure, top**) other foot and drifted into the (**ship, line, plant**) for the chairlift.

"Hey, Peter, are (**who, cat, you**) all set for an enormous day?" (**asked, stood, fence**) Stacy. She glided up beside him (**if, and, ten**) pulled her goggles up onto her (**noise, under, hat**).

"This is the best snow of (**so, the, dish**) year," insisted Peter, "and we're supposed (**to, at, we**) get more tomorrow. It's fabulous that (**who, this, hurt**) is our vacation week."

The two (**under, light, of**) them continued to talk as the (**chairlift, ship, round**) line moved forward. It wasn't long (**at, name, before**) the two of them were waiting (**not, for, week**) a chair. When it arrived, they (**said, dropped, bottom**) back slightly as the chair scooped (**them, why, feed**) up and started moving toward the (**fruit, stick, top**) of the mountain.

As they neared (**my, the, hit**) summit, the two boarders turned slightly (**in, until, hat**) the chair to prepare for getting (**as, off, cry**). When the surface of the snow (**was, parted, this**) close enough, they stood up on (**girl, and, their**) boards and pushed away from the (**pony, lift, rush**).

"Let's drop into the sunny side (**of, so, pig**) the bowl and make a few (**woods, black, turns**) to warm up before we head (**down, after, cover**) to the terrain park," suggested Stacy.

"(**When, That, Start**) sounds pretty good," agreed Peter. "While (**to, move, we**) were on the lift, I saw (**Sarah, bell, middle**) and her brothers heading that way. (**Plant, Story, Maybe**) we can catch up with them."

(**Try, Mad, The**) two of them scooted down a (**hardly, nearby, fright**) slope and then came to a (**stop, wing, cry**). They sat on the snow and (**strapped, neared, real**) in the other boot. Using the (**dance, angle, warm**) of the slope to help them (**wave, stand, aunt**) up, they rose and made a (**sat, ship, few**) slow turns. Spotting Sarah and her (**present, brothers, winter**) a few hundred yards down the (**hill, pen, drop**), they headed almost straight down the (**mountain, pocket, number**), looking forward to a great day (**from, with, bird**) good friends.

Number Correct __________ Number of Errors __________

# CORE Reading Maze Comprehension 6-A

**Name**__________________________ **Grade**______ **Date**____________________

Not So Boring

Sighing deeply, Jill sat on the bench in the park. A few of her school friends (**been, were, scent**) lounging on the grass. Spending time (**in, off, shy**) the park was something they did (**floor, ruler, almost**) every evening during the summer, and (**green, tonight, course**), they were waiting for a local (**DJ, bat, fear**) to put on some music.

"This (**bird, fact, town**) is so boring," said Jill, and (**next, most, pine**) of the others agreed, adding that (**there, else, case**) was nothing to do other than (**wish, cow, hang**) out in the park.

"I don't (**know, plan, spill**)," suggested Larry, "how about hiking to (**ran, the, fold**) top of the cliff? We all (**call, harm, like**) to do that, and what about (**name, tonight, blaze**)? We're going to get to dance (**to, up, bud**) music that we picked out."

Rita (**think, flower, nodded**) her head and smiled. "The best (**miss, hike, belt**) is the one we take after (**the, sit, cart**) last day of school. What about (**catch, dark, rafting**) down the river? I think that's (**open, even, while**) better than hiking the cliff, and (**it's, lines, age**) a lot easier. Besides, our parents (**step, wait, neat**) for us and have a picnic (**sadly, throat, afterward**)."

Almost everyone agreed with Rita except (**every, wear, Gary**), who argued for cross-country skiing across (**less, the, bay**) lake. "Skiing across Lake Washington is (**something, party, hold**) that most people have never done. (**Toe, I, Cab**) love calling my cousin in Texas (**and, why, top**) telling her how much fun it (**bow, lap, is**) every time we do it."

By (**if, now, tie**), Jill was rethinking her comment. "Okay, (**under, argue, maybe**) this isn't as boring a place (**as, so, cane**) I suggested. After all, we're only (**hot, a, side**) few hours from New York City, (**low, dart, and**) all of us have taken the (**bus, air, main**) there with our parents. Remember when (**those, ugly, we**) went in for that ice-skating show? (**Above, From, Seem**) now on, when I do that (**logged, room, boring**) thing, maybe you should remind me (**to, in, as**) think before I start complaining."

Number Correct __________ Number of Errors __________

# CORE Reading Maze Comprehension 6-B

**Name**____________________________ **Grade**______ **Date**____________________

The Morning News

As he walked in front of the camera, Matthew felt a little nervous. Even though this was just the (**school, cold, ever**) news broadcast, he was still worried. (**To, Add, He**) didn't like speaking in front of (**cover, groups, joke**), and now he would be speaking (**almost, in, sun**) front of thousands of people. He (**wouldn't, paint, song**) see them, but they could see (**by, ship, him**).

The school news broadcast was an (**deer, idea, weigh**) that started two years ago. A (**clean, need, few**) students and the technology teacher thought (**of, or, hop**) the idea while watching the local (**deer, news, cloud**). They decided a show that reported (**the, wet, hello**) news for their school and town (**reach, full, would**) be interesting to other students and (**own, the, hair**) people in the town. The students' (**spin, your, news**) broadcast was soon showing on the (**school, line, belong**) network and the local cable system.

(**Ticket, Students, Brave**) in the school took turns doing (**the, why, lion**) jobs needed to make the broadcast. (**Where, Hold, Each**) student signed up for several jobs, (**to, and, like**) names were selected at random for (**each, then, ring**) job. The newer students received training (**off, read, from**) more experienced students. Over the past (**sleepy, two, paint**) years, every student in the school (**had, show, thin**) been part of the broadcast.

Catherine (**hide, table, was**) the director of today's show. She (**sinks, hurried, soft**) around, getting things in order, including (**showing, easier, long**) Matthew where to sit. She could (**wag, big, see**) he was a little nervous, so (**bit, she, glad**) tried to help him feel more (**secretly, garden, confident**). "You always do a wonderful job (**when, around, spot**) we make presentations in class, so (**you, than, past**) won't have any problems," she said. (**Who, Stay, Their**) teacher agreed and helped straighten out (**jokes, Matthew's, painted**) collar and tie while they were (**waiting, sleepy, deeper**) for the broadcast to begin.

Everyone (**began, clock, walked**) away from the desk where Matthew (**thought, sat, doll**), and the spotlight came on. He (**tripped, magic, cleared**) his throat, waited for Catherine's signal, (**and, with, bark**) then began speaking. "Good morning, everybody. (**Why, This, Smell**) is Matthew, and I'm today's morning (**log, news, swing**) reporter."

Number Correct __________ Number of Errors __________

## CORE Reading Maze Comprehension 7-A

**Name**____________________________ **Grade**_____ **Date**____________________

The People at the Top of the Hill

Tamara wondered about the people who lived at the top of the hill. She saw them every once in (**a, is, red**) while in town, and they seemed (**youngest, interesting, listen**) in an unusual way. The man (**rode, lied, bear**) his bike almost everywhere, and when (**part, cook, he**) brought the car to town, he (**ready, always, office**) had two dogs with him. The (**block, woman, little**) worked at the hospital, and every (**once, now, keep**) in a while Tamara would see (**for, sky, her**) running on Saturday morning.

"George, what (**red, do, glad**) you know about the people who (**live, carry, short**) in the old Stevens place?" Tamara (**asked, was, foot**) tying the laces of her athletic (**kinds, play, shoes**) in preparation for an afternoon training (**bird, run, want**) with her friend.

"Not much," answered (**George, diver, shiny**), who was leaning against a tree (**sit, and, us**) stretching. "He rides his bicycle everywhere, (**over, pond, even**) in the most dreadful weather, and (**at, I, if**) think he's some kind of scientist (**save, fly, and**) does research at the university. She (**arm, dish, is**) a big deal at the hospital, (**maybe, today, rider**) even the president or whatever they (**join, call, warm**) the person who is the boss."

"(**Let's, Fix, Joke**) run up the hill and take (**if, a, or**) look at their place," suggested Tamara, (**drink, adding, chair**), "we have to do more hill (**running, skate, spring**) anyway."

The hill was steeper than (**trip, band, they**) thought, and they were breathing too (**hard, end, rest**) to talk until they reached the (**game, going, flat**) part at the top. As they (**snowed, slowed, without**) down, a voice behind them said, "(**That, Him, Oven**) hill doesn't leave much breath for (**cooked, talking, shop**), does it?"

A man on a (**money, laugh, bicycle**) pulled up beside them, breathing much (**long, more, sign**) easily than anyone should have after (**a, if, to**) climb like that. Before the two (**at, spin, of**) them could say a word, the (**cage, man, cross**) added, "Come on up to the (**fruit, house, felt**). You can get a drink of (**leaf, tiny, water**) and then run down with my (**wife, sled, cook**) You two are training for the (**loud, state, draw**) cross-country championships, right? I don't read (**minds, wishes, shut**), I just recognize you from the (**deep, sports, point**) page of the papers."

With that, (**he, on, pick**) sped ahead of them, and the (**stormy, jump, two**) runners couldn't wait to meet his (**wife, ranch, green**) and find out more about the (**classes, people, pretty**) at the top of the hill.

Number Correct __________ Number of Errors __________

## CORE Reading Maze Comprehension 7-B

**Name**______________________________ **Grade**______ **Date**____________________

### The Islanders

The ferry slowly pulled into the dock on the island. After it stopped and was tied (**recently, whisper, securely**), a few cars and dozens of (**quarters, between, passengers**) left the ferry and headed to (**except, wherever, yellow**) they were going on the island. (**As, By, Our**) soon as they had cleared the (**ferry, balloon, bright**), a few cars and some foot (**snowshoe, written, passengers**) from the island got aboard the (**kitchen, ferry, music**).

Among the passengers were a group (**so, use, of**) students who traveled every day from (**why, the, cap**) island to the mainland for school. (**Not, Him, Far**) enough people lived on the island (**to, it, tall**) justify building a school, so the (**hunter, students, penny**) crossed to the mainland by ferry. (**They, Such, Duck**) were met at the dock by (**if, leg, a**) school bus that took them the (**than, help, rest**) of the way.

The Islanders, as (**when, they, drop**) were often called, were admired by (**most, slow, nice**) of the other students at the (**teeth, being, school**) because of their different style of (**life, world, able**). There were only a few roads (**as, win, on**) the island, and almost all the (**colors, cars, dogs**) were parked beside the ferry dock. (**Why, Fit, The**) cars were used mostly when people (**smiled, went, roar**) to the mainland or for emergencies. (**Everyone, Princess, Telephone**), young and old alike, either walked (**at, or, owl**) used mountain bikes to get around.

(**A, In, Fly**) second unusual thing about living on (**what, the, log**) island was the water supply. There (**nail, buy, was**) no central source of water. Instead, (**butter, people, empty**) collected rainwater in big tanks. They (**pumped, raked, night**) it from the big tanks into (**jumping, smaller, doctor**) tanks where it was filtered and (**hunted, began, purified**) before being used. Needless to say, (**remember, conserving, presents**) water was important to everyone on (**the, ago, let**) island.

The students who lived on (**son, wear, the**) island enjoyed their quiet life and (**natural, dancing, turtle**) surroundings. They sometimes missed the things (**when, cold, that**) students on the mainland took for (**leafed, granted, family**). There were no movies or malls (**up, on, old**) the island, and it was a (**hammer, challenge, throwing**) to be part of activities after (**school, minute, whistle**). Their lives were defined by ferry (**schedules, neighbor, bicycle**), so whenever they had a chance (**if, to, way**) do something with other students their (**any, each, age**), they really enjoyed it.

Number Correct __________ Number of Errors __________

# CORE Reading Maze Comprehension 8-A

**Name**_____________________________ **Grade**_______ **Date**___________________

Basketball Saturday

On almost every Saturday morning, Henry and his friends did the same thing. As soon as there was enough (**light, bridge, warm**) to see, they met at the (**nest, park, brown**) near his house for a few (**stares, games, knock**) of basketball. Afterward, they went down (**an, mud, to**) the firehouse for a pancake breakfast.

(**About, When, Spot**) Henry arrived at the park, Christie (**was, land, few**) already there. They were usually the (**first, great, empty**) to arrive, and the rest of (**way, took, the**) players trickled in over the next (**cloudy, fifteen, stopped**) minutes. Christie was standing beside a (**picnic, kitten, threw**) table laying out enormous sheets of (**soup, round, poster**) paper. On the paper were the (**station, results, closer**) of games that had been played (**up, am, day**) to the current date.

The most (**hungry, numbered, interesting**) part of this basketball league was (**some, that, camp**) every player was a member of (**several, frightened, evening**) teams. On the same Saturday, each (**circus, slowly, player**) would be part of at least (**sky, two, get**) teams. Although it sounds confusing, the (**system, branch, already**) worked well for a number of (**sounds, reasons, terrible**). Everybody got to play on at (**least, bounced, rocky**) one winning team. Players who weren't (**if, bus, so**) good were often on a team (**down, with, ready**) some of the best players, and (**paints, nights, players**) never became angry with members of (**the, hot, face**) other teams because they would eventually (**if, put, be**) on the same team as the (**others, changes, picked**).

Henry helped Christie put the poster (**brother, string, paper**) up on the bulletin board near (**are, the, wait**) basketball court. If someone who didn't (**ring, afraid, know**) the system looked at the team (**cutting, standings, planted**), they would think that hundreds of (**players, footprints, answers**) were involved.

"Your record keeping system (**is, or, ate**) very impressive," said a voice from (**into, behind, card**) them. Henry and Christie turned to (**bat, fill, see**) one of the high school basketball (**breads, coaches, silver**) behind them. She was a regular (**visitor, haircut, widest**) to the Saturday morning games, as (**ride, face, was**) the coach of the boys' team. (**Us, In, Lay**) addition to these coaches, some of (**the, car, lion**) parents often came to the games (**try, and, sure**) joined the players for breakfast afterward.

(**Day, Jar, All**) of the players were a little (**embarrassed, snowflake, mountain**) to be playing in front of (**mouths, adults, closes**), but they also felt a sense (**of, an, fun**) pride. Over the years, many of (**rat, the, like**) players from the Saturday league were (**points, chosen, shade**) for the high school teams. Christie (**bat, lake, and**) Henry spent a few minutes talking (**with, since, well**) the coach, and then they excused (**anybody, themselves, frightened**) when other players started arriving. They (**would, hurry, bumpy**) warm up for a few minutes, (**sea, give, and**) then the first game of the (**Saturday, ground, wonder**) Morning Basketball League would begin.

Number Correct __________ Number of Errors __________

# CORE Reading Maze Comprehension 8-B

Name______________________________ Grade______ Date____________________

The Perfect Trip

The bus climbed to the top of the hill and made a sharp left turn. Everyone on the bus caught a (**chuckle, glimpse, sighing**) of one of the most spectacular (**sights, crowd, become**) they would ever experience. Before them (**tear, bow, lay**) the sea, glistening in the sunlight. (**But, Sir, The**) rocky coast here tumbled below them (**with, for, tea**) hundreds of feet. On the other (**side, note, cause**) was a sheer cliff rising for (**a, if, to**) thousand feet.

The students were on (**on, a, by**) class trip to Europe, something that (**speak, damp, none**) of them could have imagined. They (**act, milk, had**) entered a contest to come up (**down, with, stuff**) a practical solution to a problem (**up, lap, in**) their area, and their submission had (**been, speak, cellar**) the national winner. The solution they (**exercised, developed, passenger**) and implemented was so simple that (**they, sank, best**) couldn't believe no one had done (**am, it, jet**) before.

The students had requested that (**the, why, beg**) town council let them adopt a (**holiday, borrow, network**) of connected sidewalks. They would turn (**the, map, lie**) sidewalks into multiuse paths that led (**or, to, mix**) the busiest parts of town, including (**was, shy, the**) schools. With relatively little expense, the (**carvings, sidewalks, certain**) became attractive and safe places for (**rewards, charged, walkers**), skaters, and boarders. A bicycle lane (**was, for, air**) marked on the road beside each (**it, pan, of**) the sidewalks, and parking was restricted (**am, to, not**) the other side of the street.

(**Under, Catch, Within**) a matter of months, something remarkable (**had, feed, swim**) happened in the town. The number (**her, of, all**) cars had diminished considerably, and the (**basket, number, shape**) of walkers had increased more than (**tonight, bring, anyone**) had imagined. Downtown no longer had (**traffic, minute, engine**) congestion and parking problems, but it (**dry, fire, was**) busier than ever because more people (**were, fish, box**) walking. Even the school buses had (**shopped, changed, spring**) their routes and no longer came (**but, zoo, all**) the way to school. They stopped (**unless, cover, instead**) at a parking area several blocks (**away, when, swim**). Students walked the rest of the (**bed, way, cow**) to school on the multiuse path.

(**Just, Been, When**) they heard they had won the (**contest, light, silly**), the students in the class had (**if, add, a**) unanimous vote and decided to do (**a, to, nap**) tour of some towns in Europe. (**Or, It, Pat**) was these towns, with a long (**kitchen, history, welcome**) of walking and convenient public transportation, (**leaf, deck, that**) had been the inspiration for their (**journey, project, disappear**). They couldn't think of a better (**straw, nearly, place**) to take a vacation and see (**at, in, job**) person where their ideas had come (**from, past, dust**).

Number Correct __________ Number of Errors __________

# CORE Reading Maze Comprehension 9-A

**Name**________________________ **Grade**_______ **Date**________________

A Circle of Friends

The wagon train had reached the foothills of the mountains. Rather than attempting to begin the (**grinning, uphill, package**) climb with fading daylight, the wagon (**master, harness, elevator**) decided to make camp for the (**pitch, mail, night**).

With the rest of the families, (**the, how, flat**) Wilsons maneuvered their wagon into a (**leader, fortune, circle**), a formation that was the traditional (**body, way, older**) for travelers in the West to (**suppose, protect, flower**) themselves. In addition to providing a (**line, floor, call**) of defense against enemies from the (**outside, anywhere, narrow**), the circle of wagons created a (**sailor, sense, purple**) of community for the families, if (**while, fold, only**) for a night. It was almost (**as, or, pot**) if they were within the walls (**be, of, tug**) a small town, with a bonfire (**letter, burning, searched**) in the middle and people wandering (**around, above, lesson**) making small talk with one another.

(**Sugar, Scatter, Abby**) finished her chores and asked her (**brook, mother, scratch**) if she could walk among the (**hanging, other, crown**) wagons. With her regular warning to (**be, off, herd**) careful and stay inside the circle (**as, of, shy**) wagons, Mother approved her request. Abby's (**mirror, wiggle, father**) smiled and winked at her, having (**much, fine, post**) more confidence in her judgment than (**why, dot, her**) mother did.

As she wandered from (**route, speed, wagon**) to wagon exchanging greetings, Abby was (**folding, joined, reason**) by a few other young people (**eager, giant, forget**) to have something to do other (**what, than, fail**) chores. It wasn't long before a (**group, rule, learn**) of a dozen or so was (**batted, sharp, sitting**) by the central bonfire sharing their (**shelves, thoughts, possible**) about what would happen the following (**comb, stir, day**).

"The mountains seem unbelievably high," suggested (**Martin, judge, stretch**), "and from here, there seems to (**an, ice, be**) no obvious way to cross them."

"(**Father, Fellow, Squeak**) promised me that there is a (**beast, pass, must**) that is difficult but not dangerous (**when, heat, this**) time of year," replied Abby. "It (**will, lose, spray**) take us several days to reach (**were, the, fog**) summit."

"Has anyone considered the difficulty (**do, owl, of**) the walk that lies ahead of (**in, us, ear**)?" wondered Susan. "Have any of us (**attempted, circled, glances**) to scale mountains this high?"

William (**handled, plenty, laughed**), and looking around at the other (**teenagers, someone, sandwich**), said confidently, "We've walked for a (**delighted, thousand, adventure**) miles in the last few months, (**are, lip, so**) I don't think the mountains will (**be, up, seal**) much of a challenge. The real (**vegetable, matter, difficulty**) will lie beyond the summit when (**to, we, fold**) are going downhill. Who will restrain (**the, was, hour**) horses and the wagons?"

With that, (**meadows, understand, everyone**) laughed and rose to their feet. (**It, Web, Net**) was a pleasant moment before an (**evening, traveling, ascent**) that would undoubtedly be the hardest (**drip, part, cave**) of their journey.

Number Correct __________ Number of Errors __________

# CORE Reading Maze Comprehension 9-B

**Name**____________________________ **Grade**______ **Date**____________________

A Strange Place to Practice

The beach wasn't very crowded because the weather was horrible. A few people bundled up in (**out, pat, bad**) weather gear were fishing in the (**surf, dress, avoid**). They must have been very uncomfortable, (**belonging, considering, bracelet**) the crashing waves, the low temperature, (**and, for, hunt**) the blowing wind.

Snuggling into her (**apartment, raincoat, puppet**), Joanne wondered what motivated people to (**it, be, fan**) so dedicated to something that seemed (**important, awfully, whisper**) unrewarding. She almost never saw anyone (**catch, guess, early**) a fish, they were out in (**light, drum, every**) kind of weather, and they were (**almost, slowly, piece**) always alone. Every time she came (**he, win, to**) this section of beach, day or (**bird, night, slide**), at least one person was fishing (**from, bake, hall**) the shore or the jetty of (**edge, listen, rocks**) that reached several hundred yards into (**the, man, roof**) ocean.

About ten minutes later, Joanne (**backed, reached, bravest**) the jetty and scrambled up some (**huge, slow, stop**) rocks to the relatively flat part (**on, if, rag**) top. She stepped carefully from rock (**to, be, sing**) rock until she reached the far (**mill, tired, end**) of the jetty. Several of her (**lower, friends, across**) were already there, sitting with their (**backs, wave, drink**) to the driving rain. They greeted (**when, her, soon**) as warmly as possible, given the (**bundle, conditions, haystack**), and made room for her to (**sit, pole, plan**) among them.

"Whoever had the brilliant (**shadow, stove, idea**) to have rehearsal for the school (**note, play, wipe**) here should be thrown out of (**the, won, hug**) drama club," she suggested. Pausing a (**finger, moment, brushed**) for effect, she added, "Oh, it (**she, pea, was**) my idea, so I guess I (**earn, should, short**) be banned from the club, meaning (**I, of, as**) can return home."

As she pretended (**up, to, in**) get up and leave the gathering, (**health, decide, Daniel**) grumbled, "Not on your life." He (**alarmed, throat, shifted**) a bit to find a more (**comfortable, astonished, growling**) position and insisted, "Nobody gets to (**squeeze, plain, leave**) under any circumstances, especially the genius (**saw, who, rob**) suggested this location."

"Actually, this is (**a, or, say**) pretty good location to rehearse, considering (**wet, the, curl**) play is about a shipwreck in (**stormy, managed, growl**) weather," argued Elizabeth. "The weather should (**trade, cave, help**) us get into our roles more (**disappointed, thoroughly, cardboard**)."

The rain slowed down and then (**bundled, stopped, hollow**), although the wind continued to blow. (**The, Why, Bed**) six of them pulled their scripts (**they, from, flow**) under their coats and formed a (**circle, visitor, lovely**). As they did, Joanne began to (**blossom, careless, understand**) a little better what motivated the (**space, people, steer**) who were fishing. Despite the weather, (**this, why, bead**) was a beautiful spot, especially if (**dog, paid, you**) were doing something that interested you.

Number Correct __________ Number of Errors __________

# CORE Reading Maze Comprehension 10-A

**Name**____________________________ **Grade**_______ **Date**___________________

## Their First Century

The sound of so many riders clicking into bicycle pedals took Madeleine by (**surprise, weather, clean**). She had always ridden alone or (**unless, with, wall**) a few friends, and she never (**called, realized, gone**) that when hundreds of riders started (**at, card, up**), the sound would be both unusual (**and, for, cop**) satisfying.

This was Madeleine's first century, (**shy, top, the**) name given to a hundred mile (**hope, ride, hand**). She was riding with her cousin, (**hill, crow, Luke**), to raise money for cancer research. (**They, Hers, Cold**) had raised more than a thousand (**noise, dollars, stare**) each in pledges from friends, family (**bench, threw, members**), and neighbors. Now they had to (**look, bread, earn**) the pledges by actually completing the (**bark, ride, king**), an accomplishment that neither of them (**had, pump, save**) ever attempted before.

Doing the ride (**use, was, dive**) Luke's idea, and he had to (**do, hurt, early**) some serious convincing to get Madeleine (**of, bat, to**) agree to participate. He took the (**lead, creek, rest**) in training for the ride, but (**them, it, we**) wasn't long before Madeleine became enthusiastic (**about, beside, aim**) cycling. Her parents bought her a (**new, kind, form**) bicycle, which she was due for (**either, anyway, lost**), and she used her allowance to (**leak, bill, get**) some new cycling clothes and shoes. (**Yet, The, Feel**) shoes took a while to get (**used, saw, apple**) to because they had cleats on (**but, roll, the**) bottom that clipped into the pedals (**of, up, air**) her new bike. Her greatest fear (**use, hay, was**) forgetting to unclick when they came (**up, to, our**) a traffic signal, but so far, (**us, rag, she**) had avoided this embarrassment.

The first (**desk, cluster, begin**) of riders started to pedal, and (**each, chair, joke**) successive group followed along. Madeleine and (**Plant, Watch, Luke**) were in the middle of the (**all, pack, bird**) and waited for a moment to (**allow, sing, piece**) the riders ahead of them to (**jump, get, bath**) a few yards away before starting (**yet, fog, up**). They were both surprised at the (**sign, after, tingle**) of exhilaration they experienced as they (**fed, joined, lion**) the other riders, and it wasn't (**long, how, pony**) before they were pedaling at the (**cruising, buy, take**) pace for which they had trained.

(**Less, House, As**) the miles passed, Madeleine and Luke (**wrote, made, cheer**) dozens of new friends. Neither of (**he, them, want**) had ever thought about how much (**bus, pie, time**) they would have to chitchat with (**the, or, fear**) other riders, but when you have (**a, it, ran**) hundred miles to cover on a (**stone, bicycle, decide**), there's a lot of conversation going (**on, long, open**).

By late afternoon, all the cyclists (**hike, lion, were**) feeling exhausted, yet none gave the (**wider, slightest, visitor**) thought to dropping out of the (**gold, need, ride**). As they reached the crest of (**the, hard, mean**) last hill, Madeleine and Luke caught (**hat, sight, enjoy**) of the finish area a few (**grab, frown, downhill**) miles away. Their families would be (**hunt, gathered, reason**) to greet them and they began (**the, hole, dot**) descent to the finish. The cousins (**mailed, sister, had**) no doubt that they would remember (**but, this, pole**) day for the rest of their (**lives, ship, almost**).

Number Correct __________ Number of Errors __________

# CORE Reading Maze Comprehension 10B

**Name**______________________________ **Grade**_______ **Date**____________________

College Girl

"Do any of you have exciting plans for the summer vacation?" asked Mark. He and several of his friends (**throw, bench, were**) wandering along the embankment beside the (**reservoir, astronaut, contented**), one of their favorite recreational walks.

(**Doubt, Linda, Flavor**) was about to make her announcement (**when, those, firm**) Kate blurted out, "You won't believe (**such, grape, this**), but I managed to get a (**jingle, position, gradual**) at the hospital. I'm going to (**be, at, kit**) kind of an assistant to any (**up, of, ice**) the professional staff who need me, (**mostly, slowly, groan**) physicians and administrators. The position description (**exchanges, favorite, suggests**) that I'll probably be doing recordkeeping (**and, who, fact**) carrying documents from one location to (**everything, another, difficult**). I submitted my application last year, (**down, clue, but**) they said I was too young."

"(**Why, That, Size**) sounds interesting, especially because you want (**of, sun, to**) be a physician eventually," suggested Linda. "(**This, When, Cost**) will you start?"

"Approximately two weeks (**after, upon, free**) school finishes, so I'll have some (**pool, lose, time**) to visit my aunt and uncle (**in, with, ink**) California," responded Kate. She glanced at (**hive, crown, Linda**) and asked, "Didn't you say you (**load, meal, had**) some remarkable inspiration for the summer?"

(**Under, Before, Giant**) Linda could say anything, Steve answered, "(**My, Is, Dip**) brother invited me to spend the (**reason, summer, imagine**) with him at the lake. He's (**print, beard, renting**) a condominium there while he completes (**his, they, tip**) research internship for the university. I'll (**loudly, probably, tunnel**) work as a lifeguard and spend (**has, the, pale**) remainder of my time training for (**do, net, the**) rowing team."

As soon as Steve (**drifting, finished, bunch**), Linda muttered as rapidly as she (**could, spill, porch**), "All of you should be in (**bad, the, hose**) fast talking friends association. I can't (**sew, age, get**) a word in, and I really (**have, paid, dust**) some big news: I'm starting college." (**For, The, Mad**) entire group suddenly came to a (**gift, copy, halt**), turned to Linda, and looked at (**her, why, rug**) quizzically. Almost in unison, they said (**or, rip, in**) a questioning tone, "Starting college?"

With (**a, to, fog**) tinge of pride in her voice, (**arrow, Linda, wink**) answered, "The community college has a (**roomy, danger, special**) program for high school students who (**rule, have, path**) earned good grades in advanced placement (**courses, shore, upper**). I can take introductory courses in (**struggle, mathematics, pleasant**), language, chemistry, and other subjects where (**I, if, ran**) have the required qualifications. These are (**cup, hat, all**) courses that I'll have to take (**at, no, old**) matter where I attend college, so (**it, or, pin**) will save me time and money (**am, in, she**) the long run. Besides, when I (**cut, sip, get**) to college full time, I'll be (**able, clean, suit**) to take more advanced courses or (**smooth, optional, balcony**) courses in subjects in which I'm (**interested, whirled, afterward**)."

When she stopped to take a (**wheel, breath, twist**), everyone began bombarding her with questions (**and, for, tray**) expressed their admiration for what she (**let, tub, was**) planning. Kate even called her college (**sour, girl, tore**).

Number Correct __________ Number of Errors __________

# CORE READING MAZE COMPREHENSION KEY

## 2-A

| Line | | |
|---|---|---|
| 3 | the | |
| 5 | the | |
| 6 | place | He |
| 7 | who | |
| 9 | hello | |
| 10 | was | books |
| 11 | would | |
| 12 | show | |
| 13 | would | |
| 14 | two | |
| 15 | Mrs. | |
| 16 | always | today |
| 17 | Ted | |
| 18 | with | the |
| 19 | Ted | |
| 20 | Then | |
| 21 | cart | |

## 2-B

| Line | | |
|---|---|---|
| 3 | hopped | |
| 4 | mother | |
| 5 | move | |
| 6 | rabbit | |
| 7 | whispered | |
| 9 | have | |
| 10 | if | |
| 11 | By | |
| 12 | garden | over |
| 13 | pretty | |
| 14 | rabbit | |
| 16 | tapped | |
| 17 | to | |
| 18 | hopping | |
| 19 | the | |
| 20 | big | sniffed |
| 22 | you | |
| 23 | said | |

## 3-A

| Line | | |
|---|---|---|
| 3 | her | |
| 4 | onto | |
| 5 | brother | |
| 6 | first | |
| 7 | brother | |
| 8 | the | their |
| 9 | but | |
| 10 | would | |
| 11 | four | |
| 12 | of | seats |
| 13 | few | |
| 14 | Martha | |
| 15 | but | |
| 16 | the | |
| 17 | as | |
| 18 | Martha | walk |
| 19 | can | |
| 21 | I | |
| 22 | I | |
| 23 | without | the |
| 25 | said | |
| 26 | all | |

## 3-B

| Line | | |
|---|---|---|
| 3 | kites | |
| 4 | she | a |
| 6 | kite | |
| 7 | an | |
| 8 | fish | |
| 9 | it | |
| 10 | Uncle | told |
| 11 | wind | |
| 12 | away | |
| 14 | had | |
| 15 | before | She |
| 16 | and | |
| 17 | hold | |
| 18 | When | string |
| 19 | moment | |
| 20 | air | the |
| 22 | high | |
| 23 | asked | |
| 24 | Marian | |
| 25 | thing | |
| 26 | in | |

# CORE READING MAZE COMPREHENSION KEY

## 4-A

| Line | | |
|---|---|---|
| 3 | saw | |
| 4 | but | |
| 5 | and | |
| 6 | upstairs | |
| 7 | family | |
| 8 | thought | said |
| 9 | he | |
| 10 | to | |
| 11 | breath | |
| 12 | to | the |
| 13 | thought | |
| 14 | everybody | |
| 15 | Lydia | |
| 16 | side | want |
| 18 | Patrick | |
| 19 | game | |
| 20 | the | he |
| 21 | question | |
| 23 | Patrick | this |
| 24 | before | |
| 26 | Patrick | |
| 27 | few | never |
| 28 | him | |
| 29 | don't | |
| 30 | happy | |

## 4-B

| Line | | |
|---|---|---|
| 3 | outside | when |
| 4 | Grandfather | |
| 5 | fall | on |
| 6 | holding | |
| 7 | picture | |
| 8 | was | |
| 10 | I | |
| 11 | father | more |
| 12 | in | |
| 13 | about | She |
| 14 | she | |
| 16 | her | pony |
| 17 | much | |
| 18 | the | |
| 19 | always | |
| 20 | began | did |
| 21 | Father | |
| 22 | under | brought |
| 23 | in | |
| 24 | with | |
| 25 | the | hold |
| 26 | another | |
| 27 | fell | |
| 28 | just | everyone |

## 5-A

| Line | | |
|---|---|---|
| 2 | stopped | |
| 3 | by | |
| 4 | were | |
| 5 | trucks | reporter |
| 6 | truck | |
| 7 | Main | |
| 8 | clapping | a |
| 9 | sidewalks | |
| 10 | applause | but |
| 11 | Torrey | |
| 12 | original | the |
| 13 | video | over |
| 14 | an | |
| 15 | big | |
| 16 | Do | good |
| 17 | off | |
| 18 | looked | |
| 19 | weeks | |
| 20 | this | month |
| 21 | chalk | same |
| 22 | I | I |
| 23 | it | |
| 24 | eyes | |
| 25 | talking | had |
| 26 | she | was |
| 27 | knowing | |
| 28 | most | their |

## 5-B

| Line | | |
|---|---|---|
| 2 | of | |
| 3 | strap | his |
| 4 | line | |
| 5 | you | asked |
| 6 | and | hat |
| 7 | the | to |
| 8 | this | |
| 9 | of | chairlift |
| 10 | before | for |
| 11 | dropped | |
| 12 | them | top |
| 13 | the | in |
| 14 | off | was |
| 15 | their | |
| 16 | lift | |
| 17 | of | |
| 18 | turns | down |
| 19 | That | we |
| 20 | Sarah | Maybe |
| 22 | The | nearby |
| 23 | stop | strapped |
| 24 | angle | stand |
| 25 | few | brothers |
| 26 | hill | |
| 27 | mountain | with |

# CORE READING MAZE COMPREHENSION KEY

## 6-A

| Line | | |
|---|---|---|
| 2 | were | |
| 3 | in | |
| 4 | almost | tonight |
| 5 | DJ | |
| 6 | town | most |
| 7 | there | hang |
| 9 | know | the |
| 10 | like | tonight |
| 11 | to | |
| 12 | nodded | hike |
| 13 | the | rafting |
| 14 | even | it's |
| 15 | wait | |
| 16 | afterward | |
| 17 | Gary | |
| 18 | the | something |
| 19 | I | and |
| 20 | is | |
| 21 | now | maybe |
| 22 | as | a |
| 23 | and | bus |
| 24 | we | From |
| 25 | boring | |
| 26 | to | |

## 6-B

| Line | | |
|---|---|---|
| 3 | school | He |
| 4 | groups | in |
| 5 | wouldn't | |
| 6 | him | |
| 7 | idea | |
| 8 | few | of |
| 9 | news | the |
| 10 | would | |
| 11 | the | news |
| 12 | school | |
| 13 | Students | the |
| 14 | Each | and |
| 15 | each | |
| 16 | from | two |
| 17 | had | |
| 18 | was | hurried |
| 19 | showing | |
| 20 | see | she |
| 21 | confident | when |
| 22 | you | |
| 23 | Their | Matthew's |
| 24 | waiting | |
| 25 | walked | sat |
| 26 | cleared | |
| 27 | and | This |
| 28 | news | |

## 7-A

| Line | | |
|---|---|---|
| 3 | a | interesting |
| 4 | rode | |
| 5 | he | always |
| 6 | woman | once |
| 7 | her | |
| 8 | do | live |
| 9 | asked | |
| 10 | shoes | run |
| 11 | George | and |
| 12 | even | |
| 13 | I | and |
| 14 | is | maybe |
| 15 | call | |
| 16 | Let's | a |
| 17 | adding | running |
| 18 | they | hard |
| 19 | flat | |
| 20 | slowed | That |
| 21 | talking | |
| 22 | bicycle | more |
| 23 | a | |
| 24 | of man | house |
| 25 | water | wife |
| 26 | state | |
| 27 | minds | sports |
| 29 | he | two |
| 30 | wife | people |

## 7-B

| Line | | |
|---|---|---|
| 3 | securely | passengers |
| 4 | wherever | As |
| 5 | ferry | |
| 6 | passengers | ferry |
| 7 | of | |
| 8 | the | Not |
| 9 | to | students |
| 10 | They | a |
| 11 | rest | |
| 12 | they | most |
| 13 | school | |
| 14 | life | on |
| 15 | cars | The |
| 16 | went | Everyone |
| 17 | or | |
| 19 | A | the |
| 20 | was | people |
| 21 | pumped | |
| 22 | smaller | purified |
| 23 | conserving | |
| 24 | the | |
| 25 | the | natural |
| 26 | that | |
| 27 | granted | on |
| 28 | challenge | |
| 29 | school | schedules |
| 30 | to | |
| 31 | age | |

# CORE READING MAZE COMPREHENSION KEY

### 8-A

| Line | | |
|---|---|---|
| 3 | light | park |
| 4 | games | |
| 5 | to | |
| 6 | When | was |
| 7 | first | the |
| 8 | fifteen | |
| 9 | picnic | poster |
| 10 | results | up |
| 12 | interesting | that |
| 13 | several | |
| 14 | player | two |
| 15 | system | |
| 16 | reasons | least |
| 17 | so | with |
| 18 | players | the |
| 19 | be | |
| 20 | others | |
| 21 | paper | |
| 22 | the | know |
| 23 | standings | players |
| 25 | is | |
| 26 | behind | see |
| 27 | coaches | visitor |
| 28 | was | In |
| 29 | the | and |
| 31 | All | embarrassed |
| 32 | adults | of |
| 33 | the | chosen |
| 34 | and | with |
| 35 | themselves | |
| 36 | would | |
| 37 | and | Saturday |

### 8-B

| Line | | |
|---|---|---|
| 3 | glimpse | sights |
| 4 | lay | |
| 5 | The | for |
| 6 | side | a |
| 7 | a | none |
| 8 | had | |
| 9 | with | in |
| 10 | been | developed |
| 11 | they | |
| 12 | it | |
| 13 | the | |
| 14 | network | the |
| 15 | to | the |
| 16 | sidewalks | |
| 17 | walkers | was |
| 18 | of | to |
| 20 | Within | had |
| 21 | of | |
| 22 | number | anyone |
| 23 | traffic | |
| 24 | was | were |
| 25 | changed | |
| 26 | all | instead |
| 27 | away | way |
| 29 | When | contest |
| 30 | a | a |
| 31 | It | history |
| 32 | that | |
| 33 | project | place |
| 34 | in | from |

### 9-A

| Line | | |
|---|---|---|
| 3 | uphill | master |
| 4 | night | |
| 5 | the | |
| 6 | circle | way |
| 7 | protect | line |
| 8 | outside | |
| 9 | sense | only |
| 10 | as | of |
| 11 | burning | around |
| 13 | Abby | mother |
| 14 | other | be |
| 15 | of | |
| 16 | father | much |
| 17 | her | |
| 18 | wagon | |
| 19 | joined | eager |
| 20 | than | group |
| 21 | sitting | |
| 22 | thoughts | day |
| 23 | Martin | |
| 24 | be | |
| 25 | Father | pass |
| 26 | this | will |
| 27 | the | |
| 28 | of | us |
| 29 | attempted | |
| 31 | laughed | teenagers |
| 32 | thousand | |
| 33 | so | be |
| 34 | difficulty | we |
| 35 | the | |
| 36 | everyone | It |
| 37 | ascent | |
| 38 | part | |

### 9-B

| Line | | |
|---|---|---|
| 3 | bad | surf |
| 4 | considering | |
| 5 | and | |
| 6 | raincoat | |
| 7 | be | awfully |
| 8 | catch | |
| 9 | every | almost |
| 10 | to | night |
| 11 | from | rocks |
| 12 | the | |
| 13 | reached | |
| 14 | huge | on |
| 15 | to | end |
| 16 | friends | backs |
| 17 | her | |
| 18 | conditions | sit |
| 19 | idea | |
| 20 | play | the |
| 21 | moment | was |
| 22 | should | I |
| 23 | to | Daniel |
| 24 | shifted | comfortable |
| 25 | leave | |
| 26 | who | |
| 27 | a | the |
| 28 | stormy | |
| 29 | help | thoroughly |
| 31 | stopped | |
| 32 | The | from |
| 33 | circle | |
| 34 | understand | people |
| 35 | this | you |

# CORE READING MAZE COMPREHENSION KEY

## 10-A

| Line | | |
|---|---|---|
| 2 | surprise | |
| 3 | with | |
| 4 | realized | up |
| 5 | and | |
| 6 | the | |
| 7 | ride | Luke |
| 8 | They | dollars |
| 9 | members | |
| 10 | earn | ride |
| 11 | had | |
| 12 | was | do |
| 13 | to | lead |
| 14 | it | |
| 15 | about | new |
| 16 | anyway | get |
| 17 | The | used |
| 18 | the | of |
| 19 | was | to |
| 20 | she | |
| 21 | cluster | each |
| 22 | Luke | |
| 23 | pack | allow |
| 24 | get | up |
| 25 | tingle | joined |
| 26 | long | cruising |
| 28 | As | made |
| 29 | them | time |
| 30 | the | a |
| 31 | bicycle | on |
| 33 | were | |
| 34 | slightest | ride |
| 35 | the | sight |
| 36 | downhill | |
| 37 | gathered | the |
| 38 | had | this |
| 39 | lives | |

## 10-B

| Line | | |
|---|---|---|
| 3 | were | reservoir |
| 5 | Linda | when |
| 6 | this | position |
| 7 | be | of |
| 8 | mostly | |
| 9 | suggests | |
| 10 | and | another |
| 11 | but | |
| 12 | That | to |
| 13 | When | |
| 14 | after | |
| 15 | time | in |
| 16 | Linda | had |
| 18 | Before | My |
| 19 | summer | |
| 20 | renting | his |
| 21 | probably | the |
| 22 | the | |
| 23 | finished | could |
| 24 | the | |
| 25 | get | have |
| | The | |
| 26 | halt | her |
| 27 | in | |
| 28 | a | Linda |
| 29 | special | |
| 30 | have | courses |
| 31 | mathematics | |
| 32 | I | all |
| 33 | no | it |
| 34 | in get | able |
| 35 | optional | |
| 36 | interested | |
| 37 | breath | |
| 38 | and | was |
| 39 | girl | |

# Appendix

# CORE Reading Assessment Profile, Grade K

Name____________________________________ School Year___________

| | Fall | Winter | Spring |
|---|---|---|---|
| **CORE Phoneme Deletion Test** | | ____/20 | ____/20 |
| **CORE Phonological Segmentation Test** | ____/23 | ____/23 | ____/23 |
| **CORE Phonics Survey—Alphabet Skills** | | | |
| • Letter names—uppercase | ____/26 | ____/26 | ____/26 |
| • Letter names—lowercase | ____/26 | ____/26 | ____/26 |
| • Consonant sounds | | ____/21 | ____/21 |
| • Long vowel sounds | | ____/5 | ____/5 |
| • Short vowel sounds | | ____/5 | ____/5 |
| **CORE Phonics Survey — Reading and Decoding Skills**<br>• Short vowels in CVC words | | ____/15 | ____/15 |
| **CORE Graded High Frequency Word Survey**<br>Benchmark: 9–10<br>Strategic: 6–8<br>Intensive: 0–5 | ____/10 | ____/10 | ____/10 |
| **San Diego Quick Assessment of Reading Ability**<br>Independent level: 1 error<br>Instructional level: 2 errors<br>Frustration level: 3+ errors | | | |

# CORE Reading Assessment Profile, Grade 1

Name________________________________ School Year__________

| | Fall | Winter | Spring |
|---|---|---|---|
| **CORE Phoneme Deletion Test** | ____/20 | ____/20 | ____/20 |
| **CORE Phonological Segmentation Test** | ____/23 | ____/23 | ____/23 |
| **CORE Phonics Survey—Reading & Decoding Skills** | | | |
| • Short vowels in CVC words | ____/15 | ____/15 | ____/15 |
| • Consonant blends with short vowels | | ____/15 | ____/15 |
| • Short vowels, digraphs, and –tch trigraphs | | ____/15 | ____/15 |
| • R-controlled vowels | | ____/15 | ____/15 |
| • Long vowel sounds | | ____/15 | ____/15 |
| • Variant vowels | | ____/15 | ____/15 |
| • Low frequency vowel and consonant spellings | | ____/15 | ____/15 |
| • Multisyllabic words | | ____/24 | ____/24 |
| **CORE Graded High-Frequency Word Survey**<br>Benchmark: 21–24<br>Strategic: 18–20<br>Intensive: 0–17 | | | |
| **MASI-R Oral Reading Fluency Measures**<br>Benchmark:<br>50th percentile, in WCPM, +/– 10 | | **wcpm** _____<br>Target=23 | **wcpm** _____<br>Target=53 |
| **San Diego Quick Assessment of Reading Ability**<br>Independent level: 1 error<br>Instructional level: 2 errors<br>Frustration level: 3+ errors | | | |
| **CORE Vocabulary Screening** | ____/____ | ____/____ | ____/____ |

# CORE Reading Assessment Profile, Grade 2

Name________________________________ School Year__________

| | Fall | Winter | Spring |
|---|---|---|---|
| **CORE Phoneme Deletion Test**<br>(Administer if indicated by results on other tests.) | ____/20 | ____/20 | ____/20 |
| **CORE Phoneme Segmentation Test**<br>(Administer if indicated by results on other tests.) | ____/15 | ____/15 | ____/15 |
| **CORE Phonics Survey—Reading & Decoding Skills**<br>(Administer E – K as diagnostics if indicated.) | | | |
| • Short vowels in CVC words | ____/15 | ____/15 | ____/15 |
| • Consonant blends with short vowels | ____/15 | ____/15 | ____/15 |
| • Short vowels, digraphs, and –tch trigraphs | ____/15 | ____/15 | ____/15 |
| • R-controlled vowels | ____/15 | ____/15 | ____/15 |
| • Long vowel spellings | ____/15 | ____/15 | ____/15 |
| • Variant vowels | ____/15 | ____/15 | ____/15 |
| • Low frequency vowel and consonant spellings | ____/15 | ____/15 | ____/15 |
| • Multisyllabic words | | ____/24 | ____/24 |
| **CORE Graded High Frequency Word Survey**<br>Benchmark: 21–24<br>Strategic: 18–20<br>Intensive: 0–17 | | | |
| **MASI-R Oral Reading Fluency Measures**<br>Benchmark:<br>50th percentile, in WCPM, +/– 10 | **wcpm** _____<br>Target=51 | **wcpm** _____<br>Target=72 | **wcpm** _____<br>Target=89 |
| **San Diego Quick Assessment of Reading Ability**<br>Independent level: 1 error<br>Instructional level: 2 errors<br>Frustration level: 3+ errors | | | |
| **CORE Vocabulary Screening** | ____/____ | ____/____ | ____/____ |
| **CORE Reading Maze Comprehension** | ____/____ | ____/____ | ____/____ |

# CORE Reading Assessment Profile, Grade 3

Name_________________________________ School Year__________

| | Fall | Winter | Spring |
|---|---|---|---|
| **CORE Phoneme Deletion Test**<br>(Administer if indicated by results on other tests.) | ____/20 | ____/20 | ____/20 |
| **CORE Phoneme Segmentation Test**<br>(Administer if indicated by results on other tests.) | ____/15 | ____/15 | ____/15 |
| **CORE Phonics Survey—Reading & Decoding Skills**<br>(Administer E – K as diagnostics if indicated.) | | | |
| • Short vowels in CVC words | ____/15 | ____/15 | ____/15 |
| • Consonant blends with short vowels | ____/15 | ____/15 | ____/15 |
| • Short vowels, digraphs, and –tch trigraphs | ____/15 | ____/15 | ____/15 |
| • R-controlled vowels | ____/15 | ____/15 | ____/15 |
| • Long vowel spellings | ____/15 | ____/15 | ____/15 |
| • Variant vowels | ____/15 | ____/15 | ____/15 |
| • Low frequency vowel and consonant spellings | ____/15 | ____/15 | ____/15 |
| • Multisyllabic words | ____/24 | ____/24 | ____/24 |
| **CORE Graded High Frequency Word Survey**<br>Benchmark: 21–24<br>Strategic: 18–20<br>Intensive: 0–17 | | | |
| **MASI-R Oral Reading Fluency Measures**<br>Benchmark:<br>50th percentile, in WCPM, +/– 10 | **wcpm** _____<br>Target=71 | **wcpm** _____<br>Target=92 | **wcpm** _____<br>Target=107 |
| **San Diego Quick Assessment of Reading Ability**<br>Independent level: 1 error<br>Instructional level: 2 errors<br>Frustration level: 3+ errors | | | |
| **CORE Vocabulary Screening** | ____/____ | ____/____ | ____/____ |
| **CORE Reading Maze Comprehension** | ____/____ | ____/____ | ____/____ |

# CORE Reading Assessment Profile, Grades 4-8

Name______________________________ School Year__________

| | Fall | Winter | Spring |
|---|---|---|---|
| **CORE Reading Maze Comprehension** | ___/___ | ___/___ | ___/___ |
| **MASI-R Oral Reading Fluency Measures**<br>(Through Grade 6 only.)<br>See Grade Level Norms for Benchmark<br>WCPM @ 50th percentile | ___/___ | ___/___ | ___/___ |
| **CORE Vocabulary Screening** | ___/___ | ___/___ | ___/___ |
| **San Diego Quick Assessment of Reading Ability**<br>Independent level: 1 error<br>Instructional level: 2 errors<br>Frustration level: 3+ errors | | | |
| **CORE Graded High-Frequency Word Survey**<br>(Grades 3, 4. Administer to other grades only if indicated.)<br>Benchmark: 21–24<br>Strategic: 18–20<br>Intensive: 0–17 | | | |
| **CORE Phoneme Deletion Test**<br>(Administer if indicated by results on other measures.) | ___/20 | ___/20 | ___/20 |
| **CORE Phoneme Segmentation Test**<br>(Administer if indicated by results on other measures.) | ___/15 | ___/15 | ___/15 |
| **CORE Phonics Survey—Reading & Decoding Skills**<br>(Administer E – K as diagnostics if indicated.) | | | |
| • Short vowels in CVC words | ___/15 | ___/15 | ___/15 |
| • Consonant blends with short vowels | ___/15 | ___/15 | ___/15 |
| • Short vowels, digraphs, and -tch trigraphs | ___/15 | ___/15 | ___/15 |
| • R-controlled vowels | ___/15 | ___/15 | ___/15 |
| • Long vowel spellings | ___/15 | ___/15 | ___/15 |
| • Variant vowels | ___/15 | ___/15 | ___/15 |
| • Low frequency vowel and consonant spellings | ___/15 | ___/15 | ___/15 |
| • Multisyllabic words | ___/24 | ___/24 | ___/24 |

# CORE Reading Assessment Profile, Grades 9-12

Name________________________________ School Year__________

| | Fall | Winter | Spring |
|---|---|---|---|
| **CORE Reading Maze Comprehension** | ___/___ | ___/___ | ___/___ |
| **San Diego Quick Assessment of Reading Ability**<br>Independent level: 1 error<br>Instructional level: 2 errors<br>Frustration level: 3+ errors | | | |
| **CORE Phoneme Segmentation Test**<br>(Administer only if indicated.) | ___/20 | ___/20 | ___/20 |
| **CORE Phonics Survey—Reading & Decoding Skills**<br>(Administer E – K as diagnostics if indicated.) | | | |
| • Short vowels in CVC words | ___/15 | ___/15 | ___/15 |
| • Consonant blends with short vowels | ___/15 | ___/15 | ___/15 |
| • Short vowels, digraphs, and –tch trigraphs | ___/15 | ___/15 | ___/15 |
| • R-controlled vowels | ___/15 | ___/15 | ___/15 |
| • Long vowel spellings | ___/15 | ___/15 | ___/15 |
| • Variant vowels | ___/15 | ___/15 | ___/15 |
| • Low frequency vowel and consonant spellings | ___/15 | ___/15 | ___/15 |
| • Multisyllabic words | ___/24 | ___/24 | ___/24 |
| **CORE Graded High-Frequency Word Survey**<br>(Administer only if indicated.) | | | |

# Class Record: Kindergarten Phonological Awareness Assessments

Teacher______________________________ School Year__________

| | CORE Phonological Segmentation Test | | | | | | | | | CORE Phoneme Deletion Test | | | | | |
|---|---|---|---|---|---|---|---|---|---|---|---|---|---|---|---|
| | Part A | | | Part B | | | Part C | | | Part A | | | Part B | | |
| STUDENTS Tested in | F | W | S | F | W | S | F | W | S | F | W | S | F | W | S |
| Possible Points | 5 | 5 | 5 | 8 | 8 | 8 | 10 | 10 | 10 | | 5 | 5 | 5 | 5 | 5 |
| 1. | | | | | | | | | | | | | | | |
| 2. | | | | | | | | | | | | | | | |
| 3. | | | | | | | | | | | | | | | |
| 4. | | | | | | | | | | | | | | | |
| 5. | | | | | | | | | | | | | | | |
| 6. | | | | | | | | | | | | | | | |
| 7. | | | | | | | | | | | | | | | |
| 8. | | | | | | | | | | | | | | | |
| 9. | | | | | | | | | | | | | | | |
| 10. | | | | | | | | | | | | | | | |
| 11. | | | | | | | | | | | | | | | |
| 12. | | | | | | | | | | | | | | | |
| 13. | | | | | | | | | | | | | | | |
| 14. | | | | | | | | | | | | | | | |
| 15. | | | | | | | | | | | | | | | |
| 16. | | | | | | | | | | | | | | | |
| 17. | | | | | | | | | | | | | | | |
| 18. | | | | | | | | | | | | | | | |
| 19. | | | | | | | | | | | | | | | |
| 20. | | | | | | | | | | | | | | | |
| 21. | | | | | | | | | | | | | | | |
| 22. | | | | | | | | | | | | | | | |
| 23. | | | | | | | | | | | | | | | |
| 24. | | | | | | | | | | | | | | | |
| 25. | | | | | | | | | | | | | | | |

# Class Record: Kindergarten Reading Assessments

Teacher________________________________ School Year__________

| | CORE Phonics Surveys | | | | | | | | | | | | | | | | | | CORE Graded High-Frequency Word Survey | | | San Diego Quick Assessment of Reading Ability | | |
|---|---|---|---|---|---|---|---|---|---|---|---|---|---|---|---|---|---|---|---|---|---|---|---|---|
| | A. Letter Names Uppercase | | | B. Letter Names Lowercase | | | C. Consonant Sounds | | | D. Long Vowel Sounds | | | D. Short Vowel Sounds | | | E. Short Vowels in CVC Words | | | | | | | | |
| STUDENTS — Tested in | F | W | S | F | W | S | F | W | S | F | W | S | F | W | S | F | W | S | F | W | S | F | W | S |
| Possible Points | 26 | 26 | 26 | 26 | 26 | 26 | | 21 | 21 | | 5 | 5 | | 5 | 5 | | 15 | 15 | | 10 | 10 | | | |
| 1. | | | | | | | | | | | | | | | | | | | | | | | | |
| 2. | | | | | | | | | | | | | | | | | | | | | | | | |
| 3. | | | | | | | | | | | | | | | | | | | | | | | | |
| 4. | | | | | | | | | | | | | | | | | | | | | | | | |
| 5. | | | | | | | | | | | | | | | | | | | | | | | | |
| 6. | | | | | | | | | | | | | | | | | | | | | | | | |
| 7. | | | | | | | | | | | | | | | | | | | | | | | | |
| 8. | | | | | | | | | | | | | | | | | | | | | | | | |
| 9. | | | | | | | | | | | | | | | | | | | | | | | | |
| 10. | | | | | | | | | | | | | | | | | | | | | | | | |
| 11. | | | | | | | | | | | | | | | | | | | | | | | | |
| 12. | | | | | | | | | | | | | | | | | | | | | | | | |
| 13. | | | | | | | | | | | | | | | | | | | | | | | | |
| 14. | | | | | | | | | | | | | | | | | | | | | | | | |
| 15. | | | | | | | | | | | | | | | | | | | | | | | | |
| 16. | | | | | | | | | | | | | | | | | | | | | | | | |
| 17. | | | | | | | | | | | | | | | | | | | | | | | | |
| 18. | | | | | | | | | | | | | | | | | | | | | | | | |
| 19. | | | | | | | | | | | | | | | | | | | | | | | | |
| 20. | | | | | | | | | | | | | | | | | | | | | | | | |
| 21. | | | | | | | | | | | | | | | | | | | | | | | | |
| 22. | | | | | | | | | | | | | | | | | | | | | | | | |
| 23. | | | | | | | | | | | | | | | | | | | | | | | | |
| 24. | | | | | | | | | | | | | | | | | | | | | | | | |
| 25. | | | | | | | | | | | | | | | | | | | | | | | | |

# Class Record: Grade 1 Phonological Awareness Assessments

Teacher______________________________ School Year____________

| | | CORE Phonological Segmentation Test | | | | | | | | | CORE Phoneme Deletion Test | | | | | | | | |
|---|---|---|---|---|---|---|---|---|---|---|---|---|---|---|---|---|---|---|---|
| | | Part A | | | Part B | | | Part C | | | Part A | | | Part B | | | Part C | | |
| STUDENTS | Tested in | F | W | S | F | W | S | F | W | S | F | W | S | F | W | S | F | W | S |
| | Possible Points | 5 | 5 | 5 | 8 | 8 | 8 | 10 | 10 | 10 | 5 | 5 | 5 | 5 | 5 | 5 | 5 | 5 | 5 |
| 1. | | | | | | | | | | | | | | | | | | | |
| 2. | | | | | | | | | | | | | | | | | | | |
| 3. | | | | | | | | | | | | | | | | | | | |
| 4. | | | | | | | | | | | | | | | | | | | |
| 5. | | | | | | | | | | | | | | | | | | | |
| 6. | | | | | | | | | | | | | | | | | | | |
| 7. | | | | | | | | | | | | | | | | | | | |
| 8. | | | | | | | | | | | | | | | | | | | |
| 9. | | | | | | | | | | | | | | | | | | | |
| 10. | | | | | | | | | | | | | | | | | | | |
| 11. | | | | | | | | | | | | | | | | | | | |
| 12. | | | | | | | | | | | | | | | | | | | |
| 13. | | | | | | | | | | | | | | | | | | | |
| 14. | | | | | | | | | | | | | | | | | | | |
| 15. | | | | | | | | | | | | | | | | | | | |
| 16. | | | | | | | | | | | | | | | | | | | |
| 17. | | | | | | | | | | | | | | | | | | | |
| 18. | | | | | | | | | | | | | | | | | | | |
| 19. | | | | | | | | | | | | | | | | | | | |
| 20. | | | | | | | | | | | | | | | | | | | |
| 21. | | | | | | | | | | | | | | | | | | | |
| 22. | | | | | | | | | | | | | | | | | | | |
| 23. | | | | | | | | | | | | | | | | | | | |
| 24. | | | | | | | | | | | | | | | | | | | |
| 25. | | | | | | | | | | | | | | | | | | | |

# Class Record: Grade 1 CORE Phonics Survey

Teacher_______________________________________ School Year____________

| | Part E: Short Vowels in CVC Words | | | Part F: Consonant Blends w/ Short Vowels | | | Part G: Short Vowels, Digraphs and -tch Trigraph | | | Part H: R-Controlled Vowels | | | Part I: Long Vowel Spellings | | | Part J: Variant Vowels | | | Part K: Low-Frequency Vowel and Consonant Spellings | | | Part L: Multisyllabic Words | | |
|---|---|---|---|---|---|---|---|---|---|---|---|---|---|---|---|---|---|---|---|---|---|---|---|---|
| Tested in | F | W | S | F | W | S | F | W | S | F | W | S | F | W | S | F | W | S | F | W | S | F | W | S |
| STUDENTS Possible Points | 15 | 15 | 15 | 15 | 15 | 15 | 15 | 15 | 15 | 15 | 15 | 15 | 15 | 15 | 15 | 15 | 15 | 15 | 15 | 15 | 15 | 24 | 24 | 24 |
| 1. | | | | | | | | | | | | | | | | | | | | | | | | |
| 2. | | | | | | | | | | | | | | | | | | | | | | | | |
| 3. | | | | | | | | | | | | | | | | | | | | | | | | |
| 4. | | | | | | | | | | | | | | | | | | | | | | | | |
| 5. | | | | | | | | | | | | | | | | | | | | | | | | |
| 6. | | | | | | | | | | | | | | | | | | | | | | | | |
| 7. | | | | | | | | | | | | | | | | | | | | | | | | |
| 8. | | | | | | | | | | | | | | | | | | | | | | | | |
| 9. | | | | | | | | | | | | | | | | | | | | | | | | |
| 10. | | | | | | | | | | | | | | | | | | | | | | | | |
| 11. | | | | | | | | | | | | | | | | | | | | | | | | |
| 12. | | | | | | | | | | | | | | | | | | | | | | | | |
| 13. | | | | | | | | | | | | | | | | | | | | | | | | |
| 14. | | | | | | | | | | | | | | | | | | | | | | | | |
| 15. | | | | | | | | | | | | | | | | | | | | | | | | |
| 16. | | | | | | | | | | | | | | | | | | | | | | | | |
| 17. | | | | | | | | | | | | | | | | | | | | | | | | |
| 18. | | | | | | | | | | | | | | | | | | | | | | | | |
| 19. | | | | | | | | | | | | | | | | | | | | | | | | |
| 20. | | | | | | | | | | | | | | | | | | | | | | | | |
| 21. | | | | | | | | | | | | | | | | | | | | | | | | |
| 22. | | | | | | | | | | | | | | | | | | | | | | | | |
| 23. | | | | | | | | | | | | | | | | | | | | | | | | |
| 24. | | | | | | | | | | | | | | | | | | | | | | | | |
| 25. | | | | | | | | | | | | | | | | | | | | | | | | |

# Class Record: Grade 1 Reading Assessments

Teacher______________________________ School Year____________

| | MASI-R Oral Reading Fluency Measures | | | CORE Graded High-Frequency Word Survey | | | CORE Vocabulary Screening | | |
|---|---|---|---|---|---|---|---|---|---|
| STUDENTS — Tested in / Possible Points | F | W | S | F 24 | W 24 | S 24 | F | W | S |
| 1. | | | | | | | | | |
| 2. | | | | | | | | | |
| 3. | | | | | | | | | |
| 4. | | | | | | | | | |
| 5. | | | | | | | | | |
| 6. | | | | | | | | | |
| 7. | | | | | | | | | |
| 8. | | | | | | | | | |
| 9. | | | | | | | | | |
| 10. | | | | | | | | | |
| 11. | | | | | | | | | |
| 12. | | | | | | | | | |
| 13. | | | | | | | | | |
| 14. | | | | | | | | | |
| 15. | | | | | | | | | |
| 16. | | | | | | | | | |
| 17. | | | | | | | | | |
| 18. | | | | | | | | | |
| 19. | | | | | | | | | |
| 20. | | | | | | | | | |
| 21. | | | | | | | | | |
| 22. | | | | | | | | | |
| 23. | | | | | | | | | |
| 24. | | | | | | | | | |
| 25. | | | | | | | | | |

# Class Record: Grades 2 and 3 Phonemic Awareness Assessments

Teacher______________________________ School Year__________

| | CORE Phoneme Deletion Test | | | | | | | | | | | | CORE Phoneme Segmentation Test | | |
|---|---|---|---|---|---|---|---|---|---|---|---|---|---|---|---|
| | Part A | | | Part B | | | Part C | | | Part D | | | | | |
| STUDENTS — Tested in | F | W | S | F | W | S | F | W | S | F | W | S | F | W | S |
| Possible Points | 5 | 5 | 5 | 5 | 5 | 5 | 5 | 5 | 5 | 5 | 5 | 5 | 15 | 15 | 15 |
| 1. | | | | | | | | | | | | | | | |
| 2. | | | | | | | | | | | | | | | |
| 3. | | | | | | | | | | | | | | | |
| 4. | | | | | | | | | | | | | | | |
| 5. | | | | | | | | | | | | | | | |
| 6. | | | | | | | | | | | | | | | |
| 7. | | | | | | | | | | | | | | | |
| 8. | | | | | | | | | | | | | | | |
| 9. | | | | | | | | | | | | | | | |
| 10. | | | | | | | | | | | | | | | |
| 11. | | | | | | | | | | | | | | | |
| 12. | | | | | | | | | | | | | | | |
| 13. | | | | | | | | | | | | | | | |
| 14. | | | | | | | | | | | | | | | |
| 15. | | | | | | | | | | | | | | | |
| 16. | | | | | | | | | | | | | | | |
| 17. | | | | | | | | | | | | | | | |
| 18. | | | | | | | | | | | | | | | |
| 19. | | | | | | | | | | | | | | | |
| 20. | | | | | | | | | | | | | | | |
| 21. | | | | | | | | | | | | | | | |
| 22. | | | | | | | | | | | | | | | |
| 23. | | | | | | | | | | | | | | | |
| 24. | | | | | | | | | | | | | | | |
| 25. | | | | | | | | | | | | | | | |

# Class Record: Grades 2 and 3 CORE Phonics Survey

Teacher_________________________ School Year_____________

| STUDENTS | Part E: Short Vowels in CVC Words | | | Part F: Consonant Blends w/ Short Vowels | | | Part G: Short Vowels, Digraphs and -tch Trigraph | | | Part H: R-Controlled Vowels | | | Part I: Long Vowel Spellings | | | Part J: Variant Vowels | | | Part K: Low Frequency Vowel and Consonant Spellings | | | Part L: Multisyllabic Words | | |
|---|---|---|---|---|---|---|---|---|---|---|---|---|---|---|---|---|---|---|---|---|---|---|---|---|
| Tested in | F | W | S | F | W | S | F | W | S | F | W | S | F | W | S | F | W | S | F | W | S | F | W | S |
| Possible Points | 15 | 15 | 15 | 15 | 15 | 15 | 15 | 15 | 15 | 15 | 15 | 15 | 15 | 15 | 15 | 15 | 15 | 15 | 15 | 15 | 15 | 24 | 24 | 24 |
| 1. | | | | | | | | | | | | | | | | | | | | | | | | |
| 2. | | | | | | | | | | | | | | | | | | | | | | | | |
| 3. | | | | | | | | | | | | | | | | | | | | | | | | |
| 4. | | | | | | | | | | | | | | | | | | | | | | | | |
| 5. | | | | | | | | | | | | | | | | | | | | | | | | |
| 6. | | | | | | | | | | | | | | | | | | | | | | | | |
| 7. | | | | | | | | | | | | | | | | | | | | | | | | |
| 8. | | | | | | | | | | | | | | | | | | | | | | | | |
| 9. | | | | | | | | | | | | | | | | | | | | | | | | |
| 10. | | | | | | | | | | | | | | | | | | | | | | | | |
| 11. | | | | | | | | | | | | | | | | | | | | | | | | |
| 12. | | | | | | | | | | | | | | | | | | | | | | | | |
| 13. | | | | | | | | | | | | | | | | | | | | | | | | |
| 14. | | | | | | | | | | | | | | | | | | | | | | | | |
| 15. | | | | | | | | | | | | | | | | | | | | | | | | |
| 16. | | | | | | | | | | | | | | | | | | | | | | | | |
| 17. | | | | | | | | | | | | | | | | | | | | | | | | |
| 18. | | | | | | | | | | | | | | | | | | | | | | | | |
| 19. | | | | | | | | | | | | | | | | | | | | | | | | |
| 20. | | | | | | | | | | | | | | | | | | | | | | | | |
| 21. | | | | | | | | | | | | | | | | | | | | | | | | |
| 22. | | | | | | | | | | | | | | | | | | | | | | | | |
| 23. | | | | | | | | | | | | | | | | | | | | | | | | |
| 24. | | | | | | | | | | | | | | | | | | | | | | | | |
| 25. | | | | | | | | | | | | | | | | | | | | | | | | |

# Class Record: Grades 2 and 3 Reading Assessments

Teacher______________________________ School Year____________

| | MASI-R Oral Reading Fluency Measures | | | CORE Graded High-Frequency Word Survey | | | CORE Vocabulary Screening | | | CORE Reading Maze Comprehension Test | | | San Diego Quick Assessment of Reading Ability | | |
|---|---|---|---|---|---|---|---|---|---|---|---|---|---|---|---|
| STUDENTS — Tested in / Possible Points | F | W | S | F 24 | W 24 | S 24 | F | W | S | F | W | S | F | W | S |
| 1. | | | | | | | | | | | | | | | |
| 2. | | | | | | | | | | | | | | | |
| 3. | | | | | | | | | | | | | | | |
| 4. | | | | | | | | | | | | | | | |
| 5. | | | | | | | | | | | | | | | |
| 6. | | | | | | | | | | | | | | | |
| 7. | | | | | | | | | | | | | | | |
| 8. | | | | | | | | | | | | | | | |
| 9. | | | | | | | | | | | | | | | |
| 10. | | | | | | | | | | | | | | | |
| 11. | | | | | | | | | | | | | | | |
| 12. | | | | | | | | | | | | | | | |
| 13. | | | | | | | | | | | | | | | |
| 14. | | | | | | | | | | | | | | | |
| 15. | | | | | | | | | | | | | | | |
| 16. | | | | | | | | | | | | | | | |
| 17. | | | | | | | | | | | | | | | |
| 18. | | | | | | | | | | | | | | | |
| 19. | | | | | | | | | | | | | | | |
| 20. | | | | | | | | | | | | | | | |
| 21. | | | | | | | | | | | | | | | |
| 22. | | | | | | | | | | | | | | | |
| 23. | | | | | | | | | | | | | | | |
| 24. | | | | | | | | | | | | | | | |
| 25. | | | | | | | | | | | | | | | |

# Class Record: Grades 4 through 8 Reading Assessments

Teacher______________________________ School Year____________

| | CORE Reading Maze Comprehension Test | | | MASI-R Oral Reading Fluency Measures (through Grade 6 only) | | | CORE Vocabulary Screening | | | CORE Graded High-Frequency Word Survey* (Grade 4 only) | | | San Diego Quick Assessment of Reading Ability | | | Diagnostic tests as needed | | | | | |
|---|---|---|---|---|---|---|---|---|---|---|---|---|---|---|---|---|---|---|---|---|---|
| | | | | | | | | | | | | | | | | Test: | | | Test: | | |
| STUDENTS Tested in | F | W | S | F | W | S | F | W | S | F | W | S | F | W | S | | | | | | |
| Possible Points | | | | | | | | | | 24 | 24 | 24 | | | | | | | | | |
| 1. | | | | | | | | | | | | | | | | | | | | | |
| 2. | | | | | | | | | | | | | | | | | | | | | |
| 3. | | | | | | | | | | | | | | | | | | | | | |
| 4. | | | | | | | | | | | | | | | | | | | | | |
| 5. | | | | | | | | | | | | | | | | | | | | | |
| 6. | | | | | | | | | | | | | | | | | | | | | |
| 7. | | | | | | | | | | | | | | | | | | | | | |
| 8. | | | | | | | | | | | | | | | | | | | | | |
| 9. | | | | | | | | | | | | | | | | | | | | | |
| 10. | | | | | | | | | | | | | | | | | | | | | |
| 11. | | | | | | | | | | | | | | | | | | | | | |
| 12. | | | | | | | | | | | | | | | | | | | | | |
| 13. | | | | | | | | | | | | | | | | | | | | | |
| 14. | | | | | | | | | | | | | | | | | | | | | |
| 15. | | | | | | | | | | | | | | | | | | | | | |
| 16. | | | | | | | | | | | | | | | | | | | | | |
| 17. | | | | | | | | | | | | | | | | | | | | | |
| 18. | | | | | | | | | | | | | | | | | | | | | |
| 19. | | | | | | | | | | | | | | | | | | | | | |
| 20. | | | | | | | | | | | | | | | | | | | | | |
| 21. | | | | | | | | | | | | | | | | | | | | | |
| 22. | | | | | | | | | | | | | | | | | | | | | |
| 23. | | | | | | | | | | | | | | | | | | | | | |
| 24. | | | | | | | | | | | | | | | | | | | | | |
| 25. | | | | | | | | | | | | | | | | | | | | | |

*or if indicated

# Class Record: Grades 9 through 12 Reading Assessments

Teacher____________________________________ School Year____________

| | CORE Reading Maze Comprehension Test (through Grade 10 only) | | | Diagnostic tests as needed | | | | | | | | |
|---|---|---|---|---|---|---|---|---|---|---|---|---|
| | | | | Test: | | | Test: | | | Test: | | |
| STUDENTS Tested in / Possible Points | F | W | S | | | | | | | | | |
| 1. | | | | | | | | | | | | |
| 2. | | | | | | | | | | | | |
| 3. | | | | | | | | | | | | |
| 4. | | | | | | | | | | | | |
| 5. | | | | | | | | | | | | |
| 6. | | | | | | | | | | | | |
| 7. | | | | | | | | | | | | |
| 8. | | | | | | | | | | | | |
| 9. | | | | | | | | | | | | |
| 10. | | | | | | | | | | | | |
| 11. | | | | | | | | | | | | |
| 12. | | | | | | | | | | | | |
| 13. | | | | | | | | | | | | |
| 14. | | | | | | | | | | | | |
| 15. | | | | | | | | | | | | |
| 16. | | | | | | | | | | | | |
| 17. | | | | | | | | | | | | |
| 18. | | | | | | | | | | | | |
| 19. | | | | | | | | | | | | |
| 20. | | | | | | | | | | | | |
| 21. | | | | | | | | | | | | |
| 22. | | | | | | | | | | | | |
| 23. | | | | | | | | | | | | |
| 24. | | | | | | | | | | | | |
| 25. | | | | | | | | | | | | |

# Performance Criteria for Fluency and Fluency Scores: A Discussion

By Ken W. Howell

Most of us are clear about the definition of *oral reading*. Nevertheless, within education (including school psychology) there is often confusion around the concepts and terminology related to *fluency*. Therefore, in order to say what the MASI-R curriculum-based and criterion-referenced measures are actually measuring, here is a quick primer on Fluency.

## What Is Oral Reading Fluency?

Fluency is defined as the number of responses made, or items (words in the case of the MASI-R) completed, during a unit of time. The formula for finding fluency is the same as it is for rate: total number ÷ time. When using the passages supplied in the MASI-R to measure Oral Reading Fluency (ORF), the unit of time is 1 minute and results are reported as per minute data (e.g., 200 words in 2 minutes would be: 200 ÷ 2 = 100 wpm). Correct performance and error performance are reported as separate behaviors. For example, a 1 minute timing with 47 words read correctly and 6 read incorrectly would be reported as 47 ÷ 1 = 47 wpm correct (i.e., wcpm) and 6 ÷ 1 = 6 wpm incorrect (i.e., wepm), not 53 words per minute with 89% accuracy. This is because the MASI-R is a Curriculum-Based Measure (CBM), which is a standardized measure, and CBM reading administration and scoring conventions include the use of per minute data. CBM conventions additionally call for the use of three one-minute samples taken from each of three passages, so that decisions are not made from a single sample or multiple samples taken from a single passage.

What do fluency scores actually represent? Fluent oral reading is one of several ways students can react to print. In general, students who react to a passage by reading it accurately and quickly also understand it better than students who react by reading it slowly and/or inaccurately. The literature documenting this relationship is extensive and indicates a linkage between fluency and comprehension that is both causal and reciprocal. For examples of this type of research, see the chapter by Torgesen, & Hudson titled "Reading fluency: critical issues for struggling readers" in the 2006 book *Reading Fluency: The Forgotten Dimension of Reading Success*, or the 2001 article "Oral Reading Fluency as an Indicator of Reading Competence: A Theoretical, Empirical, and Historical Analysis" by Fuchs, Fuchs, Hosp and Jenkins. (See Resources for details.)

Still, some educators seem to have difficulty seeing the importance of fluency as an indicator of proficiency and a target for instruction. This is unfortunate because, like content, proficiency is an essential part of any learning expectation or objective. One indication that proficiency is a common learning expectation is that students are routinely located and described according to positions along proficiency sequences within content areas. For example, after having read the same passage, we may routinely say one student reads better than the other because she or he is more accurate. Similarly, even if both students have 100% accuracy, we may say one student reads better than another because she or he finishes the passage with equal accuracy in less time. This means that students who have 100% accuracy when reading can still do better.

The next question is: "Does increased fluency mean anything?" As we have noted, fluency is a universally recognized proficiency dimension, but when it comes to reading, fluency is much more than an indicator of expertise. A lack of fluency has critical effects on the reader and his or her reading. It is easy to think of the critical effects of fluency: Remember the last time you were trying to make a left turn and the driver in front of you didn't immediately accelerate when the green arrow light came on? Remember how long you waited for your checked luggage last time you flew? Those are mere inconveniences compared to the problems of a student reading at half of the rate of his or her peers. Even if that student's comprehension skills are fine, she or he will only have access to half of the ideas and information than the other students.

## Why Measure Oral Reading Fluency?

Assessments function in education to inform decision-making. Types of educational decisions include screening decisions, problem-solving decisions (sometimes called *diagnostic*), summative decisions, and formative decisions (sometimes called *progress monitoring*). ORF can have a role in any of these assessment functions, as long as it is employed within the appropriate constraints and guidelines of good practice. ORF functions as an indicator of important, but less easily observed behaviors, skills and processes (the most obvious of these being proficiency in silent reading).

Oral Reading Fluency is categorized in CBM as a general outcome measure. General outcome measures make use of the fairly complex and interactive tasks found at the upper levels of some skill sequences (even if a sequence is not strictly hierarchical). These are tasks that depend on the use of many lower-level skills, or prerequisites. Given success on a general outcome measure, one can reasonably infer success on the prerequisites. Therefore, as a general outcome measure for reading, ORF becomes a proxy for multiple reading skills and processes and a starting point for investigating reading problems and for monitoring reading progress. When students read passages accurately and fluently, it can be assumed that they have mastered the other skills and processes required, but not explicitly being observed, during passage reading. When they don't read passages accurately and fluently, it may mean that something about the instruction, curriculum and/or learning environment needs to be adjusted in order to teach the student missing skills or knowledge.

## What Do ORF Scores Mean?

Curriculum-based measurement (CBM) is not informal assessment; it is rigorous, precise, and there are standardized administration and scoring conventions. Norms for CBM ORF have been established. In addition, many curriculum-based measures are criterion-referenced and have established behavioral standards. The following is a set of expected performance levels for Oral Passage Reading based on sampling and research related to the minimum reading fluency levels expected for the successful application of passage reading:

| Grade Rate | Correct Rate | Error Accuracy | Expected |
|---|---|---|---|
| 6 | 140 | 0–7 | 100–95% |
| 5 | 140 | 0–7 | 100–95% |
| 4 | 140 | 0–7 | 100–95% |
| 3 | Early 100<br>Late 140 | 0–7 | 100–95% |
| 2 | Early 40<br>Late 100 | 0–5 | 100–95% |
| 1 | Early 30<br>Late 50 | 0–3 | 100–95% |

For most students who are successful, Oral Reading Fluency reaches a plateau, at least in terms of rate, somewhere between 145 and 160 wpm in the sixth grade. That level of rate remains stable across increasingly difficult levels and kinds of text as the student progresses through higher grades. However, changes in the inflection, contour and prosody of fluency are still expected. For all practical purposes, there isn't a ceiling for silent reading, but middle-school students should reach silent rates in excess of 500 wpm without loss of meaning. Ultimately, students must learn to control and adjust their rate to meet the demands of the text and their purpose for reading.

Accuracy for successful students is typically from 3 to 7 errors per minute (or + 95% accuracy). That is fewer than 5 errors before the student reaches the 100th word mark on the Teacher Record. When untimed and asked to read carefully, successful readers make few, if any, errors (i.e., + 97% accuracy). This means that setting reading objectives with criterions of 80 or 85% accuracy is inappropriate.

## What's Next?

If a student does not reach the criterion that has been established, consider using the following problem-solving sequence from the Howell & Nolet text referenced in Resources, page A21.

**Problem Solving When Assessing Reading Fluency**

| If... | Then... |
|---|---|
| Oral reading skills are acceptable | Go on to comprehension |
| Oral reading skills are not acceptable | Consider the age and accuracy of the student |
| The student is K–2 or an older student who decodes few words | Check basic decoding skill |
| Basic decoding skills are unacceptable | Focus instruction on the missing basic decoding skills |
| Basic decoding skills are acceptable | Use assisted monitoring to see if the student can correct his or her own errors |
| The student is Grade 2 or above and decodes fairly well | Check to see if oral reading is accurate but slow |
| Oral reading is inaccurate | Use assisted monitoring to see if the student can correct his or her own errors |
| Oral reading is slow but accurate | See if the student's rate improves when re-reading |
| The student's rate increased by about 40% on second reading | Build fluency (e.g., repeated readings) |
| The student's rate did not increase by about 40% on second reading | Elicit an error sample |
| You have used assisted monitoring and found that the student does not correct his/her own errors | Emphasize self-monitoring within active reading instruction |
| You have used assisted monitoring and found that the student does correct his or her own errors | Elicit an error sample |
| The student's errors do not increase as the passages get harder | Use balanced reading instruction |
| The student's errors do increase as the passages get harder | Categorize errors |
| There are no patterns to the errors | Use balanced reading instruction |
| There are non-phonic error patterns (e.g., omissions, insertions, reversals) | Correct the patterns (treat them as 'bad habits' and use pre-correction with self-monitoring) |
| There are phonics error patterns | Do a thorough evaluation of the student's knowledge of phonic skills. Consider the age & instructional history of the student. Use active reading instruction |
| There are specific sound and blending errors | Emphasize decoding skills |
| There are sight-word errors | Include sight words in the instructional program |
| The student seldom self-corrects meaningful errors | Emphasize self monitoring |

## Resources for Using ORF and Other CBM Measures

AIMSweb (2007). *Aimsweb training workbooks for early reading, reading, spelling, writing, early numeracy, and math.* http://aimsweb.com

Fuchs, L. S., Fuchs, D., Hosp, M. K., and Jenkins, J. R. (2001). Oral Reading Fluency as an indicator of reading competence: A theoretical, empirical, and historical analysis. *Scientific Studies of Reading,* Vol. 5, No. 3, 239–256.

Hosp, M. K., Hosp, J. L., & Howell, K. W. (2007). *The ABCs of CBM: A practical guide to implementing curriculum-based measurement.* New York: Guilford.

Howell, K. W., & Nolet, V. (2000). *Curriculum-based evaluation: Teaching and decision making* (3rd ed.). Belmont, CA: Wadsworth.

Intervention Central CBM Warehouse
www.interventioncentral.org/htmdocs/interventions/cbmwarehouse.php

National Center on Student Progress Monitoring
www.studentprogress.org

Torgesen, J. & Hudson, R. (2006). Reading fluency: critical issues for struggling readers. In S. J. Samuels & A. Farstrup (Eds.), *Reading fluency: The forgotten dimension of reading success.* Newark, DE: International Reading Association Monograph of the British Journal of Educational Psychology.

# Assessment-Driven Instruction: A Systems Approach

*by Linda Diamond*

While many schools and districts use assessment data to determine student needs, only a few are utilizing the data to differentiate support for teachers, make decisions about intervention programs, and monitor program implementation. Some districts use assessment data to determine system-wide professional development needs, allocate coaching time, identify students who need frequent progress monitoring, and purchase and implement intensive intervention programs designed to support at-risk students. Schools using this approach recognize the power of assessment-driven instruction. They use a variety of tests for different purposes, with particular attention to progress monitoring tests focused on critical reading indicators.

Reading skills assessed in the early grades are discrete. These specific skills tend to be the foundation for long-term outcomes such as comprehension. Because these early skills are vital to the development of reading proficiency, assessment needs to be frequent and ongoing. In the upper grades, assessment is necessary to monitor progress and to identify causes of reading weakness. Unlike the early primary-grade measures—phonemic awareness, decoding, and fluency—upper-grade assessment often starts with comprehension and fluency, and then works backward to the earlier foundational skills in order to pinpoint gaps. Given the urgency of preparing students to read and helping struggling, older readers, early screening is essential. With the right tools given at the right times, we can make accurate predictions of which students will be at risk for reading failure, and we can effectively monitor students who have been failing but who are receiving intervention (Torgesen, 2004). So what are the right tools and under what conditions do we use them?

## Types of Assessment(s)

Within their schools, educators need to organize their assessment toolkits around four broad types of assessment instruments: screening tests, progress monitoring tests (CBM, for example), outcome measures such as a state's end-of year test, and diagnostic tests. In all cases, educators need to understand the test purpose and how to use the resulting information.

**Screening tests** provide information about the knowledge and skill base of the student. They can determine the most appropriate starting point for instruction and for planning instructional groups and interventions. In the primary grades, screening tests should measure phonological awareness, phonics, fluency, vocabulary, and comprehension. In the upper grades, comprehension and fluency may be the first screening tests, but only as a starting point. Follow-up diagnostic assessments can be used to target areas for instruction based on any apparent weaknesses. Early screening tests should measure skills that most accurately predict future reading proficiency. For example, since the correlation between letter identification in Kindergarten and reading scores in first grade has been found to be fairly high, .52 (Snow et al., 1998), a test that measures this skill early is vital. Tests of oral reading fluency requiring as little as a few minutes to administer are also strong predictors of later reading skill. Fuchs, Fuchs, Hosp, and Jenkins (2001) reported that a brief oral fluency measure was a better gauge of reading comprehension than short reading comprehension tests. In their study with middle school age students with reading difficulties, the correlation between oral reading fluency and comprehension was .91 (Fuchs et al., 2001). Recent data from Florida shows a correlation between third graders' performance on the Dynamic Indicators of Basic Early Literacy Skills (DIBELS) oral fluency measure and the Florida Comprehensive Assessment Test of .70 (Buck and Torgesen, 2003). Given the reliability of these new early screening measures, educational systems must incorporate these tests into their total assessment package. These same tests, in many cases, can also serve as ongoing progress-monitoring assessments to ensure students are on track and instructional interventions are working.

**Progress monitoring** assessment should be ongoing. Examples of progress monitoring assessment include curriculum-embedded tests or tests such as those provided with DIBELS. AIMSweb, a similar system, developed by Edformation, measures the same foundational skills as does DIBELS but includes other assessments for writing and math up through eighth grade. These tests are used to regularly assess student performance on a number of important predictive reading measures. In addition to external progress monitoring tools which can help determine whether students are learning to read on a predictable schedule, it is also important to track program implementation. Most good reading programs have their own unit or theme progress monitoring tests. These program tests serve to verify the extent to which teachers are effectively using their programs and students are learning what has been taught. They answer the question, "Are teachers effectively teaching the selected reading program?" These curriculum-embedded tests, along with effective external progress monitoring tests, help a school or district determine whether the program itself, the teacher training, and the implementation of instruction and intervention are effective.

**Outcome assessment** is often used at the end of the school year. It provides data about exiting accomplishments and is useful for planning the next major segment of instruction for individual students. It most effectively provides programmatic information for large groups of students. Its greatest use is to validate the quality of a school's program and implementation.

**Diagnostic assessment** instruments are most often used after progress monitoring or screening tests reveal a pattern of weakness. Diagnostic tests such as the Woodcock Reading Mastery Test, Durrell Analysis of Reading Difficulty, and Stanford Diagnostic Reading Test, pinpoint specific weaknesses to target intervention.

All these different tests form the assessment toolkit all districts and schools need. Yet, even more vital, is the knowledge to use the information immediately and effectively.

## Using the Data

The data obtained from screening and progress-monitoring tests will help us determine student achievement in three tiers: Tier 1-benchmark, Tier 2-strategic, and Tier 3-intensive learners. These designations match the way Reading First describes a model for prevention and intervention and is the basis for the new Response to Intervention model for identifying special education students. The terms are descriptive of students based on their performance. While it is easiest to think about the need for intervention for individual students, the success and failure of large groups of students is dependent on the effectiveness of the teachers and the materials or programs available. Therefore, in addition to determining which students are truly in need of intensive or strategic interventions, we can also use the progress-monitoring tests that accompany most newer reading programs, data from screening and progress monitoring tests, and classroom observation to help us identify areas or topics in which teachers and schools need specialized assistance. Using data from multiple sources in this way will assist coaches and administrators to determine the extent to which teachers are successfully implementing their core reading programs, effectively monitoring student progress, and skillfully providing additional assistance. So how does such a comprehensive use of data look at all three levels in a school system: the student, the teacher, and the school unit?

### At the Individual Student Level

Test data at the student level will help identify *advanced students*, those who are consistently above the benchmark targets and do very well in the grade-level materials and are able to handle the materials designated as challenge, enrichment, or advanced. These students also benefit from enrichment and more in-depth work in order to continually grow and to avoid boredom. Test data revealing students at the *benchmark level* will reassure teachers that those students are on track to meet grade-level targets. Occasionally, they may need some reteaching, but generally this interruption in their overall positive trajectory of learning is only a minor setback. When data reveals students at the *strategic level,* those who are struggling with some concepts and content and often perform one or even up to two grade levels below, teachers can use the information to plan and provide support during small-group time. In addition, diagnostic tests can identify specific skills for intervention. Often assistance to these students can occur within the regular classroom with added time, adjustments to pace, and increased explicitness and intensity of focus. These students could be regrouped for a portion of their time to have targeted instruction. In addition to 90 minutes or more of a core program, they will need even more time for focused instruction. It is important that this additional instruction be carefully coordinated with the core program instruction. These students need more frequent progress monitoring and diagnostic assessments to pinpoint areas of weakness—monthly or twice a month assessment with the appropriate tests.

Students who score at the *intensive level* are those chronically low-performing students who are far below benchmark on progress monitoring assessments. These students need extended intensive and specialized instruction in small groups. For these youngsters, smaller class size will enable the teacher to focus on their needs, even groups as small as one teacher to three or five students. For students in Grades K–3 in this category, the materials in some new programs designated for reteaching, preteaching, and intervention may be sufficient. However, it is likely that other, more specialized, intensive interventions are even more appropriate. These students need very frequent progress monitoring (weekly or every two weeks) and diagnostic tests to carefully pinpoint weaknesses and set up a specific instructional plan of remediation.

### Teachers and Classrooms

Classrooms where almost all of the students are meeting *benchmarks* on multiple measures (about 80% of the students) may need relatively limited support. Teachers who are achieving positive results with a large number of students can be models for others. Support for these teachers may take the form of ideas to challenge students and extend the curriculum. The focus can also be on helping the teachers plan for the few students who are not meeting benchmarks. Clearly the quality of instruction in the core classroom is the first issue to consider when identifying students for interventions or special education. In fact, the Response to Intervention model presumes effective core instruction.

Classrooms where about one-third of the students are not meeting targets may need *strategic* support. If the teacher has the appropriate materials and has received adequate training on the program, then poor performance by large numbers of students may signal that the teacher needs help. The curriculum-embedded tests will show which program skills are not being mastered by large numbers of students, and the external progress monitoring tests will clarify the reading predictor skills on which students are struggling. Using that information, the coach can work with the classroom teacher or groups of teachers to review program routines, practice the components that are indicated, and observe teaching. For example, if one-third of the students are performing poorly on the program word recognition tasks, the teachers can meet with the coach for a review of the program's blending procedures and the components that reinforce these skills. If many students fail to meet oral fluency targets, then a coach can provide review and practice in the use of the decodable books, repeated reading and partner reading, or assist the teachers to augment an insufficient program with such materials. Teachers in classrooms fitting this profile may need more support and focused assistance from their administrators and coaches in order to implement an effective program. Although the students will certainly need added assistance, an underlying issue may be the difficulty the teacher is having in effective implementation, rather than the individual student's learning challenges.

Finally, classrooms in which over half of the students are chronically failing to meet targets can be thought of as requiring *intensive* support. The teachers in classrooms fitting this profile need ongoing assistance both from the administrator and from a coach to use the selected program and any added, specialized materials effectively to meet student needs.

For homogeneously grouped, or leveled, classrooms, contrary to the general perception, even students performing at the intensive and strategic levels at the start of the year should be able to meet basic reading targets, although the pace of instruction may need to be adjusted, and the students may be in specialized programs. In fact, if these students receive extra instructional time, additional practice on the skills covered, and increased intensity of instruction, they too learn to read on schedule. It will, however, be more demanding of the teacher's expertise. In a classroom in which all students need *intensive* support, one would expect that the teacher would have a smaller group, more time with these students, and provide extra expert instruction. If a large number of students in such a classroom fail to make appropriate progress toward meeting benchmarks and do not show improvement on more frequent progress monitoring measures, then whatever was done did not work. The point is that with effective, research-based instruction, coupled with appropriately targeted materials, all students, with the exception of 2–5% (Lyon, 2005; Torgesen, 2004), should be successfully learning how to read.

### Whole Schools

Beyond the individual school level, the district can utilize these same concepts and data to identify whole schools in need of intensive or strategic support and the degree of autonomy the school will have. For example, schools with many students performing in the intensive range may be expected to work very closely with district staff and have limited decision-making autonomy. Schools that have a large number of students performing at strategic levels may be able to negotiate a certain amount of autonomy with the district but will benefit from direct assistance. Schools that have large numbers of students successfully meeting benchmarks may have a great degree of autonomy as long as they continue to meet targets and as long as they also address the needs of students who are not reaching high performance levels. Table 1 offers a systems approach to the use of assessment data.

## TABLE 1:

| LEVEL | Individual Students (Within a Well-Implemented Classroom) | Classroom Unit | School Unit |
|---|---|---|---|
| **Advanced** | Students consistently exceed the targets and can handle advanced materials.<br>**Intervention:** Need challenge, extension and enrichment.<br>**Assessment:** 3 times a year.<br>**Materials:** Standard core program plus enrichment. | 75–80% of students are exceeding the benchmarks. Teachers may mentor others.<br>**Intervention:** Use of enrichment and challenge materials.<br>**Assessment:** 3 times a year and collected 3 times by district.<br>**Materials:** Standard core program plus enrichment. | Almost all classrooms have most students exceeding the benchmarks; school has significant decision-making autonomy.<br>**Intervention:** Use of enrichment and challenge materials.<br>**Assessment:** 3 times a year and collected 3 times by district.<br>**Materials:** Standard core program plus enrichment. |
| **Benchmark** | Students performing at this level are making good progress, occasionally needing reteaching.<br>**Intervention:** Generally none needed, reteach as problems show up.<br>**Assessment:** 3 times a year.<br>**Materials:** Standard core program. | 75–80% of students are making good progress and there is evidence the teacher is skillfully instructing all students.<br>**Intervention:** Videotaped lessons to serve as models for others. Good classrooms for visits.<br>**Assessment:** 3 times a year and collected 3 times by district.<br>**Materials:** Standard core program. | 75–80% of the classrooms are meeting the targets. Schools may be freed from certain regulations and have a high degree of autonomy.<br>**Intervention:** The school may serve as a good demonstration site for others to visit.<br>**Assessment:** 3 times a year and collected 3 times by district.<br>**Materials:** Standard core program. |
| **Strategic** | Students performing at this level are not meeting benchmark targets on one or more indicators.<br>**Intervention:** Direct instruction with teacher in smaller group 1: 5–7 including adjustments of pace and complexity.<br>**Assessment:** Diagnostic tests to pinpoint problems and target intervention. Assess students every 2–4 weeks.<br>**Materials:** Core program plus specialized, supplemental materials. | About one-third of the students are not meeting benchmarks on multiple measures.<br>**Intervention:** Assistance to the teacher on program components and supplemental materials and added support for struggling students. The coach can support these teachers with model lessons and constructive coaching.<br>**Assessment:** Data regularly monitored by coach/principal; district reviews data 3 times a year.<br>**Materials:** Core program plus specialized, supplemental materials. | Many classrooms have large numbers of students performing at strategic levels.<br>**Intervention:** These schools will need to receive directed assistance from central administration. Principal may benefit from visits to model sites and mentoring.<br>**Assessment:** Data regularly monitored by district liaison.<br>**Materials:** Core program plus specialized, supplemental materials |
| **Intensive** | Individual students who perform at chronically low levels in otherwise effective classrooms can be considered to need intensive assistance.<br>**Intervention:** Students in Grades K–3 may be able to use the intervention components of the existing program during teacher-directed small-group time. These students will regularly need at least 30 minutes focused on their targeted areas of weakness. Some may require a change of program and outside support. Grade 4–8 students will need a separate, intensive intervention replacing their base program.<br>**Assessment:** Assess every 1–2 weeks and use diagnostic tests to pinpoint areas of weakness.<br>**Materials:** Special supplementary materials or intensive intervention programs. | Over half of the students are not meeting benchmark indicators on multiple measures.<br>**Intervention:** Supportive and frequent coaching. Administrative intervention as needed. Extra support to use supplemental and intervention materials and program components skillfully.<br>**Assessment:** More frequent data collection and study by coach/principal/district.<br>**Materials:** Special supplementary materials or intensive intervention programs. | Many classrooms have large numbers of students performing at intensive levels. These schools warrant intensive and directed assistance and may, as a consequence, have limited autonomy.<br>**Intervention:** Principals may seek assistance from district staff. District leadership will provide close supervision and scrutiny of these schools.<br>**Assessment:** More frequent data collection and study by district.<br>**Materials:** Special supplementary materials or intensive intervention programs. |

## Assessment-Driven Instruction: A Systems Approach

The following flow charts also are useful to determine the locus of intervention: the school, the teachers, or the students.

## Flowchart for Heterogeneous Classrooms

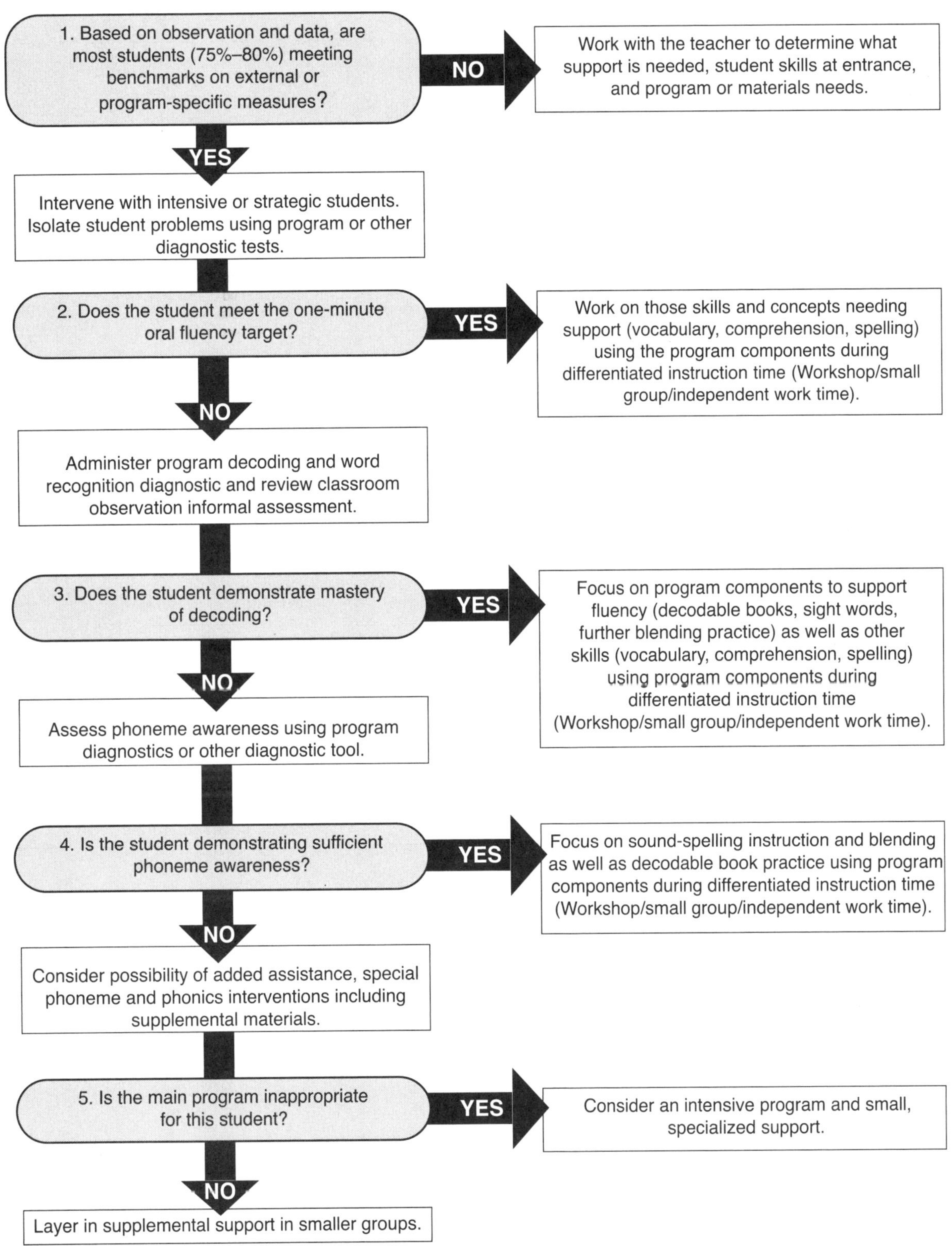

## Flowchart for Homogeneous Classrooms

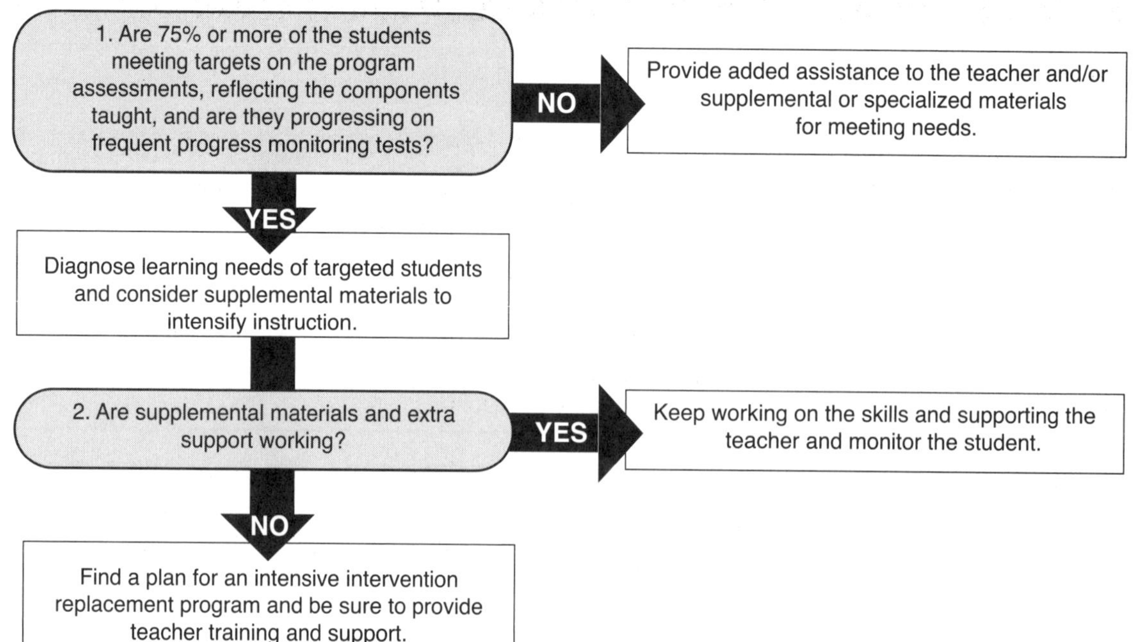


### A Final Word of Caution

Sometimes in leveled classrooms teachers have whole groups of children who have historically received inadequate instruction and have seriously low skills. These teachers will need a great deal of assistance to meet the needs of these students. However, with good programs, supportive coaches and administrators, and effective professional development, virtually all students should be able to learn to read and write. The data will inform our practices and help the entire system meet the ambitious but vital national goal of making all children readers.

### References:

Buck, J. and Torgesen, J. (2003). The Relationship Between Performance on a Measure of Oral Reading Fluency and Performance on the Florida Comprehensive Assessment Test. Tallahassee, FL: Florida Center for Reading Research.

Fuchs, L.S., Fuchs, D., Hosp, M.K., and Jenkins, J.R. (2001), Oral reading fluency as an indicator of reading competence: A theoretical, empirical, and historical analysis. *Scientific Studies of Reading*, 5, 239–256.

Germann, G. and Shinn, M. AIMSweb. Edformation Inc.: Eden Prairie, MN 55344.

Good, R.H. Dynamic Indicators of Basic Early Literacy Skills (DIBELS), University of Oregon.

Lyon, G.R. (2005). Literacy Leadership Summit. Consortium on Reading Excellence. March 2005.

Snow, C. E., Burns, M.S., and Griffin, P., Eds. (1998). "Predictors of Success and Failure in Reading" in *Preventing Reading Difficulties in Young Children.* Washington, D.C.: National Academy Press.

Torgesen, J. (2004). Avoiding the Devastating Downward Spiral. *American Educator*, Fall 2004, 6–45.

Torgesen, J. (2004). Early Screening is at the Heart of Prevention. *American Educator*, Fall 2004, 14-16

**Linda Diamond** is the CEO of CORE (Consortium on Reaching Excellence in Education), a technical assistance organization. She develops CORE's professional services and products. Mrs. Diamond was the Director of Curriculum, Staff Development and Evaluation for the Alameda City Unified School District, an elementary and middle school principal, and Direct Instruction teacher for struggling secondary readers. She is a national speaker on reading instruction and the co-author of *Assessing Reading: Multiple Measures* and the *Teaching Reading Sourcebook.*

# Resources for Assessing Reading

## Phonological Awareness Tests

*AIMSweb® Test of Early Literacy* (TEL), Edformation, Inc. Harcourt Assessment, Inc., San Antonio, TX.

*Comprehensive Test of Phonological Processing* (CTOPP), R. K. Wagner, J. K. Torgesen, and C. A. Rashotte. PRO-ED, Inc., Austin, TX.

*DIBELS: Dynamic Indicators of Basic Early Literacy Skills, Sixth Edition*, R. H. Good III, R. A. Kaminski, L. C. Moats, D. Laimon, S. Smith, and S. Dill. Sopris West, Longmont, CO.

*Fox in a Box: An Adventure in Literacy*, CTB/McGraw-Hill. CTB/McGraw-Hill, Monterey, CA.

*Indicadores Dinámicos del Éxito en la Lectura* (IDEL), D. L. Baker, R. H. Good, N. Knutson, and J. M. Watson (Eds.). University of Oregon Center on Teaching and Learning, Eugene, OR.

*Letter Sound Fluency Test*, D. Fuchs and L. S. Fuchs. Vanderbilt University, Nashville, TN.

*Lindamood Auditory Conceptualization Test, Third Edition* (LAC-3), P. C. Lindamood and P. Lindamood. PRO-ED, Austin, TX.

*Phonemic Awareness Literacy Screening* (PALS). University of Virginia, Charlottesville, VA.

*Phonemic-Awareness Skills Screening* (PASS), L. Crumrine and H. Lonegan. PRO-ED, Austin, TX.

*Test of Auditory Analysis Skills* (TAAS), J. Rosner. Academic Therapy Publications, Novato, CA.

*Test of Auditory Processing Skills, Third Edition* (TAPS-3), N. A. Martin and R. Brownell. Academic Therapy Publications, Novato, CA.

*Test of Phonological Awareness, Second Edition: PLUS* (TOPA-2+), J. K. Torgesen and B. R. Bryant. PRO-ED, Austin, TX.

## Reading Tests

*AIMSweb® Reading Curriculum-Based Measurement* (R-CBM), Edformation, Inc. Harcourt Assessment, Inc., San Antonio, TX.

*AIMSweb® Spanish Reading Curriculum-Based Measurement*, Edformation, Inc. Harcourt Assessment, Inc., San Antonio, TX.

*Burns/Roe Informal Reading Inventory: Preprimer to Twelfth Grade, Fifth Edition*, P. C. Burns and B. D. Roe. Houghton Mifflin Company, Boston, MA.

*Diagnostic Assessments of Reading* (DAR), *Second Edition*, F. G. Roswell, J. S. Chall, M. E. Curtis, and G. Kearns. Riverside/Houghton Mifflin Company, Boston, MA.

*Diagnostic Screening Test: Reading, Third Edition*, T. D. Gnagey and P. A. Gnagey. Slosson Educational Publications, Inc., East Aurora, NY.

*DIBELS: Dynamic Indicators of Basic Early Literacy Skills, Sixth Edition*, R. H. Good, III, R. A. Kaminski, L. C. Moats, D. Laimon, S. Smith, and S. Dill. Sopris West, Longmont, CO.

*Durrell Analysis of Reading Difficulty, Third Edition* (DARD), D. D. Durrell and J. H. Catterson. Harcourt Assessment, Inc., San Antonio, TX.

*Ekwall and Shanker Reading Inventory, Third Edition*, E. E. Ekwall and J. L. Shanker. Allyn & Bacon, Needham Heights, MA.

*Fox in a Box: An Adventure in Literacy*, CTB/McGraw-Hill. CTB/McGraw-Hill, Monterey, CA.

*Gates-MacGinitie Reading Tests, Fourth Edition*, W. H. MacGinitie, R. K. MacGinitie, K. Maria, and L. G. Dreyer. Riverside Publishing, Itasca, IL

*Gates-McKillop-Horowitz Reading Diagnostic Test, Second Edition*, A. I. Gates, A. S. McKillop, and E. C. Horowitz. Teachers College Press, New York, NY.

*Gilmore Oral Reading Test*, J. V. Gilmore and E. C. Gilmore. Harcourt Assessment, Inc., San Antonio, TX.

*Gray Oral Reading Tests* (GORT-4), J. L. Wiederholt and B. R. Bryant. PRO-ED, Austin, TX.

*Indicadores Dinámicos del Éxito en la Lectura* (IDEL), D. L. Baker, R. H. Good, N. Knutson, and J. M. Watson (Eds.). University of Oregon Center on Teaching and Learning, Eugene, OR.

*McCall-Crabbs Standard Test Lessons in Reading*, W. A. McCall, L. C. Schroeder, and R. P. Starr. Teachers College Press, New York, NY.

*Phonics-Based Reading Test* (PRT), R. Brownell, Academic Therapy Publications, Novato, CA.

*Slosson Oral Reading Test-Revised* (SORT-R), R. L. Slosson and C. L. Nicholson. Slosson Educational Publications, Inc., East Aurora, NY.

*Slosson Test of Reading Readiness* (STRR), L. A. Perry and G. J. Vitali. Slosson Educational Publications, Inc., East Aurora, NY.

*Spadafore Diagnostic Reading Test* (SDRT), G. J. Spadafore. Academic Therapy Publications, Novato, CA.

*Standardized Reading Inventory* (SRI-2), P. L. Newcomer. PRO-ED, Austin, TX.

*Stanford Diagnostic Reading Test, Fourth Edition* (SDRT 4), B. Karlsen and E. F. Gardner. Harcourt Assessment, Inc., San Antonio, TX.

*Test of Early Reading Ability* (TERA-3), D. K. Reid, W. P. Hresko, and D. D. Hammill. PRO-ED, Austin, TX.

*Test of Reading Comprehension, Third Edition* (TORC-3), V. L. Brown, D. D. Hammill, and J. L. Wiederholt. PRO-ED, Austin, TX.

*Test of Silent Contextual Reading Fluency* (TOSCRF), D. D. Hammill, J. L. Wiederholt, and E. A. Allen. PRO-ED, Austin, TX.

*Test of Silent Word Reading Fluency* (TOSWRF), N. Mather, D. D. Hammill, E. A. Allen, and R. Roberts. PRO-ED, Austin, TX.

*Test of Word Reading Efficiency* (TOWRE), J. K. Torgesen, R. K. Wagner, and C. A. Rashotte. PRO-ED, Austin, TX.

*Woodcock Reading Mastery Tests-Revised* (WRMT-R), R. W. Woodcock. AGS Publishing, Circle Pines, MN.

## Vocabulary

*Sight Reading and Math*, Success for All Foundation. Success for All Foundation, Inc., Baltimore, MD.

*Basic Reading Inventory*, J. L. Johns. Kendall/Hunt Publishing Company, Dubuque, IA.

*Comprehensive Receptive and Expressive Vocabulary Test, Second Edition* (CREVT-2), G. Wallace and D. D. Hammill. PRO-ED, Austin, TX.

*Expressive One-Word Picture Vocabulary Test, 2000 Edition* (EOWPVT), R. Brownell. Academic Therapy Publications, Novato, CA.

*Expressive Vocabulary Test, Second Edition* (EVT-2), K. T. Williams. AGS Publishing, Circle Pines, MN.

*Monitoring Basic Skills Progress* (MBSP), L. Fuchs, C. Hamlett, and D. Fuchs. PRO-ED, Inc., Austin, TX.

*Peabody Picture Vocabulary Test, Fourth Edition* (PPVT-4), L. M. Dunn and D. M. Dunn. AGS Publishing, Circle Pines, MN.

*Receptive One-Word Picture Vocabulary Test, 2000 Edition* (ROWPVT), R. Brownell. Academic Therapy Publications, Novato, CA.

*The WORD Test 2: Elementary*, L. Bowers, R. Huisingh, C. LoGiudice, and J. Orman. LinguiSystems, East Moline, IL.

## Achievement Tests with Reading Subsets

*BRIGANCE Comprehensive Inventory of Basic Skills, Revised* (CIBS-R), A. H. Brigance and F. P. Glascoe. Curriculum Associates, Inc., North Billerica, MA.

*Criterion Test of Basic Skills* (CTOBS-2), J. Evans, K. Lundell, and W. Brown. Academic Therapy Publications, Novato, CA.

*Kaufman Test of Educational Achievement, Second Edition* (KTEA-II), A. S. Kaufman and N. L. Kaufman. AGS Publishing, Circle Pines, MN.

*Peabody Individual Achievement Test-Revised,* F. C. Markwardt, Jr. AGS Publishing, Circle Pines, MN.

*Wechsler Individual Achievement Test, Second Edition,* The Psychological Corporation. Harcourt Assessment, Inc., San Antonio, TX.

*Wide Range Achievement Test 3,* G. S. Wilkinson. Psychological Assessment Resources, Inc., Lutz, FL.

*Woodcock-Johnson III,* R. W. Woodcock, K. S. McGrew, N. Mather, and F. A. Schrank. Riverside Publishing, Itasca, IL.

*Woodcock Language Proficiency Battery-Revised* (WLPB-R), R. W. Woodcock. Riverside Publishing, Itasca, IL.

1300 Clay Street
Suite 600
Oakland, CA 94612
1-510-540-4200
FAX 1-510-540-4242

**For information about** CORE
**Call Toll Free** 1-888-249-6155

CORE works collaboratively with schools and districts to implement effective research-based reading instruction by providing training seminars and workshops; site-based coaching; and system-building support.

### CORE Teaching Reading Sourcebook—2nd Edition

A comprehensive, Grades K–12 sourcebook covering the what, the why, the when, and the how of teaching reading. Includes research-based information as well as practical, hands-on teaching models for all aspects of explicit reading instruction. The new features in the Updated Second Edition seamlessly connect and clarify the Sourcebook's alignment to the Common Core State Standards.
**8-1/2 x 11 softcover, 864 pp. [8690-1]**

### CORE Assessing Reading: Multiple Measures—2nd Edition

A collection of assessments for the comprehensive monitoring of reading skill development for Grades K–12.
**8-1/2 x 11 softcover, 216 pp. [8464-8]**

## send prepaid orders to:

**ARENA PRESS**
20 Leveroni Court
Novato, CA 94949-5746

1-800-**422-7249** • FAX: 1-888-**287-9975**
www.Academic Therapy.com
www.HighNoonBooks.com

| QUANTITY | PRODUCT NO. | TITLE | UNIT PRICE | TOTAL |
|---|---|---|---|---|
| | 8690-1 | CORE Teaching Reading Sourcebook—2nd Edition | 75.00 | |
| | 8464-8 | CORE Assessing Reading: Multiple Measures—2nd Edition | 45.00 | |

**For ordering and price information,**
**Call Toll-Free:**
1-800-**422-7249**
**Call between 8:30 AM–4:00 PM Pacific Time**

**SUBTOTAL** ______
**Sales Tax (CA, KY & IN residents only)** ______
**TOTAL ENCLOSED (U.S. Funds)** ______

❑ Check or Money Order Enclosed
❑ Credit Card:
❑ VISA ❑ MasterCard ❑ AmEx

Exact Name on Card: ______
CC #: ______
Expiration Date: ______
Signature: ______

**SHIP TO: (Please Print)**

**NAME** ______
**ORGANIZATION** ______
**ADDRESS** ______
**CITY** ______ **STATE** ______ **ZIP** ______
**PHONE** ______